CAREER OPPORTUNITIES IN THE MUSIC INDUSTRY

CAREER OPPORTUNITIES IN THE MUSIC INDUSTRY

Shelly Field

Facts On File Publications
New York, New York ● Oxford, England

Career Opportunities in the Music Industry

Library of Congress Cataloging in Publication Data

Field, Shelly.
   Career opportunities in the music industry.

   Includes index.
   1. Music—Vocational guidance.   2. Music—Economic aspects.   I. Title.
ML3795.F497 1986   780′.23′73   84-8195
ISBN 0-8160-1126-5
ISBN 0-8160-1535-x **PB**
Printed in the United States of American
10 9 8 7 6 5 4 3 2 1

*This book
is dedicated to my parents
Ed and Selma Field
who gave me every opportunity,
supported all my decisions
and always let me be me.*

CONTENTS

SECTION 9—ARENAS, FACILITIES, HALLS, AND CLUBS

SECTION 10—EDUCATION

SECTION 11—TALENT AND WRITING

SECTION 12—CHURCH MUSIC

SECTION 13—MISCELLANEOUS CAREER OPPORTUNITIES IN MUSIC

SECTION 14—APPENDICES

PREFACE

How to Use this Book

Purpose

There are literally thousands upon thousands of people who want to get into the music business, yet most people have no idea *how* to get into the industry. Up to this point, there has been no single source describing the major job opportunities in music.

This book was written for everyone who wants to be in the music business but doesn't know how to get in. The 79 jobs discussed in this book encompass not only performing, but also the business and educational occupations in the music business. This industry needs secretaries, receptionists, publishers, tour managers, teachers, therapists, librarians, attorneys, accountants, executives, writers, publicists, salespeople, and more. The trick is to find your skills and use them to get you in the door of the music business. Once in, you have a good chance of moving into other positions as you climb the career ladder in the industry.

Read through the book and find out what you are qualified for, or how you can obtain training in the field you want to get into. You can then work toward one of the most interesting, most rewarding, and most exciting careers in the world — a career in music.

Sources of Information

Information was obtained through interviews, questionnaires, and a wide variety of books, magazines, newsletters, etc. Some information came from personal experience in the industry. Other data were obtained from friends and business associates in various phases of the music business.

Among the people interviewed were individuals in all aspects of the music industry. These include record company executives, radio station personnel, tour managers, personal managers, accountants, booking agents, church musicians, and performers. Employment agencies were contacted, as well as schools, personnel offices, unions, trade associations, orchestras, etc.

Organization of Material

Career Opportunities in the Music Industry is divided into thirteen general employment sections. These sections are: Recording and the Record Business; Radio; On the Road; Music Retailing and Wholesaling; The Business End of the Industry; Instrument Repair, Restoration, and Design; Publicity; Symphonies, Orchestras, etc.; Arenas, Facilities, Halls, and Clubs; Education; Talent and Writing; Church Music; and Miscellaneous Career Opportunities In Music. Within each of these sections are descriptions of individual careers.

There are two parts to each job classification. The first part offers job information in a chart form. The second part presents information in a narrative text.

In addition to the basic career description is additional information on unions/associations and tips for entry. Ten appendices are offered to help locate information you might want or need to get started in the music business.

The music industry is one with widespread appeal. Everyone dreams about reaching a star. For some, the star is becoming a popular recording artist; for others, a well known songwriter. Still others who love music, whatever the genre, are delighted to work in the recording business or in music education.

With talent, a few breaks, connections, training, being in the right place at the right time, a little bit of luck, or a combination of just a few of the preceding, you too can find your star in the music business. Persevere!

SHELLY FIELD
April, 1985

ACKNOWLEDGMENTS

I would like to thank every individual, company, union, and association that provided information, assistance, and encouragement for this book.

I begin with my editor, Kate Kelly, whose interest provided the initial impetus. Others whose help was invaluable include the Academy of Country Music; Alverno College; American Federation of Musicians; American Society of Music Copyists; American Symphony Orchestra League; Arista Records; Warren Bergstrom, Monticello Central School; Broadcast Music Inc.; B'nai B'rith Vocational Service; Linda Bonsante; Cantors Assembly; Dr. Jessica L. Cohen; Norman Cohen; Robert Cohen, Esq.; Fred Coopersmith; Gail Cox, Crawford Memorial Library; Robert Crothers, assistant to the president of the AFM; Daniel Dayton and W. Lynne Dayton, WSUL Radio; Julie Evans; Sara Feldberg, Crawford Memorial Library; Deborah K. Field, Esq.; Edwin M. Field; Selma G. Field; Ann Fitch; John Gatto; Sheila Gatto; Morris Gerber, Liberty Central School; Larry Goldsmith, Piano Technicians Guild; Sam Goldych, Monticello Central Schools High School Librarian; Joan Howard, Private Industry Council—Job Training Partnership Act—Employment and Training; Hudson Valley Philharmonic; Julia Jacobs; John Lawler; Bob Leone, projects director of the Songwriters Guild; Ernie Martinelli; Judy McCoy; June E. McDonald, Practising Law Institute; Phillip Mestman; Rima Mestman; Beverly Michaels, Esq.; Martin Michaels, Esq.; Music Educators National Conference; National Association for Music Therapy; National Association of Music Merchants; National Association of Recording Merchandisers; National Music Publishers Association; Jim Newton; New York State Employment Service; Florence Naistadt; Heather Dawn O'Keefe, National Music Publishers Association; Ivy Pass; Piano Technicians Guild; Practising Law Institute; Ruth Qualich, Alverno College; Harvey Rachlin; Rev. Bruce Rentz; Doug Richards; Susan G. Riley, ASOL; Sheldon Rosenberg; Gary F. Roth, BMI; Joy Shaffer, National Association for Music Therapy; Smith Employment Agency; The Songwriters Guild; Aileen Spertell, Smith Employment Agency; Karen Talmadge; The Teenagers; Dr. Ray Williams, Director of Education and Marketing, NAMM; Gordon Winarick; Dr. Diana Worby; Rachel Worby; and Johnny Worlds.

In addition, because there is such a great mystique surrounding the music business, much of the material was provided by sources who wish to remain anonymous. My thanks to them all the same.

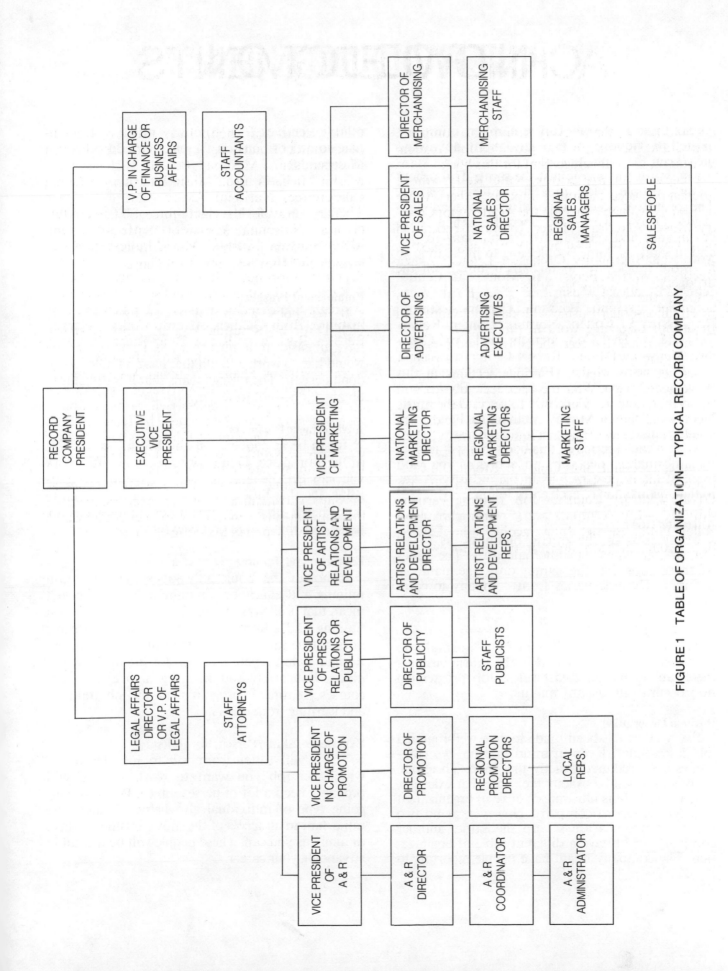

FIGURE 1   TABLE OF ORGANIZATION—TYPICAL RECORD COMPANY

INTRODUCTION

As far back as anyone can remember, music has existed in one form or another. It may not always have been the sophisticated versions that we know today, but it was music just the same. Throughout history, people made music for different reasons. The primitive people used drums to send messages. Drums were also used to dance to in ceremonies and celebrations. People sang for joy and in sadness. Some people sang to make time go by more quickly or to take their minds off the drudgery of hard, tedious work.

Over the years, music has evolved into a multibillion-dollar business. Today thousands and thousands of people work in this industry. There are many more that reap the benefits and pleasures from music.

As you read over the various sections in this book, searching to find the "perfect" job, keep in mind that there is no one way to get into the music business. There are many methods. I have given you the guidelines. You have to do the rest.

Within each section of this book you will find all the information necessary to acquaint you with most of the important jobs in the industry. A key to the organization of each entry follows:

Alternate Titles

Many jobs in the music business, as in all industry, are known by alternate titles. The duties of these jobs are the same; only the name is different. The title varies from company to company.

Career Ladder

The career ladder illustrates a normal job progression. Remember that in the music business there are no hard-and-fast rules. Job progression may occur in almost any manner.

Position Description

Every effort has been made to give well-rounded job descriptions. Keep in mind that no two companies are structured exactly the same. Therefore, no two jobs will be exactly the same. For example, note figure 1. This illustrates a table of organization of a typical record company. However, as no two record companies are set up the same, another company might have a different table of organization. The company might have people reporting to

other executives. The company might also eliminate some positions on the chart or add others. It all depends.

Salary Ranges

Salary ranges for the eighty-three job titles in this book are as accurate as possible. Salaries for a job will depend on how big a company is, where it is located, and the applicant's experience.

Employment Prospects

If you choose a job that has an EXCELLENT, GOOD, or FAIR rating, you are lucky. You will have an easier time finding a job. If, however, you would like to work at a job that has a POOR rating, don't despair. The rating means that it is difficult to obtain a job—not totally impossible.

Advancement Prospects

Try to be as cooperative and helpful as possible in the workplace. Don't try to see how little work you can do. Be enthusiastic, energetic and outgoing. Do that little extra that no one asked you to do. When a job advancement possibility opens up, make sure that you're prepared for it.

Education and Training

Although the book only gives the minimum training and educational requirement, this doesn't mean that is all you should have. Try to get the best training and education possible. A college degree does not guarantee a job in the music business, but it might help prepare a person for life in the workplace. Education and training also encompass courses, seminars, programs, on-the-job training, and learning from others.

Experience/Skills/Personality Traits

These will differ from job to job. However, whichever job you want to work at, you will probably need a lot of perseverance. Being an outgoing type of individual also helps. Contacts are important in all facets of the music business. Make as many as you can. These people will be helpful in advancing your career.

Best Geographical Location

You will note that most jobs in record companies, the business end of the industry, etc. are located in the major music capitals of New York City, Los Angeles, and Nashville. Jobs in talent and performing can also be found in other culturally active areas. Opportunities in teaching, retailing, wholesaling, etc. may be found most anywhere in the country.

Unions/Associations

Unions and trade associations offer valuable help in getting into the business, obtaining jobs, and making contacts. They may also offer scholarships, fellowships, seminars, and other programs.

Tips for Entry

Use this section for ideas on how to get a job and gain entry into the area of the business you are interested in. When applying for any job always be as professional as possible. Dress neatly. Don't wear sneakers. Don't chew gum. Don't smoke. Always have a few copies of your resumé with you. This, too, should look neat. Have it typed and presented well.

Use *every* contact you have. Don't get hung up on the idea that you want to get a job by yourself. If you are lucky enough to know someone who can help you obtain a job you want, take him or her up on it. You'll have to prove yourself at the interview and on the job. Nobody can do that for you. The last piece of advice in this section is to *be on time* for everything. This includes job interviews, phone calls, work, meetings, etc. People will remember when you're habitually late and it will work against you in advancing your career.

Have fun reading this book. Use it. It will help you find a career you will truly love. When you do get the job of your dreams, do someone else a favor and give them the benefit of your knowledge. Help them learn about the business. Good luck!

RECORDING
AND THE
RECORD BUSINESS

A&R COORDINATOR

CAREER PROFILE

Duties: Finding talent for a record company to sign; locating tunes to match with specific artists on the label's roster

Alternate Title(s): A&R Representative; Artist and Repertoire Coordinator; A&R Staffer; Talent Acquisition Rep

Salary Range: $14,000 to $55,000 +

Employment Prospects: Poor

Advancement Prospects: Fair

Best Geographical Location(s) for Position: New York, Los Angeles, Nashville

Prerequisites:

  Education or Training—High school diploma

  Experience—Experience in music or record business helpful

  Special Skills and Personality Traits—Foresight; ability to see past "raw" talent; self-confidence; enjoyment of music; ability to deal well with people

CAREER LADDER

```
┌─────────────────────────────────┐
│                                 │
│          A&R Director           │
│                                 │
└─────────────────────────────────┘

┌─────────────────────────────────┐
│                                 │
│         A&R Coordinator         │
│                                 │
└─────────────────────────────────┘

┌─────────────────────────────────┐
│     A&R Administrator;          │
│     A&R Assistant or Trainee    │
└─────────────────────────────────┘
```

Position Description

An A&R Coordinator or rep performs a variety of functions depending on the record company he or she works with and its size.

The main duty of the A&R Coordinator is to find talent for the company to sign up. He or she may do this in a number of ways. The A&R Coordinator may visit clubs and/or showcases checking out new talent. The individual may listen to tapes and demo records and/or watch videocassettes of acts performing. The A&R Coordinator may also try to sign up existing talent, such as individuals currently signed with another record label. In cases such as this, the A&R Coordinator might either wait for the act's contract to expire, or, in rare cases, try to buy out an existing contract. When A&R Coordinators are vying for an established act to sign with their company, they do everything in their power to make their contract more attractive than competing companies' contracts.

The A&R Coordinator has another important duty. He or she is often responsible for finding (or helping to find) songs for the artists signed to the record label. These can be located in a number of ways. One is by going through the masses of tapes and demos of new tunes that are mailed or brought to the record company by would-be songwriters. Another method is to listen to old hit records or classics that might be arranged in a new or current fashion. The A&R Coordinator might put a staff writer of the record company together with the artist in an effort to come up with that all-important hit tune. The new artist might also be a writer and have a healthy supply of his or her own material from which a potential tune might be selected.

Once a tune is picked, the A&R Coordinator locates a producer who will work well with the act. The A&R Coordinator might also help an unmanaged or poorly managed act find a management team, lawyers, accountants, etc.

The A&R Coordinator works very closely with the act from the moment they are signed with the label. He or she takes the act under his or her wing and tries to build it into a total artistic, creative, and commercial success.

If an act is unhappy about anything, whether it be a record not selling well or difficulties with an assigned producer, the act would talk to their A&R Coordinator.

The A&R Coordinator works closely not only with the act, but also with the various other departments in the company to assure the act the best possible chance of attaining success.

The A&R Coordinator is usually responsible to the vice-president in charge of A&R, the vice-president in charge of talent acquisition, or the A&R Director. It depends on how the particular record company is structured.

The hours for the A&R Coordinator are often irregular and long as a result of late nights at clubs seeking out talent and the nature of the job.

Salaries

Depending on the size of the record company, salaries can be quite high for this position. Salaries can range from $14,000 to $55,000+ annually. In addition, A&R Coordinators are often given bonuses for signing existing "superstar" talent or an artist who makes it big.

Employment Prospects

There are many people who want to work as A&R Coordinators. As a matter of fact, there are more people than there are positions.

If the record company requires an A&R Coordinator, they will usually try to find a qualified individual within the ranks of the company. Exceptions are made, however, when an A&R Coordinator has worked at another company and proved him or herself by finding artists who consistently hit the top.

Advancement Prospects

Once an individual gets into a record company, he or she has the opportunity to move up the career ladder. As an A&R Coordinator, the individual may move into the position of A&R Director, or the person may be hired by a bigger, more prestigious company for the same position. To move ahead, the individual must prove him or herself by signing acts that hit the top of the charts.

Education and Training

An A&R Coordinator must have at least a high school diploma. Certain labels prefer that their staff members hold a college degree. Others don't care as long as the individual can do the job.

Degrees or courses in music merchandising, the music business, communications, marketing, advertising, etc. might prove useful. In addition, there are a number of seminars, workshops, and programs put together by associations and organizations that are helpful both for their educational value and for the opportunity they provide for developing contacts.

Experience/Skills/Personality Traits

A&R Coordinators usually have worked in the music business, the record business, and/or radio prior to accepting their positions.

The A&R Coordinator must have a unique type of foresight that comes into play when watching a new act or listening to a new tune. He or she must have that special ability to see past the raw talent to the potential talent an act or record could have. The individual must have the self-confidence to stand by his or her decision and not be swayed.

Unions/Associations

A&R Coordinators may belong to the National Academy of Recording Arts and Sciences (NARAS) as associate members. They might also be members of the Country Music Association (CMA), the Gospel Music Association (GMA), or the Black Music Association (BMA).

Tips for Entry

1. If you are interested in getting into an A&R position, try to get a job in a record company performing any task possible. Many companies promote from within. An energetic, talented, bright individual can move up.
2. You might want to begin your career by checking out local talent. If you can recognize talent, you might very well find it in a local act. You might want to work with this act as a manager or agent. You will be gaining valuable experience.
3. Read the trades and books or magazines on trends in the music and record business. Trends often repeat themselves over a period of years. This information may be useful to your career.

A&R ADMINISTRATOR

CAREER PROFILE

Duties: Planning budgets for artists signed to the record label; dealing with clerical functions and administration of the A&R department.

Alternate Title(s): A&R Administration Representative

Salary Range: $13,000 to $35,000+

Employment Prospects: Poor

Advancement Prospects: Fair

Best Geographical Location(s) for Position: New York, Los Angeles, Nashville

Prerequisites:

Education or Training—High school diploma; college degree may be required or preferred by some companies

Experience—Experience in a record company is useful; bookkeeping positions are helpful

Special Skills and Personality Traits—Ability to budget; ability to work with numbers; enjoyment of music; ability to communicate both verbally and on paper

CAREER LADDER

```
┌─────────────────────────┐
│     A&R Coordinator     │
└─────────────────────────┘

┌─────────────────────────┐
│     A&R Administrator   │
└─────────────────────────┘

┌─────────────────────────┐
│  A&R Assistant or Trainee │
└─────────────────────────┘
```

Position Description

An A&R Administrator works in the A&R department along with the A&R coordinators. If the record company is a small one, he or she might assume the duties of both A&R administration and coordination. In a large record company, however, the A&R Administrator is responsible for much of the clerical function of the department.

The individual is responsible for planning budgets for the artists who are signed to the label. Working on the annual or semiannual budget for the coming year is one of the more important functins of the A&R Administrator. He or she must analyze previous budgets, current acts, and projected estimates of costs. The A&R Administrator must then come up with a working budget for the recording of the acts.

As the year progresses, the individual working in A&R administration keeps an eye on the budget in relation to the expenses. Staying within a budget means that the A&R Administrator is doing his or her job. The individual might work exclusively with one or two studios in order to build up a great volume of studio time. With this volume, the A&R Administrator can often receive discounts on time.

The A&R Administrator keeps track of all monies spent for recording studio time, session musicians, talent, and miscellaneous expenses. These costs are all logged. It is through this log that expenses for each recording act can be tracked.

The A&R Administrator also submits bills and purchase orders to the proper individuals in the accounting department. He or she must make sure that these bills are submitted and paid on time. Union regulations stipulate certain time limits for musicians' payment schedules. A late bill could result in a union dispute.

The A&R Administrator works with the A&R Coordinator in monitoring the progress of a label's recording acts in order to determine how much has been recorded, when the record will be ready for release, how much the recording has cost to date, and whether the act is within budget, etc. This information is compiled into reports that are given to various department heads in the recording company.

If the act is receiving tour support from the record company, the A&R Administrator must keep records of all monies laid out on behalf of the group. This is often recouped later from record sale monies.

The A&R Administrator is additionally responsible for obtaining all pertinent information that will be on the completed record packaging. This information includes the name of the group, the members of the group, other musicians who played on the record, producers, tunes, lengths of songs, how the songs will be sequenced on the record (if it is an LP), and any other additional material the act, its management, and the producer want on the packaging.

The A&R Administrator might have to apply for copyright materials and applications for any songs, tunes, record covers, etc. that it owns. The A&R Administrator might be responsible for applying for any mechanical rights licenses that are necessary. He or she must make sure that all this is on file.

The A&R Administrator must be very organized. He or she must keep excellent records. The individual is responsible to different people and department heads depending on the company. He or she might be responsible to one of the company's vice-presidents in charge of A&R, or might be responsible to an A&R administration supervisor.

Salaries

Salaries for A&R Administrators will vary depending on the size of the record company and the qualifications and duties of the individual. Earnings can range from $13,000 to 35,000+ per year for individuals in these positions.

Employment Prospects

The A&R department is one of the most popular departments in which to work. There are more people who desire jobs in this area than there are openings.

Record companies often promote from within. If an individual is considering a position in an A&R department, he or she may have to enter through a lower-paying job in a different department.

Advancement Prospects

An individual who has obtained a position as an A&R Administrator probably will have the oppor-

tunity to move into an A&R Coordinator position. He or she, of course, must be energetic, enthusiastic, and excellent at his or her current job.

Openings do occur as people change jobs and labels. As noted throughout this section, most record companies prefer to promote from within when there are qualified individuals.

Education and Training

Many record companies require a college degree for this position. Others just ask for a high school diploma. It depends on the label.

College courses or majors that might prove useful include business and administration. There are colleges around the country with curriculums in the music business.

There are also a number of seminars, programs, and workshops put together by record companies, associations, organizations, or colleges that are helpful both for their educational value and for the opportunity they provide for developing contacts.

Experience/Skills/Personality Traits

The individual working in A&R administration must have the ability to plan budgets for recording artists. Certain acts that the company feels will sell more records will have bigger budgets. Newer or lesser acts must have budgets developed for them that are considerably smaller.

Since most of the job is budgeting or checking bills, the ability to work with numbers is a must. Other parts of the job require the individual to write reports and to keep other departments of the company informed. The A&R Administrator, therefore, must also be able to communicate both on paper and verbally.

Unions/Associations

A&R Administrators may belong to the National Academy of Recording Arts and Sciences (NARAS) as associate members. They might also belong to the Country Music Association (CMA), the Gospel Music Association (GMA), and/or the Black Music Association (BMA), depending on their musical interests.

Tips for Entry

1. Record companies do promote within. If you want to work in the A&R department, try to get a job in a record company doing any type of work you can. Be enthusiastic and ask questions.
2. Read the trades and any other information you can lay your hands on regarding trends in the music business, record deals, etc.

3. If you are in college, see if the record company has a summer internship program for which you can get college credit.
4. If you are not in college, there are also some minority training programs available at record companies that can help you get your foot in the door. Check with the personnel departments of the individual record companies.

PROMOTION STAFFER

CAREER PROFILE

Duties: Visiting and calling radio station program directors; trying to get airplay for the label's records

Alternate Title(s): Promotion Man (or Woman); Regional Staff Promotion Person; Local Promotion Person; Record Promoter; Promotional Representative

Salary Range: $15,000 to 37,000+

Employment Prospects: Fair

Advancement Prospects: Fair

Best Geographical Location(s) for Position: New York City, Los Angeles, and Nashville for positions with major record companies; other locations for independent promoters (reps may work in various locations)

Prerequisites:

Education or Training—High school diploma

Experience—Sales jobs helpful; working in music business, radio, etc. useful

Special Skills and Personality Traits—Ability to sell; music knowledge; aggressiveness; communication skills

CAREER LADDER

```
┌─────────────────────────────────┐
│      Director of Promotion      │
└─────────────────────────────────┘

┌─────────────────────────────────┐
│       Promotion Staffer         │
└─────────────────────────────────┘

┌─────────────────────────────────┐
│   Local Promotion Person (Rep)  │
└─────────────────────────────────┘
```

Position Description

A Promotion Person working at a record company has one prime function: to get airplay for the label's records. In order to accomplish this, the Promotion Person or representative visits and calls radio station program directors and music directors.

Promotion People may be assigned a certain category of music—for example, R & B, pop, gospel, disco, etc. They are also assigned territories. There are a number of different markets in which Promotion People generally work. This is where they hope to "break" records.

The Promotion People work closely with program directors, music directors, and disc jockeys in these markets. The first thing the Promotion Person does is to set up appointments with these station people. When the label's Promotion Person goes on appointments he or she will bring a number of the label's new releases. The Promotion

Person will probably also bring along a supply of promo or press material on the artists who made the records.

The individual will sit with the radio station personnel and listen to the new releases. The Promotion Person hopes that the program director or the music director will like the song well enough to add it to the station's playlist. The rep may leave copies of the records with the radio station staff to listen to at their leisure.

Promotion People will visit a number of stations in each area covered. The individual may go to AM stations if the song that is being promoted is a single. If the record is an LP or a cut from an LP the Promotion Person probably will go to an FM station. There are also stations that handle both cuts from LP's and singles.

In this position, the individual might do quite a bit of socializing. Promotion People often take key radio station personnel out to lunch, dinner, or for drinks. They might also bring a program director to a club in order to listen to a group play a song live and gauge audience response.

The individual must do research in order to get stations to play many records. He or she may talk to Promotion People in other markets to determine how a specific tune is doing. The Promotion Person must also check with various record stores to see what kind of sales a record has in a specific area. The rep may check into the total sales of the record in the label's sales department. Any number of other methods to develop information on the reason a radio station should play a record may be employed.

At certain times, Promotion People will use the phone and mail to reach disc jockeys, program directors, and music directors. This system of mailing promotional copies of records and press material to stations and then following up with phone calls is frequently used in smaller areas. These smaller locations usually do not have the market potential to justify visits, but may be important just the same.

Salaries

Salaries for Promotion People will vary depending on the size of the record company and the experience and duties of the individual. Salaries will range from $15,000 to $37,000+ annually.

Employment Prospects

Employment prospects are fair for those people who can obtain entry into a record company. There are usually quite a number of Promotion People working for each major company. Individuals who have built up a good reputation in other record companies working in this position generally will not find any problem getting a job. Other individuals may gain entry in local promotion positions.

Advancement Prospects

A person who is a Promotion Representative has a number of options for career advancement. The individual may have a good track record for getting records listened to and put on playlists. This person is in a good position. He or she can usually obtain a better job at a larger record company. A Promotion Person may also move into the job of director of promotion.

Education and Training

As with many jobs in the recording industry, there is no major educational requirement other than a high school diploma. There are Promotion People with degrees and without them. Degrees might help an individual feel more confident about holding a job but they do not necessarily help one obtain a job. A degree may, however, help an individual to advance his or her career.

Experience Skills/Personality Traits

People working in the promotion field are generally interested in music, records, and radio. Some of these individuals have worked in one of these three areas at a prior time while others have been involved with product sales or a variety of different positions.

People in this field of endeavor need to be able to sell. While they may not be selling a product directly, they are selling the sound of a record. Promotion People are judged on how many records they can get radio stations to add to their playlist. In order to do this, it is necessary for the Promotion Person to stay on top of the music and the record industry and be well-informed about all phases of it. The person must additionally be aggressive and articulate.

Unions/Associations

Promotion People may belong to the Black Music Association (BMA), the Gospel Music Association (GMA), or the Country Music Association (CMA), depending on the type of music they promote. Additionally, they may belong to the National Academy of Recording Arts and Sciences (NARAS) as associate members.

Tips for Entry

1. There are internship programs available in many record companies. Check directly with the various companies.
2. It helps to have contacts to get into a position in a record company. If you have any, this is the time to use them.
3. There are minority training programs available in some record companies. If you qualify, check these out.
4. Enter the record company in any way possible. Apply for a position as a secretary, receptionist, mailroom clerk, etc. These companies do promote from within.

STAFF PUBLICIST

CAREER PROFILE

Duties: Handling the publicity and press needs of acts signed to a label

Alternate Title(s): Press Agent

Salary Range: $12,000 to $75,000+

Employment Prospects: Fair

Advancement Prospects: Fair

Best Geographical Location(s) for Position: New York City, Los Angeles, Nashville

Prerequisites:

Education or Training—College degree or background in journalism, communications, music business, or music merchandising helpful

Experience—Positions in music- or nonmusic-oriented publicity and public relations

Special Skills and Personality Traits—Ability to write; creativity; persuasive manner; ability to work under pressure; enjoyment of music

CAREER LADDER

```
┌─────────────────────────────┐
│    Director of Publicity     │
└─────────────────────────────┘

┌─────────────────────────────┐
│       Staff Publicist        │
└─────────────────────────────┘

┌─────────────────────────────┐
│ Music- or Nonmusic-Oriented  │
│  Publicist; Music Journalist │
└─────────────────────────────┘
```

Position Description

Publicists on staff in record companies perform many different functions. The main goal of the department is to get as much good publicity for the artists signed to the label as possible. Publicity helps the label sell records and that is the way the company produces income.

A beginning Publicist may do just clerical types of work, such as assembling press kits. He or she may start by gathering information for the press kits or by writing simple press releases.

As the Publicist gains more experience, he or she will be writing more creative press releases. Eventually the Publicist will work with the act on developing publicity strategies for their press campaign.

As a Publicist, an individual must be able to get an artist's name in the news (magazines, trades, TV, radio, etc.) as often as possible. This is accomplished by writing press releases, sending them to the correct media, talking to media about acts, arranging interviews, etc.

The Publicist often arranges a series of print interviews, radio interviews, and TV appearances in conjunction with the release of a new record.

He or she may either keep the information on the group going to the media in a shotgun approach or release information selectively. This would depend on the type of campaign that has been chosen for the act prior to the record's release.

When Publicists have something very important going on with one of their artists, they usually plan a press party or press conference to announce it. These press parties and conferences must only be used for special events. If this caution is not heeded, the media might not be interested on the next occasion, though the Publicist may really have something important to unveil. In addition, because of the great expense of these press functions, executives usually like them limited in frequency.

Publicists stay on the phone a great deal of the time, calling media and trying to interest them in what is happening with their acts. When they are not on the phone or writing releases, Publicists are often at parties or functions meeting with the press and other people important to their clients.

Publicists are usually the first ones to send out promotional copies of new records to the media and other important materials. After a new record is released the Publicist might work with the A&R department or the promotion department on a showcase booking of the group. The Publicist might then decide that this is the proper time for an all-important press party.

The Publicist working for a record company often works closely with an act's personal publicist or P.R. firm. (Acts hire personal publicists and P.R. firms because they want more attention than a label Publicist can give them.) Label Publicists often work with up to ten acts each. As a rule, label Publicists zero in on creating publicity that will potentially sell more records. Personal Publicists work to create an image for the artist that will help to sustain him or her in the business longer.

The Publicist's hours are not the regular 9 to 5 most people work. Publicists work a long regular day and then go out to parties, clubs, and other functions to mingle with the press or to listen to acts they represent.

It is also the Publicist's job to set up interviews and appearances with the media when the act goes on tour. During big tours the Publicist works with a tour publicist and other tour personnel, coordinating tour publicity.

The staff Publicist is usually responsible to the Director of Publicity at the label. All the staff publicists meet regularly with this individual to map out strategies and handle any problems that come up.

Salaries

Salaries for Staff Publicists vary depending on the size of the record label one is working for and the amount of experience the Publicist has. Salaries can range from $12,000 for a beginning Publicist or a Publicist at a small label, to $55,000 at a bigger label. Salaries for Publicists can go up to $75,000 or more yearly if the Publicist is experienced, working at a big label, and has a great deal of responsibility. This salary level is rare, though. The average salary range for a Publicist at a label would be from $25,000 to $35,000 annually.

Employment Prospects

Although it is difficult to obtain a job other than one at entry level at a record label, if an individual can get into a company and can write well, he or she has a decent chance of landing a position in the publicity department.

There is a fairly high turnover of people in this department because individuals move around to various record labels. Bigger labels sometimes have an entry level position in this department. However, the individual might do nothing but fill press kits. As one gets more experience, he or she is usually given less tedious work and more interesting projects.

It is sometimes easier for an individual to find a job as a Publicist in a record company (because you can start out in an entry level position and move out of it fairly quickly), than as a Publicist in a music-oriented P.R. firm.

Advancement Prospects

As noted throughout this section, most positions in the record business allow for advancement fairly routinely. This is especially so in nonsupervisory capacities.

Publicists who do well at their jobs move into better positions in the department, such as supervising others or handling more prestigious clients.

Publicists with a proven track record at one label can usually find a job at another label without too much trouble.

Publicists also often gain experience at a label and then strike out on their own as independent Publicists or with a P.R. firm.

Education and Training

Different positions in publicity require different amounts and types of education. Not all positions at record companies require college degrees or backgrounds. However, these applicants are often preferred.

College courses or majors that might prove useful in this type of position include public relations, marketing, advertising, music merchandising, journalism, and communications.

In addition, there are a number of seminars offered by different organizations, associations, and colleges on publicity, promotion, and public relations as related to the music business.

Experience/Skills/Personality Traits

A Publicist working in a record company must be able to work under pressure, as deadlines must be met on a constant basis.

Publicists must have the ability to write well. Creativity is a plus; it helps to come up with new angles for acts. The Publicist must constantly keep making new media contacts. These people can make or break an act.

As the Publicist must go out after working hours quite frequently, he or she must have a lot of stamina and not mind having a business life and social life wrapped in one. Enjoying and appreciating music, especially the music of the acts being promoted, is helpful, too.

Unions/Associations

Staff Publicists working in a record company may belong to the Public Relations Society of America (PRSA). This organization is one of the best-known in the publicity and public relations field. It offers seminars, booklets, a magazine, and other helpful information to members.

The individual might also belong to the National Academy of Recording Arts and Sciences (NARAS) as an associate member.

Tips for Entry

1. Find out if the record company has an internship program and try to get into it. It's worth working for nothing (or a small salary) for a summer or a short period of time if you can gain entry into one of these programs. Not only is the experience worthwhile, but you also have an excellent chance of being hired after the internship ends.

2. Prepare your resume and a few samples of your writing style. Send these with a cover letter to personnel departments or publicity directors of record companies.

3. There are a number of employment agencies specializing in public relations and publicity jobs. Call or write to them about openings in the record companies.

4. There are also a limited number of employment agencies specializing in jobs in the music business. Check these out.

5. If you have any contacts in the record business, this is the time to use them. See if they will help you get your foot in the door.

ARTIST RELATIONS AND DEVELOPMENT REPRESENTATIVE

CAREER PROFILE

Duties: Acting as a liaison between a record company and one or more of their signed artists

Alternate Title(s): Artist Relations and Development Staffer

Salary Range: $12,000 to $30,000

Employment Prospects: Poor

Advancement Prospects: Fair

Best Geographical Location(s) for Position: New York City, Los Angeles, Nashville

Prerequisite:

Education or Training—High school diploma minimum; college degree may be preferred

Experience—Experience in public relations, publicity, or artist management helpful

Special Skills and Personality Traits—Knowledge of music and record business; ability to deal effectively with people

CAREER LADDER

```
┌─────────────────────────────────────────┐
│  Artist Relations and Development Director │
└─────────────────────────────────────────┘

┌─────────────────────────────────────────┐
│         Artist Relations and             │
│      Development Representative           │
└─────────────────────────────────────────┘

┌─────────────────────────────────────────┐
│         Publicist/P.R. Counselor;        │
│                 Intern                    │
└─────────────────────────────────────────┘
```

Position Description

The Artist Relations and Development Representative is a position that is not present in every record company. Certain companies either are too small to retain people in this position, or they delegate the responsibilities normally taken care of by the Artist Relations and Development Rep to other departments.

Duties of the Artist Relations and Development Representative differ, too, depending on the company. If the record company does have this department, most often it is the Representative's responsibility to act as a liaison between the company and its artists. The Representative makes sure that the artist feels that the record company is treating him or her specially. For example, the Artist Relations and Development Rep might send roses on behalf of the record company to a female singer whose record just went gold. The Rep might make sure that a group is sent a bottle of champagne before kicking off a prestigious tour. In essence, the Artist Relations and Development

Representative makes sure that there is a good relationship developed between the artists and the record company, not only businesswise, but socially, too. The record business is unique in that business life and social life blend into one.

The Artist Relations and Development Representative keeps in close contact with the act and their management. He or she listens for potential problems that might involve the record company. When the individual hears of any developing problems, he or she takes care of them (or, if unable to solve the problems, brings them to the attention of someone who can).

The Artist Relations and Development Representative works with the act and its management to help build their career. The Reps work with all the different departments of the record company, doing such things as planning promotional concert tours in conjunction with record releases. The Rep makes sure that the tour coincides with the record release. If it turns out that a tour has to begin three weeks later than anticipated, the Rep might discuss with the record company executives the option of holding up the release for a short time.

The Artist Relations and Development Representative might also work with the publicity department or the group's P.R. firm in coordinating television, radio, and promotional public appearances.

At times, the individual will attend an act's concert and review their performance. He or she might make suggestions on how the act could improve their performance or stage presentation.

The Artist Relations and Development Representative usually becomes quite friendly with the act and its management team. He or she might remain friends with the act long after their recording contract has expired and the group has moved on to another company.

This is another position in the record industry in which long, irregular hours are maintained. To be successful at this job, an individual must really love both music and people.

Salaries

An Artist Relations and Development Representative has a salary range of $12,000 to $30,000 annually. The salary of the individual will depend on the size of the record company he or she is working with. Salary is also dependent on the individual's duties and qualifications.

Employment Prospects

Since not every record label has this position, it is often difficult to find openings. Once again, there are many people who want to work in this department of a record company and a limited number of positions.

Individuals who want to work in this type of situation but cannot find this position or cannot find an opening in this department might want to look for jobs in publicity and public relations. Then, when an opening is located, the individual will have a range of experience in the field as a backup.

Advancement Prospects

As in most positions in a record company, once an individual gets his or her foot in the door, there is a fair chance for advancement and promotion. In order to be promoted, there must be an opening in an advanced position. Individuals may direct their career into another department for advancement.

Education and Training

Although often there is no educational requirement above a high school diploma, a college degree or background might be the thing that separates one applicant from another. Courses in publicity, promotion, journalism, English, and communications might be helpful. There are also degrees offered by various colleges in music merchandising and the music business.

It is also wise to take part in any seminar or program available where you can learn, as well as develop contacts.

Experience/Skills/Personality Traits

Most individuals who work in the artist relations and development department have had some type of experience in promotion, publicity, or public relations. Others have worked in artist management.

The successful Artist Relations and Development Representative must have a knowledge of both music and the record business. He or she must attend many shows and concerts, concentrating on other acts and their stage appearances, concerts, performances, etc.

He or she must not only have the ability to deal with people, but must also like to do so. Many times an act makes strange or uncalled-for requests of the record company. The Rep must have the ability to deny such a request and still keep them relatively happy.

Unions/Associations

The Artist Relations and Development Representative in a record company might belong to the Country Music Association (CMA), the Gospel Music Association (GMA), and/or the Black Music Association (BMA), depending on the variety of musical artists he or she represents. The individual may also be an associate member of the National Academy of Recording Arts and Sciences (NARAS).

Tips for Entry

1. Attend as many seminars and programs as you can to learn the business and develop contacts.
2. As with many other record company jobs, you might have to accept an entry level position to get to the position you want. People are promoted if they have the drive and the qualifications.
3. Try to find a record company with either a summer internship program or a college internship program and request to be placed in this department. This way you will have an "in" when you finish school.

MARKETING REPRESENTATIVE

CAREER PROFILE

Duties: Overseeing specific markets; reporting sales of records to radio stations and trades

Alternate Title(s): Marketing Staffer

Salary Range: $14,000 to $25,000

Employment Prospects: Fair

Advancement Prospects: Poor

Best Geographical Location(s) for Position: New York City, Los Angeles, Nashville; record company may send rep to various other cities

Prerequisites:

Education or Training—High school diploma

Experience—Intern position helpful but not necessary

Special Skills and Personality Traits—Communication skills; understanding of and knowledge of music and record business; ability with numbers

CAREER LADDER

```
┌──────────────────────────────────────┐
│  Regional Director of Marketing;      │
│  Regional Representative              │
└──────────────────────────────────────┘

┌──────────────────────────────────────┐
│  Local Marketing Representative       │
└──────────────────────────────────────┘

┌──────────────────────────────────────┐
│  Field Merchandiser;                  │
│  Intern;                              │
│  Clerical Position in Record Company  │
└──────────────────────────────────────┘
```

Position Description

A Marketing Representative for a record company may work on a local or regional level. The prime function of the marketing department in the record company is to develop various ways to market and sell the company's records. The Marketing Representative will help execute this function.

Depending on the position held, the Marketing Representative oversees marketing activities in a certain area. A local Rep will oversee specific markets. The regional Rep will oversee entire regions. For example, a local Rep may be in charge of the marketing in Philadelphia. The regional Marketing Representative or director would be in charge of the entire northeast section of the United States, which would include Philadelphia.

Regardless of territory, the individuals have the same function and duties. The first, mentioned above, is to oversee the marketing of the records. To accomplish this, the Reps will work under the supervision of the director of marketing to assist in implementing such marketing strategies as delivering displays for a number of the label's hot acts to record shops or setting up window displays in the record stores. Other ideas might not involve stores directly. The concepts might revolve around radio station giveaway contests with the label's new records or T-shirts, bumper stickers, posters, etc. as prizes. The marketing department often offers radio stations and record shops in a specific area joint promotions, such as promotional appearances in a record shop by a hot group combined with radio station album giveaways.

The Marketing Representative is also responsible for calling and/or visiting record stores in a specific area to make sure that they have sufficient records on hand to meet possible demands. This often occurs after a group has won an award or a gold record or appeared in concert in the city.

The Marketing Representative gets reports of record sales from the various shops and stores in the specific market. He or she will call these in to the radio stations, major trades, and tip sheets. This is the method many record stores and radio stations use to develop the music charts.

The Marketing Representative reports directly to his or her supervisor. In most cases, that is the director of marketing. The local Rep may also report to the regional director of marketing. Hours are irregular. There is often a great deal of travel associated with this job.

Salaries

Salaries for Marketing Representatives vary according to the positions they hold and the companies they work for. A Marketing Rep can expect $14,000 to $25,000 annually.

Employment Prospects

If an individual can find a way into the record company, he or she has a fair chance of becoming a Marketing Representative. One of the better ways of getting a job in the marketing department is by working as in intern for the department.

Major record labels hire a fairly large number of Reps. Other labels hire a smaller number of people for these positions. Numbers depend on the size of the company.

Advancement Prospects

Marketing Representatives can advance their careers by becoming regional Reps or regional directors of marketing. The individual may be promoted to the position of marketing director or a specific type of music, such as black or R & B music, gospel music, etc. The Rep can further advance his or her career by becoming the national marketing director of a label.

Education and Training

The only education usually required to be a Marketing Representative is a high school diploma. There are individuals in the marketing department who hold bachelor's or even master's degrees. These are not necessary, but are sometimes useful. Individuals desiring a higher educational background may want to take courses in marketing, business, advertising, etc. There are a number of colleges that offer music business or music merchandising degrees. Keep in mind that these degrees do not guarantee a job, but are helpful in preparing for one.

Experience/Skills/Personality Traits

Experience in a record company is useful for work in this field. One of the best ways to get this experience is to look for an intern position in the department. These jobs give the individual an invaluable hands-on learning experience.

Marketing Representatives must also be literate, articulate, and good with numbers. Creativity is a plus. Understanding of the music business and a complete knowledge of the record industry is essential.

Unions/Associations

Marketing Representatives may belong to a number of associations. These include the Country Music Association (CMA), the Black Music Association (BMA), the Gospel Music Association (GMA), the National Academy of Recording Arts and Sciences (NARAS), and a host of others.

Tips for Entry

1. Try to find an internship in a record company's marketing department. This opportunity might come through either the record company or a college.
2. If you already have a job in a record company, possibly in the clerical end, volunteer to do some work for the marketing department. Learn the business.
3. Get a job in a large record store and make contacts with Marketing Representatives who visit and/or call the store. They might be able to get you an appointment for an interview.

CONSUMER RESEARCHER

CAREER PROFILE

Duties: Researching and analyzing consumer buying practices for the record company

Alternate Title(s): Market Researcher; Market Analyst

Salary Range: $14,000 to $25,000

Employment Prospects: Fair

Advancement Prospects: Fair

Best Geographical Location(s) for Position: New York City, Los Angeles, Nashville

Prerequisites:

Education or Training—Bachelor's degree in business usually preferred; master's degree sometimes required

Experience—Working as a research assistant or trainee in any field; conducting interviews and opinion polls

Special Skills and Personality Traits—Knowledge of research and analytical methods; ability to write reports; knowledge of music business and record industry

CAREER LADDER

```
┌─────────────────────────────┐
│     Marketing Staffer       │
└─────────────────────────────┘

┌─────────────────────────────┐
│    Consumer Researcher      │
└─────────────────────────────┘

┌─────────────────────────────┐
│ Research Assistant or Trainee│
└─────────────────────────────┘
```

Position Description

The marketing and/or sales departments of record companies hire Consumer Researchers. These people have interesting jobs. Their main function is to research consumer buying practices for the record company. After the data have been compiled, they must be analyzed by the Consumer Researcher. With this information the marketing and/or sales department can develop a better understanding of the various types of records people want to buy or have previously purchased.

The Consumer Researcher—or market researcher, as he or she is sometimes referred to—may secure information on the record-buying public in a number of ways. The first step the individual usually takes is to decide the method or methods that will be used in finding information. The Consumer Researcher may collect facts from the record company and its various departments. Information they might seek out are types of records that have sold previously; the number of records of each style that were sold during a certain

time period (e.g., pop, classical, R & B, fold, etc.), and the geographical location in which each variety sold well.

The individual might then research facts about records that were sold on other labels. This is usually much more difficult, as companies seldom like to help their competitors. However, the Consumer Researcher may talk to distributors, record shops, rack jobbers, etc. in order to gather such data.

Another method of checking out consumer buying practices is to prepare a survey. An interview might be given by the individual directly, or he or she might train a number of people in a variety of markets to handle the project. The Consumer Researcher might also choose to interview consumers by phone on their buying habits. All of the different methods may be used to secure results.

After the surveys or the interviews have been completed, the Consumer Researcher will have to tabulate and analyze the data collected. From these surveys, the individual very often can obtain information about customer opinions and tastes in record buying. This tells the marketing and/or sales department what type of records to market, the best sales locations, and more effective ways to do the job.

The Consumer Researcher in a record company must be very knowledgeable about records, target markets, the music business, and the recording industry in order to know the types of questions to ask in a survey interview or opinion poll. Individuals in this field work closely with the marketing director and the department staff. The Consumer Researcher may recommend test marketing of certain records in specific areas. In other situations, the individual may recommend for or against the release of a certain record in an area because of his or her test marketing. The head of the marketing department has the option of listening to recommendations or ignoring them. The amount of authority the Researcher has, of course, depends on the position and the structure of the department.

Salaries

Consumer Researchers working for record companies may earn $14,000 to $25,000 annually. Salaries will depend on the size of the record company, its location, and the qualifications and duties of the Consumer Researcher.

Employment Prospects

Those who are qualified have a fair chance of obtaining a job as a Consumer Researcher in a record company. Marketing and/or sales departments of major labels usually hire a good number of Consumer Researchers. Smaller labels frequently hire a limited number, too.

There is competition in every phase of the record company, especially in larger labels. The more qualified an individual is for this job, the better his or her chances for employment.

Advancement Prospects

Consumer Researchers may advance their careers in a number of ways. The individual may assume responsibility for bigger and better projects. He or she might move into a supervisory position in the research department. Another possibility for advancement is for the individual to become a member of the marketing staff—a marketing coordinator or vice-president of marketing. As in all positions in record companies, advancement really depends on the individual and on the structure of the label.

Education and Training

A good solid education is necessary for this type of job. A bachelors degree is usually required. A masters degree is sometimes preferred. Majors may be in business administration, marketing or any related field. Courses in computer technology or data processing are extremely helpful.

Experience/Skills/Personality Traits

Individuals who aspire to get into the marketing end of the recording industry may be interested in consumer research. Those who become Consumer Researchers need the know-how to delve into consumer buying habits. The Consumer Researcher must know how to analyze the data and render an understandable final report for supervisors. In order to excel at this type of job, a thorough knowledge of the music business and recording industry is essential.

Unions/Associations

There is no union for Consumer Researchers. Individuals may belong to advertising associations, such as the American Advertising Federation (AAF) or the American Marketing Association (AMA). Both these organizations provide information and assistance to people in this field.

Tips for Entry

1. Get experience in consumer research in any field.
2. Become a pollster for a new product, a corporation, a new service, etc.
3. This is one of the jobs in which a good education really helps. The more qualified you are, the better your chance of employment.
4. These jobs are often listed in the classified sections of newspapers in the major music capitals.

ADVERTISING ACCOUNT EXECUTIVE

CAREER PROFILE

Duties: Developing advertising campaigns for a record label's products

Alternate Title(s): Account Representative

Salary Range: $18,000 to $35,000+

Employment Prospects: Fair

Advancement Prospects: Poor

Best Geographical Location(s) for Position: New York City, Los Angeles, Nashville

Prerequisites:

Education or Training—College degree in advertising, marketing, or a related area preferred

Experience—Copywriter; advertising executive in nonmusic-related agency

Special Skills and Personality Traits—Creativity; ability to work under pressure; knowledge of advertising skills and technology; cognizance of music and record industry

CAREER LADDER

```
┌─────────────────────────────────┐
│      Director of Advertising     │
└─────────────────────────────────┘

┌─────────────────────────────────┐
│  Advertising Account Executive   │
└─────────────────────────────────┘

┌─────────────────────────────────┐
│     Advertising Copywriter;      │
│  Advertising Account Executive in│
│    Nonmusic-Oriented Agency      │
└─────────────────────────────────┘
```

Position Description

An Advertising Account Executive in a record company develops advertising campaigns for the label's products. The main purpose of the advertising campaign is to make the public aware that a certain record has been released and is in the stores. If the public knows about a record, it is hoped, they will buy it.

The Advertising Account Executive or representative, as he or she may be called, is usually assigned a certain number of acts and/or records to work with. This assignment generally comes from the director of the advertising department.

A lot of work goes into planning an advertising campaign for a new record. The Account Executive may study other campaigns used for the specific artist and/or record or might look over other programs. The individual will consider the act's public image and decide what type of people the advertising should hit. For example, if the Account Executive is developing a campaign for a teenage "bubble gum" recording act, the individual will gear the advertising to teenagers and other young people. If an act has put out a hard rock album, the Account Executive will probably gear the advertising to a hard rock audience.

Depending on the size and the structure of the record company, the Account Executive may not only have to develop advertising campaigns for the new records, but may also have to do the artwork and/or copywriting, too. The Advertising Representative may also have to negotiate contracts for advertising space or air time.

The Advertising Account Executive in the record company must have a total understanding of the recording industry and the acts and/or records for which he or she is developing campaigns. The individual needs to work with many of the other departments in the record company to obtain useful information and ideas for an advertising program. For example, the rep may work with the promotion or publicity departments, putting together a total campaign that includes advertising, promotional appearances in record stores, and television and radio interviews.

In this position, the individual must have the ability to know which types of advertising will be most effective for the money. He or she must decide whether ads should be run on TV or radio, in newspapers, magazines, or trades, or on billboards, etc. Decisions must also be made as to which ads should be run locally and which ads should be run nationally. Often, when a large record store or chain advertises a specific record or group of records, the label picks up the cost of the ad.

It is very important for the Advertising Account Executive to be able to stay within the budget allocated to each record.

Account Executives have frequent meetings with the director of the department. During these sessions new concepts, problems, and budgets are discussed. It is also during these times that the effectiveness of the campaigns are evaluated.

The individual in this job works long hours. He or she is responsible to the director of advertising.

Salaries

Advertising Account Executives in a record company earn from $18,000 to $35,000+ annually. Salaries will vary depending on the size of the record company and the experience and duties of the individual.

Employment Prospects

Employment prospects are fair for an individual who is trained and qualified in this area. Those who are knowledgeable about both advertising and the recording industry have better prospects. The Advertising Account Executive who has proven him or herself in this field should be able to find employment. Large and mid-size record companies usually have advertising departments. Many of the smaller labels use the services of an outside advertising agency.

Advancement Prospects

Advancement is difficult for an Advertising Account Executive working in a record company. To move up the career ladder, the individual can seek out the same type of position in a larger, more prestigious company. This type of advancement would probably mean more responsibility and a higher salary. The individual may move into the position of Director of Advertising in a record company. Many Advertising Account Executives obtain jobs in advertising agencies not affiliated with music.

Education and Training

Although it is not always required, a college degree in advertising, marketing, or a related area is usually preferred by most record companies. Degree programs in these fields may be found in many colleges and universities around the country.

There are many seminars, workshops, and additional courses in advertising and the music and recording industry that are beneficial to an Advertising Account Executive.

Experience/Skills/Personality Traits

The person working in this position must be very creative. He or she must have the ability to come up with unique, effective advertising campaigns for new records. The Account Executive must be knowledgeable about all advertising skills and technology including copywriting, the use of audiovisuals, graphics, etc.

An ability to work under intense pressure is necessary.

Many record companies prefer that the staff of their advertising department have prior experience in the field. Other companies prefer to train staff themselves.

Unions/Associations

Advertising Account Executives working in record companies may belong to the National Academy of Recording Arts and Sciences (NARAS) as associate members. Individuals might also belong to the American Advertising Federation (AAF).

Tips for Entry

1. Look for an internship in the advertising department of a record company. This is one of the best ways to learn about the business. Chances of landing a paying job with the label after the internship are good, too.

2. Get a good education or solid training. Many of the things you will need to know for this type of position are taught in a school setting. You're better off making any major mistakes working on an advertising project for school than directly on the job.

3. If you can't find a job in a record company's advertising department, look into an advertising job in a nonmusic-oriented advertising agency. After you obtain some experience, try the record labels again.

REGIONAL SALES MANAGER

CAREER PROFILE

Duties: Supervising the selling of the label's records and tapes to wholesalers and/or retail outlets; creating sales campaigns and policies; overseeing staff of department and/or region

Alternate Title(s): Regional Director of Sales; District Sales Manager

Salary Range: $25,000 to $65,000+

Employment Prospects: Poor

Advancement Prospects: Poor

Best Geographical Location(s) for Position: New York City, Los Angeles, Nashville; may also work and/or live in major market target cities such as Atlanta, Philadelphia, Chicago, Detroit, etc. This depends on the company's structure.

Prerequisites:

Education or Training—High school diploma minimum; some positions require college degree

Experience—Retail and/or wholesale sales experience, salesperson for record company

Special Skills and Personality Traits—Superb sales techniques; cognizance of record industry; knowledge of music business; ability to lead and direct others; ability to work under pressure

CAREER LADDER

```
┌─────────────────────────────┐
│   National Sales Director   │
└─────────────────────────────┘

┌─────────────────────────────┐
│   Regional Sales Manager    │
└─────────────────────────────┘

┌─────────────────────────────┐
│        Salesperson          │
└─────────────────────────────┘
```

Position Description

A Regional Sales Manager of a record company is in charge of selling the label's records to wholesalers and/or retail outlets in the specific region assigned. Depending on the structure of the company, regions might be divided into different segments of the country. The most popular divisions include the northeastern region, the southeastern region, the southwestern region, the midwest region, and the western region. It is in these markets that the greatest concentration of selling occurs.

The Regional Sales Manager must see to it that a specific amount of merchandise is sold each month. These sales quotas can run into hundreds of thousands of dollars. This "demand" selling can lead to a lot of pressure. In order to meet these huge quotas, the individual must work closely with both the national sales director and the salespeople in the region.

In this position, the individual is in charge of creating sales campaigns for his or her region. The Regional Sales Manager designs these campaigns with the help of the national sales director. Together, all the Regional Sales Managers and the national director work out the sales policies they will use in selling the product. These programs include merchandise return policies, the number of records one is required to buy in order to qualify for discounts, etc.

As a Regional Sales Manager or director of sales, the person may be responsible for interviewing, hiring, and training salespeople. Each company has different methods and techniques for selling their product.

The Regional Sales Manager must keep a close watch on how salespeople in his or her region are producing. The region usually consists of a number of cities; for example, the northeast region might include Baltimore, Boston, Hartford, New York City, Philadelphia, and surrounding areas. The Regional Sales Manager must supervise each salesperson in each of these cities.

If sales activity slacks off in any particular area, the individual must check into it, find out what is wrong, and correct the situation. It may be that the city requires additional promotion. In that case, the Regional Sales Manager would contact the promotion department. It could be that a certain record needs more of an advertising push in a specific area. The individual must know whom to contact in case of a problem and do so rapidly. Loss of sales for even one week will negatively affect the sales quota for the month.

At times, the Regional Sales Manager may feel that the salespeople in an area just aren't doing a good job. It is up to him or her to talk to the individuals, give them some pointers or a pep talk, and get them selling again.

The Sales Manager is also responsible for making sure that the salespeople in the various areas are servicing all accounts. That means that all accounts must be called upon on a regular basis, phone calls returned, and orders filled rapidly. If this is not happening, the Sales Manager is not doing a competent job.

The Regional Sales Manager works long hours, travels extensively, and works under a great deal of pressure to meet sales quotas. He or she is responsible directly to the national sales director.

Salaries

The Regional Sales Manager of a major recording company will do quite well financially. In addition to a regular salary, the individual often receives commissions on the products sold in his or her region.

Individuals working in smaller companies will earn considerably less than their counterparts from the major labels.

The Regional Sales Manager earns $25,000 to $65,000+.

Employment Prospects

Employment prospects for Regional Sales Managers in major record companies are limited. There are only a few major record companies and each has only a certain number of Sales Manager positions. Jobs are difficult to come by, but are obtainable.

Opportunities might be slightly better with smaller companies or independent labels.

Advancement Prospects

Advancement is slow. To move up the career ladder, one would probably want to become the national sales director of a label. These jobs are more limited than Regional Sales Manager positions.

If one does a really great job as a Regional Sales Manager, one advancement opportunity might be for the individual to move to a position at a bigger or more prestigious label but remain in the Regional Sales Manager position. One may also obtain a better and bigger region as a form of career advancement.

Education and Training

There are many Sales Managers of record companies with just a high school diploma. It is really all that they require. There are some positions, however, that require a bachelor's degree. For those who are currently planning on attending college, thought should be given to the new courses and degrees in music business and/or music merchandising. These degrees and courses will not obtain a job for the individual, but they will certainly help with some background and knowledge about the industry. This extra know-how might prove helpful. Many of the schools also offer internships in cooperation with record companies.

Experience/Skills/Personality Traits

A Regional Sales Manager for a record company must be familiar with the entire record industry and have a basic knowledge of the music business. The individual must have proven that he or she was a superb salesperson. An ability to lead and direct others is necessary to succeed in this business. The individual must also be able to work effectively under pressure, as it is a constant in this position.

Unions/Associations

Sales Managers working for record companies may belong to the National Association of Recording Merchandisers (NARM). This organization provides a forum for people in the recorded music industry. Individuals might also be members of the Country Music Association (CMA), the Black Music Association (BMA), and/or the Gospel Music Association (GMA).

Tips for Entry
1. These positions are generally not advertised. As a rule, the Regional Sales Managers are chosen from the ranks of salespeople working for the company. The first step to take is to obtain a job in the sales department.
2. This is another of the jobs in which contacts help. If you have them, use them to help you get an interview.
3. On occasion, the Regional Sales Manager might also be chosen from another department. Keep your eyes and ears open. Find out what is happening in the company and go for it.

SALESPERSON

CAREER PROFILE

Duties: Selling the company's records and tapes; servicing accounts

Alternate Title(s): Sales Representative

Salary Range: $16,000 to $35,000+

Employment Prospects: Fair

Advancement Prospects: Fair

Best Geographical Location(s) for Position: New York City, Los Angeles, Nashville, Atlanta, Chicago, Philadelphia, Jacksonville, Miami, Detroit, etc.

Prerequisites:

Education or Training—High school diploma minimum; some positions require bachelor's degree

Experience—Retail and/or wholesale jobs helpful

Special Skills and Personality Traits—Good sales skills; aggressiveness; reliability; knowledge of music and records; ability to work under pressure

CAREER LADDER

```
┌─────────────────────────────────┐
│                                 │
│     Regional Sales Manager      │
│                                 │
└─────────────────────────────────┘

┌─────────────────────────────────┐
│                                 │
│          Salesperson            │
│                                 │
└─────────────────────────────────┘

┌─────────────────────────────────┐
│                                 │
│     Salesperson in Related      │
│        or Unrelated Field       │
│                                 │
└─────────────────────────────────┘
```

Position Description

A Salesperson at a record company sells the label's records and tapes. He or she does this by physically visiting accounts, mailing out letters and other information, and/or making phone calls. The person's accounts may include retail stores, rack jobbers and one-stops. In order to meet the sales quota usually imposed by regional managers, the Salesperson must constantly service his or her accounts competently.

The individual should be totally knowledgeable about the company's catalog. Although a good number of records sold are new releases, the Salesperson must be aware of the label's older releases, too. The retailer, rack jobber, and one-stops might ask the Salesperson questions regarding a new release's sales in other areas of the country. The individual, therefore, should stay informed about as many record-related matters as possible.

After discussing any questions the buyer might have and talking about the new releases available, the Salesperson will take the order. He or she will let the purchaser know what costs are, the types of discounts available, and how much of the product it is necessary to purchase in order to qualify for the discounts. The Salesperson may also talk about any special promotions that are available to the retailer.

The Salesperson will probably visit a number of accounts each day. Certain days may be set aside for handling correspondence and/or phone work. Depending on the structure of the company, the Salesperson might have other duties in retail shops. These duties might include taking inventory of the company's records and tapes, suggesting which records and tapes should be reordered, setting up in-store displays or window displays, etc.

Once a Salesperson has received an order, the individual must call it in to be filled. The individual must check back periodically to make sure that orders have been received on time. If they have not, the individual must bring the matter to the attention of the regional sales manager and have it taken care of.

The Salesperson talks to and/or sees the regional sales manager on a regular basis. The Salesperson must attend periodic sales and strategy meetings.

Salaries

Salespeople are compensated in various ways. They may earn a straight salary, a salary plus a commission on sales made, or a commission against a basic salary.

It is difficult to estimate the yearly earnings of a Salesperson in a record company because of the different salary structures, the sizes of various record companies, and the amount of product sold.

Generally, a salary for a Salesperson working for a record company might range from $16,000 to $35,000+.

Employment Prospects

Employment prospects are fair for those interested in working as a record company Salesperson. Good Salespeople are hard to find in any industry, and this includes the record business. The opportunities for people to work for major companies in locations other than the three major music capitals expands the prospects. Major record companies employ large numbers of Salespeople in all the music markets, which include New York City, Los Angeles, Nashville, Memphis, Atlanta, Philadelphia, Chicago, Jacksonville, Miami, Detroit, Baltimore, and a host of others.

Advancement Prospects

If a Salesperson shows superior selling skills, he or she may be promoted to regional sales manager or another supervisory position. Selling skills are proven to management when Salespeople meet and exceed their monthly quotas, obtain new accounts, and service old ones well.

Education and Training

A high school degree is the minimum educational requirement for a Salesperson in a record company. Certain positions, however, may require a bachelor's degree. Courses that can be useful include marketing, sales, music merchandising, finance, and others in related areas.

Experience/Skills/Personality Traits

Salespeople working for record companies need many of the same skills and/or experiences found in other sales jobs. The person may find that retail and/or wholesale selling experience is helpful.

A good Salesperson has good sales and interpersonal skills. He or she should be aggressive, articulate, and reliable. The individual needs to be able to work under heavy pressure in order to meet sales quotas. The person working in this situation also needs a knowledge of music and records to be effective on the job.

Unions/Associations

Salespeople working for a record company might be members of the National Association of Recording Merchandisers (NARM). NARM is an association that provides a forum for those in the recorded music business.

Tips for Entry

1. Apply to a field office of a major record company. These may be located in Philadelphia, Jacksonville, Miami, Chicago, Detroit, Baltimore, or one of a host of other cities, depending on the structure of the record company.
2. Send a resumé and a cover letter directly to the record company. You might want to send one to the national sales director and one to the personnel department to make sure the proper person sees it.
3. If you do send your resumé or a letter, try to find out the person's name you are sending it to. Try to send it to a specific name, such as Mr. John Jones, Director of Sales, etc.
4. Remember to include all your sales achievements, not just music-oriented ones. If you had a 90% conversion rate selling vacuum cleaners door to door, chances are you will be a great Salesperson for any product.

FIELD MERCHANDISER

CAREER PROFILE

Duties: Distributing and explaining merchandising promotions to record shops and departments in specific markets

Alternate Title(s): Merchandising Rep

Salary Range: $12,500 to $20,000

Employment Prospects: Fair

Advancement Prospects: Fair

Best Geographical Location(s) for Position: Major markets are New York City, Los Angeles, and Nashville. The individual may also work in other cities, including Atlanta, Memphis, Miami, San Francisco, Philadelphia, Boston, Chicago, Detroit, and others

Prerequisites:

Education or Training—High school degree minimum

Experience—Some type of sales experience helpful

Special Skills and Personality Traits—Pleasant personality; knowledge of music and/or the record industry; communication skills; good rapport with people

CAREER LADDER

```
┌─────────────────────────────────────┐
│      Merchandising Coordinator;      │
│           Salesperson;               │
│      Marketing Representative;       │
│   Merchandising Representative       │
└─────────────────────────────────────┘

┌─────────────────────────────────────┐
│                                     │
│         Field Merchandiser          │
│                                     │
└─────────────────────────────────────┘

┌─────────────────────────────────────┐
│             Intern;                 │
│         Clerical Position           │
└─────────────────────────────────────┘
```

Position Description

A Field Merchandiser works for the record company in the marketing, merchandising, sales, or promotion department, depending on the structure of the company. The individual in this position travels to record stores and the record departments of stores in his or her territory. The Field Merchandiser distributes promotional displays, posters, contests, and merchandising aids to these locations. Displays might include record or tape holders, posters, window displays, pictures, or album covers. Additional possibilities would be contest entry blanks, T-shirts, buttons, bumper stickers, and other merchandising items relating to the label's acts.

The individual may physically set up the displays or may just give the owner or manager of the shop or department advice on how to set it up, describe where it would be most effective, etc. If there is a promotion under way, such as an album giveaway, the Field Merchandiser will explain the promotion in detail to the manager or owner. If the record company has set up an in-store appearance or a promotional concert in the area, the individual may bring in concert tickets, flyers, posters, or other items and make sure that everything is moving according to schedule.

The Field Merchandiser travels for the majority of his or her working days. The individual keeps in close contact with the supervisor of the department. The Field Merchandiser is also required to attend staff meetings. At these meetings, new promotions and merchandise are discussed. The talk may also turn to which retailers are using the merchandising displays and which ones are not. Ideas are often exchanged concerning better methods to entice shop owners and managers into using the merchandise.

The individual in this position may also check the store's inventory of the label's records while attending to other tasks. If a supply is low, the Field Merchandiser will contact the salesperson or sales manager responsible for servicing the area.

Salaries

Field Merchandisers can expect to earn a salary of $12,500 to $20,000 per year. Salaries will vary for individuals depending on the size of the record company, the location, the experience of the Field Merchandiser, and his or her exact duties.

Employment Prospects

Employment prospects are fair for Field Merchandisers. The individual has opportunities to work not only in the major markets of New York City, Los Angeles, and Nashville, but in other regions as well. These might include Atlanta, Memphis, Miami, San Francisco, Philadelphia, Boston, Chicago, Detroit, Baltimore, and Houston, among others.

Advancement Prospects

A Field Merchandiser may move up the career ladder to be a marketer, a merchandising coordinator, a salesperson, a sales manager, etc. The possibilities are limitless.

Education and Training

There is no specific educational requirement for this job. A high school degree is sufficient in some positions. If the individual wants to advance his or her career, additional training may be useful. In many companies, this position is looked on as an entry level job. A background in business, marketing, or music merchandising may prove helpful.

Experience/Skills/Personality Traits

It helps a Field Merchandiser to have some type of sales experience prior to taking the job, although it is not always necessary. Possessing a pleasant personality and establishing a good rapport with people makes the job easier. Being articulate is a plus. A knowledge of the music and/or record industry is essential.

Unions/Associations

Field Merchandisers may belong to the National Association of Recording Merchandisers (NARM). This organization represents people that work in recorded music. While regular membership is open to record shops, distributors, rack jobbers, etc., associate membership is open to others who work in the industry.

Tips for Entry

1. Try to obtain a job in a large record store in a major market for a short time. In this position, you will often have the opportunity to meet Field Merchandisers, salespeople, promotion people, etc. Get to know them and ask about the proper person to talk to about a job in the company.
2. If you do work in a record shop or department that deals directly with record company personnel, your boss (the store owner or manager) might be able to help you. Ask the management person whether they would make a call on your behalf to the company person they deal with from the record label to inquire about setting up an interview for you.
3. If there is an opportunity open to obtain an internship in the marketing or merchandising department, grab it.

INTERN

CAREER PROFILE

Duties: Performing tasks in specific departments of a record company while learning the business under the direction of management.

Alternate Title(s): Trainee

Salary Range: $0 to $12,000

Employment Prospects: Fair

Advancement Prospects: Good

Best Geographical Location(s) for Position: New York City, Los Angeles, Nashville

Prerequisites:

Education or Training—High school diploma minimum; other requirements depend on position

Experience—No experience required

Special Skills and Personality Traits—Eagerness to learn; desire to enter record industry; brightness; aggressiveness; knowledge of music and/or recording business; other skills dependent on specific position

CAREER LADDER

```
┌──────────────────────────────┐
│                              │
│    Staffer in Department     │
│                              │
└──────────────────────────────┘

┌──────────────────────────────┐
│                              │
│           Intern             │
│                              │
└──────────────────────────────┘

┌──────────────────────────────┐
│     Clerical Position;       │
│         Student              │
│                              │
└──────────────────────────────┘
```

Position Description

An Intern working in a record company will perform many of the same duties as other people on staff. The Intern works under the direction of a department head, manager, or director. One of the advantages of obtaining an Intern position in a specific department is that the individual has the opportunity to learn the ropes from experienced people.

There are Interns in almost every department of a record company. In certain companies, one becomes an Intern in a specific department. In others, the individual's internship involves working in various departments of the company. Duties will depend on the department to which one is assigned. For instance, an Intern working in the publicity/press relations department may address envelopes for invitations to press parties, make calls to check whether various people will be attending press parties, and help make arrangements for the press function. As he or she gains experience the Intern might begin writing press

releases, attending meetings to work out publicity campaigns, calling the media to discuss a good story, etc.

An Intern working in the marketing department might work on consumer research surveys, tabulate data, and/or call radio stations and the trades with information about the number of records sold in a specific market. As time goes on, the Intern may learn to develop marketing campaigns, go out with field reps, or help the director create a sales incentive program.

The Intern usually begins by handling a lot of the tedious work that no one else wants to do. As he or she becomes more experienced, the individual learns how to perform more difficult tasks. Only the simplest of projects is performed without direct supervision.

Whether or not the Intern is getting paid a salary, he or she is expected to function like a paid employee. This includes arriving at work on time and not taking time off unnecessarily. It is to the

Intern's advantage to learn as much as possible through instruction, asking questions, and just working in a hands-on situation.

The individual is responsible to the supervisor or department head to whom he or she is assigned. If the Intern is using the program as part of a college credit experience, a paper on the work experience might be expected.

The Intern has a fairly good chance of becoming a member of the company staff after the internship has concluded.

Salaries

Interns may work and not earn a penny. If they do earn a salary, it is usually quite small. An individual who has obtained an internship through a college might get college credit for his or her work. If the person is working as an Intern and is lucky enough to receive a salary, it probably would range from $5,000 to $12,000.

Employment Prospects

Despite the low pay or even lack of a salary, many people want to work as Interns. Individuals seeking internships can find them in almost every department of every major record company. Smaller labels tend to offer fewer opportunities.

Although many of these internship programs may be located directly through the record company, there are a number that can be obtained through schools and colleges in return for college credit and hands-on experience.

Advancement Prospects

One of the major reasons so many people try to become Interns in this industry is that it almost guarantees a job in the record company. After all the training and instruction given to the individual, the company most likely will want to keep the intern in its employ. The person must, of course, be a good employee and learn the trade. Interns can advance their careers very quickly in most departments. They may first be promoted to staffers, and then become coordinators, supervisors, or directors in various departments.

Education and Training

To become an intern in a record company the only educational requirement may be a high school diploma. If an individual is currently in college, he or she may be able to have the school set up a internship program with a company for college credit. The person may be working toward a degree in any subject that can be made relevant to a semester or summer in a record company. Majors might include business, advertising, music, communications, journalism, the social sciences, prelaw, etc.

Experience/Skills/Personality Traits

Interns do not really need any experience. What is required is the desire to enter the record industry and an eagerness to learn all about it.

Individuals who are chosen to be Interns generally are bright and aggressive and have pleasant personalities. A knowledge of music and/or the recording business is a plus.

Unions/Associations

Interns do not usually belong to any union while working in a record company. They may, however, join associations relevant to the department in which they are working.

Tips for Entry

1. If you are in college, the school may know of some Intern positions in record companies. If the school has a music business or merchandising degree or offers courses, they might have an internship program already established with a record company.
2. You might consider writing a few of the major companies to see if you can work out an internship program.
3. If you live in one of the music capitals, you might want to visit the record companies personally to see if you can get an internship in one of the departments.
4. Interns are often chosen from the ranks of clerical workers in the office. Talk to the head of the department with which you want to work.

CAMPUS REPRESENTATIVE

CAREER PROFILE

Duties: Promoting record label's products on campus for students

Alternate Title(s): Student Representative; Label Representative; College Representative; Campus Rep

Salary Range: $1,000 to $3,500+

Employment Prospects: Poor

Advancement Prospects: Good

Best Geographical Location(s) for Position: Major campuses around the country

Prerequisites:

Education or Training—Working toward a bachelor's degree

Experience—Working with campus concerts; member of student activities or union board

Special Skills and Personality Traits—Enjoyment of music; ability to work without direct supervision; responsibility; knowledge of music and/or recording industry; desire to get into music business

CAREER LADDER

```
┌─────────────────────────────────┐
│   Record Company Intern;         │
│   Staff Member in Record Company │
└─────────────────────────────────┘

┌─────────────────────────────────┐
│   Campus Representative          │
└─────────────────────────────────┘

┌─────────────────────────────────┐
│   Student                        │
└─────────────────────────────────┘
```

Position Description

A Campus Representative is a student who is hired by a record company to promote that label's products on the campus. The student may work with or without pay. Products promoted may include the company's records, merchandising material, or concerts.

The student usually does his or her work in the campus bookstore, record shop, or student union. The individual will set up a display provided by the record company. There are a variety of displays or booths the Representative might set up. One might be a merchandising booth. This would be loaded with merchandising material related to the label's acts. It might include T-shirts, bumper stickers, pins, buttons, and posters. Another type of display might be a point-of-purchase exhibit. This might be set up in a record store or bookstore and contain the label's records. These displays are often quite elaborate.

The student may be responsible for checking the inventory of the records in the campus shop or in the shops surrounding area. When stock gets low,

the Rep notifies the distribution department. Conversely, if stock is not moving, the Representative might let the label know, so they can do some extra promotion in the area.

There are many other functions the individual might perform. These all depend on the specific label. At times, the Campus Rep may interview other students to find out how they feel about the label's records, acts, etc. This information would be relayed back to the correct department of the company.

Another duty of the Campus Representative may be to sell concert tickets for the label's acts when they perform on campus or in the immediate area. He or she might also put up posters or flyers in the area to promote the show. The individual may line up interviews with specific media personalities for the acts when they come to the college for a concert. The Rep could even interview the act him or herself for the campus paper, a local paper, or a radio station.

The job of Campus Representative is sought out by individuals aspiring to get into the recording industry. A position like this allows a person to pay dues while still in school. The position almost guarantees entry into a record company.

Salaries

Campus representatives may work with or without payment. When they do earn a salary, it usually isn't very high. A salary for a student in this position runs between $1,000 and $3,500+ a year.

The reason most people vie for this type of job is that it often leads to a position in the record company after graduation.

Those individuals who do not receive a salary will usually get free records, tapes, T-shirts, posters, and concert tickets.

Employment Prospects

The position of Campus Representative is not easy to obtain, but is possible. The problem is that not all labels use the services of such individuals. Once one finds a company that has a college department, though, prospects get better.

A person may also try to create a position such as this with any record company, even if it does not currently have Campus Representatives.

Advancement Prospects

Advancement prospects are fairly good for those who are Campus Representatives. Once a person works for a label, he or she has an excellent chance of obtaining a job after graduation. The label feels that the person has proven him or herself and is part of the company.

People who have worked in this job may advance to almost any position in the record company. It is important to remember that the hard part of getting a job in a record company is getting in. Advancement is easier to accomplish especially if the individual is bright and aggressive and wants to move up the career ladder.

Education and Training

Campus Representatives, as a rule, are concurrently attending a college or university in hopes of graduating and earning a degree. There are many different fields an individual might be study-

ing. These include communications, music, business, finance, journalism, advertising, marketing, or music merchandising. The list of majors is not limited to these and could be endless.

Experience/Skills/Personality Traits

Record companies usually choose bright, aggressive people to fill these positions. As many of these jobs pay either nothing or only a small salary, the person must really want to get into the record business. A knowledge of the industry and the music business, even if only basic, is helpful. An ability to work without direct day-to-day supervision is necessary.

Unions/Associations

Students who have these jobs do not have to belong to any union or associations. However, if they are interested in the music business, they probably belong to the student union or activity board of the college, work on school concert committees, and might represent the school at the National Entertainment Conference (NEC) and/or the National Entertainment and Campus Activities Association (NECCA). Both these organizations work to help all parties involved in booking concerts on campuses.

Tips for Entry

1. Campus Representative jobs may be obtained through the record company's college department. Call or write and inquire about these positions. If you do call, follow up with a letter and your resumé.
2. If the company does not have a college department, write to the public relations department, personnel director, or president of the company asking about Campus Representative positions.
3. In the event that a label does not use the services of a Campus Rep, don't let this stop you. Call, write, and/or set up an appointment for an interview to create a job for yourself. It sometimes works.

ARRANGER

Position Description

An Arranger's main function is to arrange the various parts of a musical composition. This is accomplished by determining voice, instrument, harmonic structure, rhythm, tempo, and tone balance to achieve the desired effect.

A talented Arranger can take a song and, through creative arranging, turn it into a hit tune. A good Arranger will be aware of current music trends. Trying to record a tune to the disco beat of the 1970's might not work in the 1980's.

One of the functions of the Arranger is to transcribe a musical composition for an orchestra, band, choral group, or individual artist in order to adapt the tune to a style different from the one in which it was originally written.

The Arranger may, in addition to working on new tunes, work on new arrangements of some old hits or classics. Arranged well, these tunes (sometimes called "cover records") often outsell the original versions.

The Arranger who works for a recording artist will work closely with the act and the producer. He or she will be on hand before recording even begins to hear how his or her arrangements sound in rehearsals. Last-minute changes are not uncommon.

In addition to working with recording artists, Arrangers may work with artists arranging music for concerts. Other Arrangers work with such services as Muzak, which arranges and orchestrates much of the music heard in dentist's offices, doctor's offices, and department stores.

Music Arrangers who work for music publishers are responsible for developing new and/or different ways to write and play music. The music Arranger might even go into television. In this type of job, the individual might be responsible for putting together music for skits or musical guests on comedy or variety shows.

One working as a music Arranger might get into the motion picture business, scoring and/or arranging music for the title tune and the music throughout the film. The opportunities are endless once the Arranger gets in the door.

Most Arrangers work freelance. Therefore, the more jobs they get, the more they earn. Hours for this type of position are extremely irregular. Recording sessions do not usually go from nine to five (although they might run from 9:00 P.M. to 5:00 A.M.).

Staff Arrangers employed by music publishers have a more regular workday.

Arrangers are usually musicians first. Many Arrangers perform with an act and arrange much of the act's material. They might also write much of the music the act records.

Salaries

Arrangers who have not yet hit stardom and success may make so little arranging that they must work other jobs to make ends meet. Once an Arranger gets his or her foot in the door, he or she can expect to make from $10,000 to $15,000 yearly.

Others who have attained more success in arranging may earn up to $30,000 annually. Salaries depend, of course, on how much work one gets. Fees for Arrangers of movies, television, or recordings are usually paid according to the scale set by the American Federation of Musicians (AFM).

In some instances, Arrangers are paid a royalty on each piece of music or record sold, in addition to their fee.

Top Arrangers may demand and receive fees well over scale payments, as well as royalties. These people may earn between $50,000 and $75,000+ yearly.

Employment Prospects

It is not difficult for an Arranger to break into the profession on a small scale. Arranging tunes for groups who have not yet made it is a good example of the work one may do. Money for this type of employment is usually low. It does give the aspiring Arranger a start, though.

Arrangers have opportunities to work for the recording industry, TV, motion pictures, shows, music publishers, or print-music licensees. Other opportunities include working for an individual artist or group of artists, arranging materials for recordings or concerts.

Advancement Prospects

Advancement as an Arranger comes in working for more prestigious groups. As the individual's talent is recognized, he or she will have more opportunities. Composing and arranging one's own material for a Broadway show or a top group is probably a situation most Arrangers hope for.

Education and Training

No formal education is required to become an Arranger. Some type of training is usually necessary, however. This training can be garnered in a conservatory or college or through private study.

The Arranger must be knowledgeable and be able to implement all phases of orchestration. He or she must be educated (either formally or informally) in areas of composition, harmony, arranging, and theory.

Most people aspiring to be an Arranger have studied at least one instrument, either privately, at conservatory or college classes, or a combination of both.

Experience/Skills/Personality Traits

Arrangers begin as musicians. They need to play at least one instrument well. The ability to play more than one is a plus.

Quite frequently, Arrangers have tried composing on some level, either amateur or professional. The Arranger must have the ability to read and write music. Talented Arrangers—those who become most successful—are creative individuals who can develop their ideas into musical arrangements.

A good musical "ear" is a necessity, as are versatility and familiarity with current musical trends.

Unions/Associations

Arrangers may belong to the American Federation of Musicians (AFM). This is a bargaining union that sets payment scales for arrangements.

Arrangers may also be members of the National Academy of Recording Arts and Sciences (NARAS). This organization gives out the Grammy awards each year.

Many Arrangers additionally belong to the American Society of Music Arrangers.

Tips for Entry

1. As a member of the American Federation of Musicians (AFM), you will receive their publication, *The International Musician*. This paper has a number of opportunities and openings listed in it.
2. Hanging around recording studios might help you learn about the profession and develop contacts.
3. Write as much music as you can. Write for up-and-coming groups, yourself, etc.

4. You might want to arrange some tunes and try sending them to publishers.
5. You might want to form your own group and arrange for them.

6. Any type of experience in this field helps. Consider donating your talent (writing and arranging) to a local production or school or college musical.

RECORD PRODUCER

CAREER PROFILE

Duties: Producing records for recording acts; helping select songs to be recorded; supervising recording sessions

Alternate Title(s): None

Salary Range: $12,500 to $250,000+

Employment Prospects: Fair

Advancement Prospects: Fair

Best Geographical Location(s) for Position: New York City, Los Angeles, Nashville

Prerequisites:

Education or Training—Music training useful; recording school helpful

Experience—Studio experience helpful

Special Skills and Personality Traits—Good musical "ear"; knowledge of music business; musical creativity; love of music; ability to select hit tunes

CAREER LADDER

```
┌─────────────────────────────┐
│                             │
│    Major Record Producer    │
│                             │
└─────────────────────────────┘

┌─────────────────────────────┐
│                             │
│       Record Producer       │
│                             │
└─────────────────────────────┘

┌─────────────────────────────┐
│        Musician;            │
│        Arranger;            │
│        Talent Scout         │
└─────────────────────────────┘
```

Position Description

The Record Producer's main job is to produce a record. If the individual is very successful and lucky, he or she will come out of a recording session with a hit record. There are a number of different responsibilities within this job classification, some creative and others business-oriented.

The Record Producer first helps a group or artist select the tune or tunes to be recorded. Once an act has rehearsed and is ready to record, the Producer will locate a suitable studio in which to record and arrange for studio time. The Producer may then choose an engineer, hire an arranger, and contact a contractor who will find background musicians and vocalists for the job.

The Producer will make sure that all those hired arrive at the studio on time. The individual is also in charge of making sure that those who have been hired are paid promptly.

During the recording session the Producer will work closely with the engineer. The person in this position advises the engineer of any specific sounds or feelings he or she is trying to create. The Pro-

ducer will supervise the entire recording session, making decisions about when to do a take over, what takes to use, etc.

The Producer usually adds a personal touch to the recording. This is sometimes a special sound effect or the way a tune is ended. Often, it is a blend of instruments or vocal harmony. It is not unusual for a Producer to place his or her trademark on records.

It is up to the Producer to try to keep the recording within the budget agreed upon. Going over budget often costs the label or artist thousands of dollars extra.

After the recording has been made, the Producer is often in charge of "mixing" it to perfection. Although the Producer doesn't always do this job personally (special engineers or mixers are often hired), he or she always supervises this function. Success or failure in the mixing process can be what makes or breaks a record.

If the tunes recorded are for an album, the Producer may help choose the order in which they are placed on the LP. He or she will also help to choose the single from the album.

The Producer is involved with all aspects of the record. When the recording and mixing have been completed, the Producer's job does not end. Though the creative process is almost over, the Record Producer must attend to many of the business aspects of producing.

The Producer is responsible for clearing mechanical licenses, making sure that all copyrights are checked, and providing completed consent forms and releases from artists, engineers, photographers, etc. who worked on the LP (if they are to receive credit on the record). At this point the Producer must also submit receipts and paid bills to the record company.

The Record Producer may work on staff for a label or be an independent Producer, freelancing his or her talent. The Producer on staff at a record company is responsible to the A&R department head. The Producer who freelances may be responsible directly to the label or to the artist. This depends on the arrangement made beforehand.

Salaries

Record Producers on staff at a record company may earn a salary plus royalties on records produced.

Producers who freelance as independents are paid a fee for their services by either the label or the artist. In addition, they are always paid royalties on works they produce. The amount of the royalties differ from Producer to Producer. Successful Record Producers can negotiate for larger royalty payments. This money is often advanced to the individual.

Staff Producers may earn $12,500 to $45,000+, depending on the label. Very successful Independent Producers may earn up to $250,000+ annually.

Employment Prospects

All records have Producers. The record is sometimes produced by a member of the group that recorded it. At other times, the record may be produced by the engineer. Records may also be produced by a staff Producer working at a record company or by an independent Producer who freelances his or her talent.

On some records there is more than one producer. For example, there may be an executive Producer and a coproducer. Another possibility is for an artist to produce part of the record in conjunction with the executive Producer.

There are quite a few possibilities for employment in this field. However, one must first get in the door.

Advancement Prospects

The way a Producer advances in the recording industry is by working on records that become hits. As a Producer's efforts yield records that hit the charts, he or she becomes more valuable.

When a Producer attains success, many different options open. The Producer may go to a position at a better label, demand more money, work with more prestigious acts, or freelance as an independent Producer.

Education and Training

There is no college requirement to become a Producer, although many Producers do possess college degrees. Music training is useful. Some people attend a sound recording school for a short period to learn more about the recording process.

This is another of the careers in which a knowledge of the music business is quite helpful, as it makes it easier to get into the industry. This knowledge can be obtained through formal education or by working in various jobs in the music business.

Experience/Skills/Personality Traits

The most important qualification for a Record Producer is the ability to pick hit tunes. Every recording group or artist wants a number one song. This is how they gain recognition and make money. Record Producers who can, indeed, pick the tunes and have a proven track record doing so will be successful.

Record Producers must have a good musical "ear" and the ability to know what will sound good. Naturally, the Producer must love music, as he or she will be listening to it for a good part of the day.

The Record Producer must be able to hear raw talent and have the ability to foresee how it will sound if properly arranged and recorded.

Unions/Associations

Record Producers may be active or associate members in the National Academy of Recording Arts and Sciences (NARAS). This is the association that gives out the Grammy awards each year.

Record Producers might also belong to any of the music associations, including the Country Music Association (CMA), the Black Music Association (BMA), and the Gospel Music Association (GMA).

Tips for Entry

1. Try to find a job in a recording studio as a floor manager, engineer, studio set-up worker, receptionist, etc. to gain opportunity to watch Producers at work.
2. One way of getting into producing is to find a group with a song they want to record. Put some of your own money into the recording of a master you produce and try to sell both the record and the group to a major label.
3. As with many careers in the music business, you should check with some recording studios or even a major label to see if you can intern or apprentice in return for learning the skills.

RECORDING ENGINEER

CAREER PROFILE

Duties: Operating the sound board and other electrical equipment during the recording of music

Alternate Title(s): Mixer; Recording Assistant

Salary Range: $7,800 to $100,000 +

Employment Prospects: Fair

Advancement Prospects: Fair

Best Geographical Location(s) for Position: New York City, Los Angeles, Nashville

Prerequisites:

Education or Training—College or technical school background in sound engineering or recording technology; apprenticeship in studio in lieu of schooling

Experience—Experience in studio necessary

Special Skills and Personality Traits—Good musical "ear"; electronic and mechanical inclination; appreciation of music; stamina; ability to work under a great deal of pressure

CAREER LADDER

```
┌─────────────────────────────────────────┐
│   Top Freelance Recording Engineer;     │
│        Engineer-Producer;               │
│          Chief Engineer                 │
└─────────────────────────────────────────┘

┌─────────────────────────────────────────┐
│                                         │
│          Recording Engineer             │
│                                         │
└─────────────────────────────────────────┘

┌─────────────────────────────────────────┐
│                                         │
│          Recording Assistant            │
│                                         │
└─────────────────────────────────────────┘
```

Position Description

It is the Recording Engineer's job to operate the sound board and all the other electrical equipment necessary when making a recording.

This is not, however, the only responsibility of the Recording Engineer. In a large studio there are usually a number of different engineers working on a session. These include the recording assistant or set-up Engineer, the main Recording Engineer, and possibly another Engineer who helps with the mixing after tracks have been recorded.

Prior to a recording session, one of the Engineers (usually the recording assistant) prepares the studio before the act arrives. As recording time is booked by the hour (and it is very expensive), no one wants to waste time waiting for the instruments to be set up or the mikes to be placed, turned on, and checked.

The Recording Engineer must discuss with the act and/or his or her producer how they want the end product to sound. It then becomes the Engineer's responsibility to make the record into the sound image the act wants.

He or she does this during the recording session by operating the sound board and the other electrical equipment and electronic devices. The different audio controls used create different sounds. After a track has been recorded, the Engineer plays it back. The Engineer, the act, and the producer then discuss the recording and any changes they would like. For example, recording might need more base, more treble, a faster or slower tempo, etc. This information is noted for later use.

After all the tracks have been recorded, the Engineer will mix them down to either two or four tracks. Mixing is not just a skill, but an art the Recording Engineer must learn. He or she decides how loud or soft a specific track should be and then balances it correctly. The individual might feel that another instrument is needed. The Engineer would talk over this suggestion with the producer to get his or her opinion. If the producer agrees, another track with the instrument is recorded. This new track is then mixed down with the others to become, eventually, the master tape.

Through the entire recording process the Recording Engineer works closely with the producer and the act. He or she discusses the sound with these individuals and tries to put their ideas into the final product.

In certain studios, the Recording Engineer must not only know how to work the equipment, but also how to repair it when it breaks down. As a rule, many Recording Engineers know how to take apart and put together most of the equipment they work with.

Engineers keep up with the latest electronic and recording technology. They are constantly striving to improve their talent in the engineering process.

Recording Engineers work long, irregular hours. Many Engineers begin work at 9 or 10 P.M. and work until the next morning with one act. In the afternoon, they often have to return to the studio with another client. The job requires a lot of stamina.

Recording Engineers must have the ability to work with people with whose musical ideas they disagree. The Recording Engineer is usually responsible directly to the producer and act or to the chief Engineer in the studio.

Recording Engineers can be on staff at a record company or a recording studio. They can also work by the hour. Better-known Recording Engineers work freelance. Their business is obtained through word-of-mouth.

Salaries

Salaries vary for Recording Engineers according to the situation for which they have been hired. Recording Engineers who are just beginning (called recording assistants or studio set-up workers) usually make close to the minimum wage.

As the Recording Engineer gains experience he or she will be better compensated. A lot depends on whether the individual is on staff, paid by the number of hours per week that he or she works, or a freelance Engineer.

Salaries for those individuals who are on staff range from $7,800 to $25,000 per year. Recording Engineers who are well-known and freelance often make up to $50,000 yearly. In addition to being paid a fee by the act or record company he or she is working with, the individual is also usually paid a percentage of the monies given to the recording studio for renting the studio time. This percentage varies.

Top Recording Engineers who work with popular recording acts can make $100,000+ annually.

Employment Prospects

As with most jobs in the recording industry, things are very competitive. However, if an individual doesn't mind starting at the bottom, he or she may eventually get a job in a recording studio. A person with talent, personality, patience, and perseverance may obtain a position as a Recording Engineer, or at least as an assistant.

Advancement Prospects

It is often necessary to knock on a lot of doors, make a great number of calls, and mail many resumés before you get your foot in the door. Once this is done, however, a person who works hard and has a lot of talent and a little bit of luck will advance his or her career.

Engineers select different roads for advancement. One is to become a chief Engineer. This individual is in charge of the entire studio and supervises all recordings that take place in that studio.

Another method of advancement is for the individual to become a top freelance Recording Engineer. Top recording groups, record companies, and producers will usually seek such a person out to work with them on sessions.

Another method of advancement selected by Engineers is to become an engineer-producer. This individual will produce records as well as engineer them.

Education and Training

There are a variety of ways to train for a position as a Recording Engineer: through college courses in sound engineering, for example, or in a technical or training school course in sound engineering or recording technology.

A third method of training for this position is to work as an apprentice in a recording studio. Many times, the individual in this position does not get paid or is paid a minimum salary. He or she learns the business from the bottom up. By being in this environment and asking questions, he or she will pick up the major engineering methods. Eventually, he or she will become a recording assistant and learn even more.

Experience/Skills/Personality Traits

As noted above, experience in a studio is one aid to becoming a Recording Engineer. In addition, the Engineer must have a good musical "ear" to be effective at his or her job.

The ability to work under a great deal of pressure is important to the Recording Engineer. He or she might have to work with three or four different recording acts a day. Each act usually is set on how the record should sound. The Engineer must be able to communicate and translate their verbal ideas onto tape.

Unions/Associations

Recording Engineers may be active members of the National Academy of Recording Arts and Sciences (NARAS). This is the association that gives out the Grammy awards each year.

Depending on the type of music the individual works with, he or she might be a member of the Country Music Association (CMA), the Gospel Music Association (GMA), and/or the Black Music Association (BMA). These associations work to promote their specific variety of music.

Recording Engineers may represent a recording studio as a member of the Society of Professional Audio Recording Studios (SPARS).

Tips for Entry

1. If you can afford to, you might consider offering your services free to a recording studio in exchange for learning the business. When they feel you know enough, they might put you on salary.

2. Check to see what organizations are offering in the ways of seminars for Recording Engineers. These seminars might help you make important contacts as well as learn more about the industry.

3. Check with various record companies (the larger ones) to see if they offer an internship program in the recording engineering department. It isn't uncommon for the record company to hire an intern after the internship ends.

RECORDING STUDIO SET-UP WORKER

CAREER PROFILE

Duties: Arranges sound recording equipment in studio before recording begins

Alternate Title(s): Recording Assistant; Assistant Engineer

Salary Ranges: $7,000 to $12,000

Employment Prospects: Fair

Advancement Prospects: Fair

Best Geographical Location(s) for Position: New York City, Los Angeles, Nashville

Prerequisites:

Education or Training—Technical school background in sound recording may be helpful, but not required; on-the-job training

Experience—Prior work with electrical equipment useful

Special Skills and Personality Traits—Knowledgeable in electronics; dependable; mechanically inclined; appreciative of music; able to get along with people

CAREER LADDER

```
┌─────────────────────────────────┐
│                                 │
│            Engineer             │
│                                 │
└─────────────────────────────────┘

┌─────────────────────────────────┐
│                                 │
│  Recording Studio Set-Up Worker │
│                                 │
└─────────────────────────────────┘

┌─────────────────────────────────┐
│                                 │
│     Clerk in Recording Studio   │
│                                 │
└─────────────────────────────────┘
```

Position Description

Recording Studio Set-Up Workers do as the name implies—set up equipment. Individuals employed in this type of position have the responsibility of physically setting up the recording studio before a recording session takes place.

As recording time is usually very expensive, companies and/or individuals renting the studio do not want to waste their own time setting up their instruments, mikes, etc. The Studio Set-Up Worker handles this task.

Once a block of time is booked by an act, the Recording Studio Set-Up Worker goes to work. He or she receives work orders indicating which instruments will be used, where they will be placed, how many mikes will be needed, etc.

Using this work order as a guide, the Set-Up Worker begins. In addition to setting up the instruments and mikes, the individual must position other pieces of equipment, such as consoles, isolation booths, tape machines, amps, music stands, and chairs.

Some of this equipment is moved by hand. The rest is loaded onto dollies and handtrucks. Each piece must be in the correct position before the recording session begins.

The Studio Set-Up Worker helps connect all the equipment to the correct electrical lines, following instructions. If there is a breakdown of any particular piece of equipment during the session, the Studio Set-Up Worker will replace it or fix it as quickly as possible. If there is a short in any of the electrical lines, the Set-Up Worker may help repair the problem.

After the recording session is completed, the Set-Up Worker dismantles all the equipment, instruments, and mikes and puts them in their proper places. If anything has broken or is not in good working order, he or she either fixes it or reports it as broken so that it can be repaired or replaced.

In some studios the Set-Up Worker is also responsible for maintaining the tape library. In this job, the Set-Up Worker needs to be totally organized. A lost tape can create a real problem for a studio.

The Studio Set-Up Worker may assist the engineer during a recording. He or she is usually responsible to that individual.

Salaries

Salaries for Recording Studio Set-Up Workers are considerably lower than those of engineers. The Set-Up Worker often earns only a minimum salary. Beginning Set-Up Workers may only earn around $7,000 yearly. With added experience, the individual may earn up to $12,000 annually. Salaries do not usually go much over this figure.

Employment Prospects

A Studio Set-Up Worker may find it easier to obtain a job in a studio than an engineer would. In some small studios, Set-Up Worker positions are considered entry level. In others, individuals must begin as clerks, receptionists, or gofers.

Advancement Prospects

If a Recording Studio Set-Up Worker watches what is going on in the studio and asks questions, he or she has a reasonable chance for promotion to an assistant engineer or engineer. The main thing that is necessary for advancement is skill.

Education and Training

People spend a great deal of money to rent recording time and do not always want to use their time and money to train an aspiring engineer. Many individuals in the industry feel that because a certain degree of training and skill are required, the person who wants to get into engineering should attend a technical school or college in order to learn the basics of the craft.

There are others who feel that on-the-job training is the best way to learn. A Studio Set-Up Worker with virtually no experience in recording may obtain a job in a studio and by watching and asking questions receive the same, if not better, training.

Experience/Skills/Personality Traits

Many Studio Set-Up Workers first walk into a studio and obtain jobs as receptionists, secretaries, gofers, etc. After a short time, if someone leaves and a position opens, the person who is in the right place at the right time gets the job. Others enter the engineering field as Studio Set-Up Workers.

Set-Up Workers do need to know the basics of electronics and to be mechanically inclined. As they are around music on a constant basis, an appreciation of music helps. Dependability and getting along well with those who book studio time can help the Studio Set-Up Worker advance his or her career.

Unions/Associations

Recording Studio Set-Up Workers do not usually belong to any union or specific trade association at this point in their career.

Tips for Entry

1. Check different studios to see if the opportunity to learn the business can be gotten in exchange for working free in the studio. After you have learned enough, they may put you on salary.
2. Some of the larger recording companies offer internship programs in recording. If you are a beginner, they'll start you as a Set-Up Worker and you can move up the career ladder from there.
3. Certain recording associations and organizations give seminars on different facets of the recording business. Check this out.
4. Positions in this field are often advertised in the classified ads in cities that have recording studios.
5. Knock on the door of as many recording studios as you can. Be persistent.

ORCHESTRATOR

CAREER PROFILE

Duties: Transposing music from one instrument or voice to another in order to accommodate a particular musician or group; writing scores for an orchestra, band, choral group, individual instrumentalist, or vocalist

Alternate Title(s): None

Salary Range: Earnings depend on how much orchestrating is done; it is impossible to estimate earnings

Employment Prospects: Fair

Advancement Prospects: Fair

Best Geographical Location(s) for Position: New York City, Los Angeles, Boston, and other cultural and/or metropolitan areas

Prerequisites:

Education or Training—Training in music theory and notation

Experience—Experience copying music and/or arranging

Special Skills and Personality Traits—Knowledge of music theory; ability to transpose music; accuracy; reliability; neatness; understanding of music

Position Description

An Orchestrator's prime function is to write the scores for an orchestra, band, choral group, individual instrumentalist, or vocalist. In this position, the person transposes the music from one instrument or voice to another to accommodate a particular musician or musical group. For example, an Orchestrator might be asked to transpose a score for a song into a key more suited to a vocalist.

When accomplishing this function, the individual does not usually alter the musical quality, harmony, or rhythm. He or she just scores the composition so that it is consistent with the instrumental and vocal capabilities of the artists.

Although many Orchestrators work with the compositions of composers and arrangers, sometimes the individual is asked to work as the arranger. For instance, the Orchestrator may be asked to transcribe a composition while adapting it to another style of music. An example is when an

individual changes the style of a pop tune to an "easy listening" instrumental version. This type of work often requires additional knowledge or training.

The Orchestrator may also function in the capacity of a copyist, transcribing musical parts onto staff or manuscript paper from a score written by an arranger. The individual performing as an Orchestrator can work full-time or part-time. He or she may be responsible for orchestrating, arranging, and/or copying as part of a job.

Salaries

Salaries for Orchestrators will vary depending on how much work they do and under what conditions. Orchestrators may be paid according to fees set by the American Federation of Musicians (AFM). In certain situations, the individual may be paid by the hour. These situations include work where the Orchestrator must do adjustments, alterations, additions, or takedowns of the score. Time rates are also used when page rates are not practical.

Effective December 1, 1985, the hourly rate for Orchestrators will be $25.52. These rates are set by the American Federation of Musicians (AFM), the union for Orchestrators.

Rates will vary for work done by the page depending on the type of arrangement orchestrated and what needs to be done. For example, an individual Orchestrating a tune in which incomplete material is given will receive $16.00 per page effective December 1, 1985. The same rate would apply for scoring a piano part from a lead or melody sheet of music.

If the individual scores for voices, depending on the circumstances, he or she will receive $7.02 per page effective December 1, 1985.

Employment Prospects

Employment prospects are fair for Orchestrators. They may work for orchestras, bands, choral groups, individual instrumentalists, or vocalists. Individuals may work for, with, or as arrangers in the recording field. They may also do orchestration for television, films, and theater.

Advancement Prospects

Advancement for an Orchestrator may occur when the individual becomes so well known that he or she is constantly busy. People in this job may become successful composers and musicians in their own right. They may also go on to work in the music publishing field as music editors.

Education and Training

As in many music jobs, there is no formal education required in order to become an Orchestrator. The individual must know how to write scores for orchestras, bands, choral groups, etc., and/or how to transpose them from one instrument to another. This knowledge might be acquired at a conservatory, college, or university, or through private study. The skills needed might also be self-taught.

Experience/Skills/Personality Traits

As an Orchestrator, an individual must have a thorough knowledge of music theory. He or she needs the ability to transpose music. The person must be accurate and have neat handwriting. Reliability is a must for success in this job. Additionally, the Orchestrator must have a good understanding of music.

Unions/Associations

Orchestrators may belong to the American Federation of Musicians (AFM). This union sets the minimum rate scale for Orchestrators.

Tips for Entry

1. These positions are often advertised in the classified section of newspapers in major cultural centers.
2. Put up your business card or a flyer in music and instrument repair stores.
3. Talk to the orchestra(s) in your area to see if they have part- or full-time work.
4. If you are just beginning, volunteer to do some of this work for a local theater putting on a musical. It will give you invaluable experience and will add to your resumé.

COPYIST

CAREER PROFILE

Duties: Transcribing musical parts onto staff paper from scores

Alternate Title(s): None

Salary Range: It is impossible to estimate salary; earnings vary depending on the amount of copying done

Employment Prospects: Good

Advancement Prospects: Fair

Best Geographical Location(s) for Position: Major cultural and music centers for most jobs; other cities may also have positions

Prerequisites:

Education or Training—Training in music notation and theory

Experience—Music background useful; writing music helpful

Special Skills and Personality Traits—Knowledge of music notation; knowledge of music theory; neatness; accuracy

Position Description

A music Copyist transcribes musical parts onto staff or manuscript paper from a score. This score may have been done by an arranger, composer, or orchestrator. The Copyist reproduces the various parts for instruments and/or voices.

The individual utilizes his or her knowledge of music notation and experience and background in music to accomplish this task. The function of the Copyist is to make it easier for the musician or vocalist to play or sing his or her part. It is important for the person copying the music to do so neatly and accurately. If not, it will be extremely difficult for the artist to perform properly.

At certain times, the individual will be asked to copy a corrected or changed score. At other times, the individual may copy various parts for different instruments. A very talented individual may be asked to write the music from a record or tape onto paper without seeing a copy of the music. This is a very difficult feat and requires a thorough knowledge of music theory, notations, harmony, composition, and orchestration.

The music Copyist may work full-time, either independently or for a music publisher, or part-time. As a music Copyist, the person is responsible to the individual or organization using his or her services. If that person or organization feels that the work is inaccurate, messy or illegible, or is not done on schedule, the music Copyist will not be hired again. As the amount of music work in any given area is limited, the word will get around and the individual will not be able to obtain more copying work.

Salaries

The American Federation of Musicians (AFM) sets minimum fees and wages for Music Copyists. There are different fees depending on the type of work done.

Copyists are usually paid by the page copied in relation to the score page. They are usually remunerated per page and a half produced. Rates vary depending on the parts copied.

In certain situations, the Copyist may be paid by the hour. As of December 1, 1985 the rates will be $13.15 per hour.

Employment Prospects

Employment prospects are good for music Copyists. There are opportunities for individuals who can perform this function in major music and cultural centers as well as in smaller cities. There are many groups, writers, composers, arrangers, and orchestrators who require this service.

Many Copyists do the job part-time while pursuing a career as a musician, singer, composer, etc. There are also many students who perform copying services while in school.

Advancement Prospects

Copyists may advance their careers by becoming well-known arrangers, composers, orchestrators, singers, etc. There are Copyists who go on to become music editors for music publishing companies.

Many individuals prefer to stay in copying and develop a client following.

Education and Training

There is no formal educational requirement to become a Copyist. Individuals must know how to transcribe musical parts onto manuscript paper. They must have a knowledge of music notation, music theory, etc. This knowledge may be obtained in high school or college or at private music lessons. It might also be a self-taught skill.

Experience/Skills/Personality Traits

As noted above, the Copyist must know how to transcribe music parts onto manuscript paper. The person must know and understand music notations and should be cognizant of music theory. The individual must write neatly and be accurate.

Many Copyists are musicians and aspiring songwriters and arrangers. The person performing this function usually has a great interest in music.

Unions/Associations

Copyists may belong to the American Federation of Musicians (AFM). This union sets the minimum wages music Copyists receive.

Copyists may also belong to the American Society of Music Copyists. This association provides information to Copyists.

Tips for Entry

1. You may wish to advertise your skill in a newspaper or entertainment magazine in your area.
2. Put up signs in the music stores, record shops, and showcase clubs in your area.
3. Occasionally there are positions requiring this skill advertised in the help wanted sections of newspapers.
4. You may consider talking to local acts and groups and letting them know you provide this service. They might be interested.

RADIO

MUSIC DIRECTOR

Duties: Selecting music for specific programs on radio station

Alternate Title(s): None

Salary Range: $15,000 to $75,000+

Employment Prospects: Poor

Advancement Prospects: Fair

Best Geographical Location(s) for Position: Local communities for small market stations; New York City, Los Angeles, Chicago, etc. for major market stations

Prerequisites:

Education or Training—No educational requirement; hands-on training in a radio station helpful

Experience—Working as a disc jockey for a period of time

Special Skills and Personality Traits—Knowledge of music; ability to supervise; responsibility

```
┌─────────────────────────────┐
│      Program Director        │
└─────────────────────────────┘

┌─────────────────────────────┐
│       Music Director         │
└─────────────────────────────┘

┌─────────────────────────────┐
│        Disc Jockey           │
└─────────────────────────────┘
```

Position Description

The Music Director of a radio station is responsible for selecting music for specific programs aired on the station. The individual works closely with the program director. In certain stations, the Music Director is also the program director. The Music Director might also have his or her own show, working as a disc jockey.

Music Directors as a rule began their careers in radio as disc jockeys. During the time they were D.J.'s they proved that they had expertise in selecting records and putting shows together.

The Music Director's duties vary depending on what type of format is being used by the station and the duties of the program director. He or she may spend time with the record promotional people, screening tunes for the program director to listen to. The two then discuss the records that could potentially make it in their market.

Music Directors assist the program director in most music-oriented activities. The individual helps the P.D. research the market, determine the kind of audience the station plays to, learn what the people want to hear, and get a feel for station listeners' likes and dislikes.

The individual often meets with or talks to the managers of major record stores in the area. Through these meetings, he or she can find out what's hot in record releases.

The Music Director, along with the program director, might help train new disc jockeys and help them adjust to the station's procedures. This is often done by listening to air checks, which are short tapes of the different on-air personalities recorded at various times.

The Music Director is responsible directly to the program director. He or she works long hours. When the station is short of on-air personnel, the program director might assign the Music Director to take another shift. In addition, the Music Director often takes part in special appearances or promotions. These special shows usually take place during a weekend or at night.

Salaries

Salaries for Music Directors vary depending on the size of the radio station, its location, its popularity, the duties of the Music Director, and his or her experience. Salaries tend to be highest in major markets, such as New York City, Los Angeles, Chicago, etc.

Music Directors' salaries can range from $15,000 to $75,000+ annually. In addition, many jobs offer other benefits.

Employment Prospects

Employment prospects are not good for Music Directors. Many radio stations do not employ a Music Director. They often combine the job with that of the program director.

The best place to look for a position is in a small to mid-sized station. These jobs do not usually pay good salaries. The individual, however, can gain experience, making it easier to find a position at a bigger station.

Advancement Prospects

A Music Director can advance to the position of program director at a radio station. The individual may also advance his or her career by becoming a Music Director at a better or bigger station.

Education and Training

There is no educational requirement for a job as a Music Director. If the individual does attend college, he or she should take courses in communications, journalism, music, and broadcasting. He or she should also work on the school's radio station. This will give the individual hands-on training.

There are many radio broadcasting vocational and trade schools located around the country. Although a majority of these schools are good ones, some are not. Check into the school's reputation through the state's Attorney General's office and/or the Department of Consumer Affairs.

Experience/Skills/Personality Traits

Most Music Directors begin working in radio stations as disc jockeys. If they've been to college, they also have experience working on their college radio stations.

Music Directors, as a rule, like music. They enjoy listening to records and have a knack of knowing what will be hot.

Individuals in this position must be responsible people who have the ability to supervise others.

Unions/Associations

Music Directors may belong to the National Association of Broadcasters (NAB). Depending on the job situation, they might also belong to the American Federation of Television and Radio Artists (AFTRA). Music Directors may additionally belong to the National Association of Broadcast Employees and Technicians (NABET).

Tips for Entry

1. Work in a college radio station and/or a local station to gain experience.
2. Certain larger stations have college credit internship programs. It is not unusual for a station to hire an intern after graduation.
3. Openings and positions are often advertised in the classified sections of newspapers.
4. There are also positions advertised in most of the radio- and record-oriented trades, including *Radio and Records*, *Billboard*, and *Broadcasting*.

DISC JOCKEY

CAREER PROFILE

Duties: Introducing music, commercials, and news on a radio station

Alternate Title(s): D.J.; Deejay; Jock

Salary Range: $7,500 to $150,000+

Employment Prospects: Fair

Advancement Prospects: Fair

Best Geographical Location(s) for Position: Major market stations are located in New York City, Los Angeles, Chicago, etc; small market stations are found in towns and cities around the country

Prerequisites:

Education or Training—No educational requirement; college or vocational background in communications or radio broadcasting useful

Experience—Position on school or college station helpful

Special Skills and Personality Traits—Enjoyment of music; good speaking voice; ability to project personality over the air

CAREER LADDER

```
┌─────────────────────────────────────┐
│         Program Director;            │
│  Disc Jockey at Major Market Station │
└─────────────────────────────────────┘

┌─────────────────────────────────────┐
│            Disc Jockey               │
└─────────────────────────────────────┘

┌─────────────────────────────────────┐
│             Student;                 │
│             Intern                   │
└─────────────────────────────────────┘
```

Position Description

A Disc Jockey's main responsibility is to introduce the records, commercials, news, and public announcements that are aired on a station. The Disc Jockey is expected to have some sort of style or personality he or she projects over the air waves. This personality is what makes a Disc Jockey successful and gives him or her a following.

Disc Jockeys work in time shifts. Shifts vary, but usually range from three to five hours in length. D.J.'s are usually assigned the same shift every day. Popular Disc Jockeys receive the most listened-to shifts, such as the morning drive, afternoon drive, or early evening slot.

Depending on the size of the station and its makeup, the Jock has additional responsibilities. Sometimes the D.J. is responsible for picking out the music for his or her show. This usually occurs in small market stations that have small staffs. They must, however, choose records from an approved playlist put together by the station's program or music director.

Sometimes the Disc Jockey is also the acting music or program director. This, once again, depends on the size of the station and how it is staffed. If the station is small, the Disc Jockey might also be responsible for putting the records on the turntable and working the sound controls.

During the course of his or her shift, the D.J. sometimes comes up with comments, ad libs, the weather, or information about the records he or she is introducing.

Disc Jockeys have other activities besides performing on the air. As the Disc Jockey becomes a celebrity of sorts (even in small markets), he or she is often asked to make public appearances for store promotions, station promotions, or charity events. He or she also might do voice-overs on commercials for radio or television. In addition, Disc Jockeys might act as live jocks at clubs or discos, or even host concerts in large or small facilities.

The Disc Jockey is responsible to the program director, music director, or station manager.

Salaries

Salaries for Disc Jockeys vary according to a number of factors, including the size of the station, the market, the experience of the jock, and his or her appeal.

Salaries can start at close to minimum wage for a beginner in a small market station. A Disc Jockey who is very popular may earn $150,000+ annually. In addition, Disc Jockeys may make additional income from personal appearances, voice-over commercials, and doing disco D.J. work.

Employment Prospects

Employment prospects in small market stations are fair. There is a large turnover at many of these stations because pay is so low and people want to move on to better positions.

Employment prospects get tougher as the market gets larger.

Advancement Prospects

The Disc Jockey at a small market station has an opportunity to advance to the position of program director or music director at that station or a similar station. He or she also has the option of trying to locate a position at a better station in a bigger market.

Education and Training

Although there is no educational requirement for the position of Disc Jockey, many people do get a college background. If the individual is considering college, courses in communications and broadcasting are useful. Working on the college radio station is also valuable experience. This gives the individual hands-on training.

If the person is planning on attending a broadcasting vocational or trade school, he or she should check out the reputation of the school. This can be accomplished through the state's Attorney General's office and/or the Department of Consumer Affairs. Although most of these schools have good reputations, some do not. These are the schools to avoid.

Experience/Skills/Personality Traits

Many Disc Jockeys begin their careers by participating in a high school radio club. They then move on to a college station and learn many additional radio jobs.

A Disc Jockey must have a good speaking voice and the ability to project his or her personality over the air.

The Disc Jockey must be responsible and dependable. He or she must consistently show up on time for his or her air shift.

Disc Jockeys must pass a test given by the FCC (Federal Communications Commission) in order to receive a third class radio-telephone operator's license.

Unions/Associations

Disc Jockeys may be members of the American Federation of Television and Radio Artists (AFTRA). Individuals might also belong to the National Association of Broadcasting (NAB) or be an associate member of the National Academy of Recording Arts and Sciences (NARAS). Disc Jockeys may additionally belong to the National Association of Broadcast Employees and Technicians (NABET).

Tips for Entry

1. Positions may be advertised in the classified sections of newspapers.
2. Other openings may be advertised in the radio and record trades, such as *Billboard, Broadcasting,* and *Radio and Records.*
3. See if you can get into a college internship at a radio station.
4. Work on your high school or college radio station for experience.
5. Make a demo tape and send it along with your resumé to a station's general manager or personnel director (depending on the station size). Make sure you make a few copies of the tape and always keep one.

ON THE ROAD

TOUR COORDINATOR

CAREER PROFILE

Duties: Coordinating the many facets of an act's tour

Alternate Title(s): None

Salary Range: $20,000 to $78,000+

Employment Prospects: Poor

Advancement Prospects: Fair

Best Geographical Location(s) for Position: Most tours are planned from booking agencies or management firms in New York City, Los Angeles, and Nashville

Prerequisites:

Education or Training—No formal educational requirement; college background helpful

Experience—Travel and touring experience with music acts as road manager, tour publicist, etc.

Special Skills and Personality Traits—Ability to assert authority; responsibility; organization; freedom to travel

CAREER LADDER

```
┌─────────────────────────────────┐
│   Tour Coordinator for Major Tour; │
│       Personal Manager;          │
│        Booking Agent             │
└─────────────────────────────────┘

┌─────────────────────────────────┐
│                                 │
│        Tour Coordinator          │
│                                 │
└─────────────────────────────────┘

┌─────────────────────────────────┐
│                                 │
│        Road Manager;             │
│        Tour Publicist            │
└─────────────────────────────────┘
```

Position Description

The position of Tour Coordinator is one of the most important jobs on the road. The individual in this position is responsible for coordinating all of the many facets of an act's tour. He or she oversees everything that is done by all members of the tour staff while the act is on the road. It is the duty of the Tour Coordinator to supervise not only the road personnel but the act as well.

The Tour Coordinator's job starts before the tour leaves for its first destination. He or she works with the act's management, booking agents, and publicists. The individual maps out the location of concerts and their dates and times. He or she then discusses with the publicist or tour publicist other appearances that have to be made, including radio interviews, television spots, print media interviews, special promotions, stops at record shops, etc. These are added to the list of times, dates, and locations.

The Tour Coordinator may work out what transportation will be used by which members of the entourage. Often, for example, the singers travel by plane, the musicians by private bus, and the equipment crew by truck. In instances where the group must travel two thousand miles in a day, the logical transportation would be an airplane, probably a chartered jet. The Tour Coordinator finds the best routes to take, makes reservations at hotels, and rents cars, limos, buses, and planes. As a rule, the Tour Coordinator tries to make the best arrangements as economically as possible.

The Tour Coordinator also plans the tour day by day—sometimes hour by hour—to use time as well as possible. He or she tries to get everyone where he or she is supposed to be with the least amount of effort. The road gets grueling, and sometimes the Tour Coordinator must weigh the price of flying against traveling a cheaper way and having the act come in too exhausted to put on a good show.

Once the tour leaves, the Tour Coordinator really goes into action. He or she must coordinate all the activities of the entourage. The problems of the entourage, the act, and the promoters often become the problems of the coordinator.

The Tour Coordinator works closely with the tour manager, as many of their responsibilities are interchangeable. Sometimes he or she is also the road manager. Tour Coordinators also keep in close contact with the act's management and agents. He or she lets them know if everything is going according to schedule or if the act will be late for a particular date.

If a car or bus breaks down, it is the Tour Coordinator's responsibility to make sure another means of transportation is found. If a member of the backup band gets sick while on the road, the Tour Coordinator must find a replacement. If the act has a major problem during the tour, the individual must deal with it or at least delegate someone to handle the situation.

Tours can be long (no matter how short they really are). Life on the road is not for everyone. The Tour Coordinator must be able to deal with the responsibilities of the job and the road while everyone around is under tremendous pressure. Most tours average six to eight weeks, although there are shorter and longer ones. Hours are long and irregular. The Tour Coordinator is always on call, not only for the act and the entourage, but also from management, agents, the act's family, etc.

Tour Coordinators often come off the road and are so physically and mentally exhausted that they must take a few weeks off and do nothing.

The one thing all Tour Coordinators, road managers, and road personnel have in common is a love of music and of life on the road.

Salaries

Salaries of Tour Coordinators are usually high. An individual could start at $400 per week. However, the remuneration is usually much higher. The average is between $650 and $750 per week plus either expenses or a per diem.

Experienced Tour Coordinators who work on prestigious tours often earn $1,500 per week plus expenses and bonuses.

Tour Coordinators are not always on staff and therefore may not work every week. There are some situations where the Tour Coordinator is paid a reduced salary while a group is not actively working in order to retain his or her services.

Employment Prospects

The outlook is not good for Tour Coordinators. There are few jobs in this area and more potential Tour Coordinators than positions.

With the current high price of touring, there are fewer and fewer tours going out, and when they go, they go with fewer personnel.

Advancement Prospects

As a Tour Coordinator, an individual can advance his or her career by becoming a Tour Coordinator for a better-known group or for a major, prestigious tour.

There are a few Tour Coordinators who go into personal management or booking after their experience as Tour Coordinators.

Education and Training

There is no formal educational requirement for this position. However, a college background often helps with the job. Courses in accounting, bookkeeping, psychology, publicity, and the music business are useful.

Experience/Skills/Personality Traits

Many Tour Coordinators were roadies, road managers, and publicists. There are Tour Coordinators who worked as travel agents or travel escorts but always had a love of music.

The most important trait a Tour Coordinator can have is a love of the road and travel. The individual in this position has to like living out of a suitcase. He or she also must be responsible, dependable, and able to supervise an entourage of people. The Tour Coordinator must be organized. A disorganized person can make a shambles of a tour. He or she must also have the ability to deal effectively with a crisis.

Unions/Associations

Tour Coordinators do not belong to any bargaining unions. They might, however, be members of the Touring Entertainment Industry Association (TEIA). This organization provides a forum of professionals in the touring industry.

Tips for Entry

1. This is another of the positions in the music business that you get through contacts. If you have any, use them. If you don't, develop some.
2. Advertise your availability in a small display or classified ad in one of the music trades.
3. Experience helps. If you have put together a tour for even an unknown show group, put it on your resumé.

ROAD MANAGER

CAREER PROFILE

Duties: Handling problems that occur while act is traveling; supervising equipment, sound, and light personnel

Alternate Title(s): Tour Manager

Salary Range: $10,000 to $50,000+

Employment Prospects: Poor

Advancement Prospects: Fair

Best Geographical Location(s) for Position: Major tours are usually planned in New York City, Los Angeles, and Nashville; positions may be available throughout the country

Prerequisites:

Education or Training—No formal education required

Experience—Positions as roadie or equipment manager helpful

Special Skills and Personality Traits—Responsibility; ability to work under pressure; dependability; ability to supervise, freedom to travel

CAREER LADDER

```
┌─────────────────────────┐
│                         │
│    Tour Coordinator     │
│                         │
└─────────────────────────┘

┌─────────────────────────┐
│                         │
│     Road Manager        │
│                         │
└─────────────────────────┘

┌─────────────────────────┐
│                         │
│   Equipment Manager;    │
│        Roadie           │
│                         │
└─────────────────────────┘
```

Position Description

The Road Manager of a group is the group's management representative while the act is on the road. He or she is responsible for handling many of the problems that occur while an act is traveling. The main job is to get everybody and everything where they are supposed to be and on time. Everything must be accomplished as easily as possible with the fewest problems possible.

The Road or Tour Manager is directly responsible to either the tour coordinator, the group's management, or the group itself, depending on the advance arrangement made.

At times, the Road Manager is also the tour coordinator. In these situations, he or she is responsible for all the problems on the road and for supervising not only the equipment, sound, and light personnel, but also the tour publicist, the tour photographer, the musicians, the security, and anyone else working on the tour.

It is the Road Manager's duty to make sure that the act is up in the morning, gets to any public appearances, interviews, or television or radio spots. He or she must make sure they arrive at rehearsals and concerts on time.

He or she is responsible for getting the equipment to the concert hall on time and getting it set up properly. The Road Manager supervises the sound checks, light checks, and security checks for the performances.

The Road Manager is often the liaison between the act and the promoter of a concert or club date. He or she has the responsibility of collecting any monies owed to the act before and/or after the show. The individual must make sure that riders have been followed and the promoter satisfied.

He or she is in charge of paying the entourage and all bills on the road. The Road Manager must keep all receipts, vouchers, etc. from the tour to give to the group or its management. All money must be accounted for.

The Road Manager often has to deal with problems between members of the entourage or help a member of the entourage take care of personal problems at home. Long road tours put stress on most people. The Road Manager must be the one who keeps a cool head no matter what happens.

If an individual has responsibilities that must be dealt with at home, Road Managing is definitely not the job to look for. Road Managers must like travel and must be free to be away from home for weeks or even months at a time.

Hours are long. Road Managers may work twenty hours or more a day. They are always on call. While most of the entourage is fast asleep, the Road Manager is often working throughout the day and long into the night.

Salaries

Salaries of Road Managers vary greatly according to the popularity and success of the groups they work with. Road Managers are usually paid weekly salaries. They may, however, be paid a flat rate for each tour they complete. In addition, Road Managers are paid a per diem for living expenses while on tour. In some groups, the Road Manager's room and board are paid for and the per diem is used for personal expenses. In other situations, the Road Manager's room and board must be paid out of the per diem.

A Road Manager for a touring (but not recording) group might make between $200 and $250 per week. A Road Manager for a top recording group often makes $1,000 per week plus bonuses. Road Managers' salaries are often reduced by a percentage when the act is not working. This reduction keeps the Road Manager under salary with the group. Some Road Managers do not receive any salary when their act is not on tour, and may work for other groups.

Employment Prospects

Although most touring groups employ Road Managers, positions often go to nonmusical friends of a group. The Road Manager position is one for which you have to be at the right place at the right time. In addition, you need a lot of contacts in the business to find open positions. Groups and their management tend to use individuals who have a proven track record in road management for major tours.

Advancement Prospects

Road Managers advance either by moving into the position of tour coordinator or by acting as Road Manager for a more prestigious tour. Often an individual has more clout as Road Manager for a prestigious tour than he or she would have as tour coordinator for a tour starring lesser-known musicians.

To advance, the Road Manager must prove him or herself. Management has to be totally convinced that the Road Manager is completely reliable, responsible, and effective as their representative on the road.

Education and Training

There is no formal educational requirement for the position of Road Manager. There are Road Managers who have not even completed high school. The more successful Road Managers, however, have. There are also Road Managers who have college degrees in everything from business to psychology.

Experience/Skills/Personality Traits

Most Road Managers start out as roadies. Some begin their careers as equipment personnel or tour publicists.

The Road Manager must be able to deal with problems effectively, especially when he or she is under pressure. He or she must have the capability to supervise not only the group's road crew, but also union crews present in many concert halls.

The most important trait that a Road Manager can have is responsibility. It is his or her responsibility to get personnel and equipment where and when they are supposed to be. In addition, the Road Manager must be dependable.

Unions/Associations

Road Managers may belong to a new trade organization called the Touring Entertainment Industry Association (TEIA). This association helps provide a forum for people in the touring industry. Yearly conferences are held in different sections of the country.

Tips for Entry

1. This is a position most often gotten through contacts. If you have any, use them.
2. You might want to try to get a position by putting a small ad in one of the music trades.
3. Many groups starting out have a nonmusical friend act as Road Manager. This might be a way to gain experience.
4. Check the trades to see what tours are going out. These are usually printed well in advance. Send resumés to these groups, their management, and/or their record companies.

TOUR PUBLICIST

CAREER PROFILE

Duties: Publicizing an act's tour to both fans and the media through press releases, press conferences, and special promotions

Alternate Title(s): Publicist

Salary Range: $15,000 to $55,000+

Employment Prospects: Poor

Advancement Prospects: Fair

Best Geographical Location(s) for Position: Major tours are usually planned in the music capitals of New York City, Los Angeles, and Nashville; tours may leave from other locations

Prerequisites:

Education or Training—College degree in communications, English, journalism, public relations, or music merchandising preferred

Experience—Prior position in music or nonmusic-oriented publicity

Special Skills and Personality Traits—Willingness to travel; writing skills; national media contacts; ability to work under pressure

CAREER LADDER

```
┌─────────────────────────────────┐
│   Independent Tour Publicist;    │
│   Tour Coordinator/Manager       │
└─────────────────────────────────┘

┌─────────────────────────────────┐
│        Tour Publicist            │
└─────────────────────────────────┘

┌─────────────────────────────────┐
│          Publicist              │
└─────────────────────────────────┘
```

Position Description

A Tour Publicist is a trained publicist who goes on tour with a recording act or artist. He or she is in charge of making sure that both the act's fans and the media know that the group or artist is coming to town to perform a concert.

Certain Tour Publicists set up media interviews with local television, radio, newspaper, and magazine editors before the group leaves their home base. They might also arrange press parties and press conferences. Other times a staff publicist takes care of these details. The Tour Publicist's main function occurs on the road. When the group leaves on tour, the Tour Publicist is automatically part of the entourage.

On the road, he or she attends all interviews, photography sessions, concerts, press parties, and press conferences along with the act. In addition, the Tour Publicist accompanies the act to all radio interviews or television appearances. The Tour Publicist usually spends a few minutes with the show's producer, talent coordinator, or host to discuss what he or she would like the act to talk about during the interview.

At concerts, it is the Tour Publicist who is responsible for issuing press passes to disc jockeys, music editors, photographers, etc. He or she also issues the important backstage passes. All interviews and photo sessions must be approved in advance by the Tour Publicist. He or she usually sets a specific time before or after each show for additional interviews and photo sessions.

The Tour Publicist works closely with any sponsoring radio or television stations. He or she tries to make sure the employees of the station are happy. This might entail arranging special interviews or autograph sessions, presenting records or T-shirts, etc.

The Tour Publicist, who works for a record company or publicity firm, usually calls his or her office at least once a day. The Tour Publicist is responsible to his or her superiors at the record company or the publicity firm. An independent Tour Publicist is responsible directly to the act and its management team.

Tour Publicists work for the duration of the tour. It is not a nine to five job. While the act is still sleeping at 10:00 A.M., the Tour Publicist has already been up for a few hours making calls and discussing arrangements for the upcoming day. The Tour Publicist might still be up at 3:00 A.M. at a party thrown in the act's honor. The Tour Publicist must have a lot of stamina and a great love for the job to survive on the road.

Salaries

The salary for a Tour Publicist is usually higher than that for a home-based publicist because he or she must travel for long periods of time. Tour Publicists who work for a record company or publicity firm generally receive a weekly salary plus a daily or weekly stipend to cover personal expenses. Travel expenses are paid by the act or its management firm.

Independent Tour Publicists receive a weekly or monthly fee plus all expenses. These expenses may include food, lodging, phone, and other amenities. All work-related expenses, such as printing, long-distance phone calls, mailings, etc., are paid for by the group, record company, etc.

Salaries for Tour Publicists vary according to the employer, the act, and the amount of experience that the Tour Publicist has. A beginning Tour Publicist usually makes no less than $300 per week plus expenses. An average salary for a Tour Publicist working for a fairly established music group is between $25,000 and $35,000 per year plus expenses. There are Tour Publicists who are very much in demand who can command $1,000 and up per week for certain tours.

Employment Prospects

With the expenses of traveling going up, many groups cannot go on tour as often as they used to. There are also few groups that can afford the services of a Tour Publicist. These positions are available, but only on a very limited basis. However, there are not many people who like to or can travel constantly.

Advancement Prospects

A good Tour Publicist can advance to the position of tour coordinator or tour manager. If the Tour Publicist has worked for a major record com-

pany or has experience working with a publicity firm, he or she has the option of becoming an independent Tour Publicist.

Education and Training

A Tour Publicist position usually requires much the same training as a home-based publicist. A college degree with a major in communications, journalism, English, public relations, or music merchandising is preferable. Seminars on music-oriented publicity are also helpful.

Experience/Skills/Personality Traits

The Tour Publicist must have the ability to travel and must enjoy being on the road for long stretches at a time. Tour Publicists work under more pressure than home-based publicists. Road tours sometimes create stress for people. Toward the end of a tour, for example, the entire entourage may get jumpy. They just want the tour to end. The Tour Publicist must make sure that this attitude is not displayed to the media or the fans.

The Tour Publicist must maintain a list of national media contacts to call upon while his or her client is touring.

Unions/Associations

There are no unions that represent Tour Publicists in the music field. There are a number of organizations and associations Tour Publicists can belong to. The best known is the Public Relations Society of America (PRSA), which has local chapters in major cities in the United States.

Tips for Entry

1. Place an ad in one of the music trades (classified or display) describing the type of position you're looking for. Professionals in the business read these trades and might be looking for someone to fill this type of position.

2. If you're working in a music-oriented public relations firm or a record company, talk to your superiors about this position. Often they need someone for this position. Many publicists in a company may not be free to travel for great lengths of time.

3. Send your resumé with a cover letter to record companies or music-oriented public relations firms asking about openings for Tour Publicists.

SOUND TECHNICIAN

CAREER PROFILE

Duties: Working the sound board for an act on tour; taking care of sound equipment

Alternate Title(s): Audio Technician; Sound Person; Sound Man or Woman

Salary Range: $7,500 to $30,000+

Employment Prospects: Fair

Advancement Prospects: Poor

Best Geographical Location(s) for Position: Major tours are usually planned in New York City, Los Angeles, or Nashville, although they leave from various cities; other tours are planned from cities around the country

Prerequisites:

Education or Training—No educational requirements; training in electronics or sound

Experience—Experience working sound boards and other sound equipment

Special Skills and Personality Traits—Good musical "ear"; love of music; knowledge of electronics; knowledge of sound board; freedom to travel

CAREER LADDER

```
┌─────────────────────────────┐
│  Sound Technician for Top Act; │
│       Road Manager           │
└─────────────────────────────┘

┌─────────────────────────────┐
│      Sound Technician        │
└─────────────────────────────┘

┌─────────────────────────────┐
│  Sound Technician Assistant; │
│          Roadie              │
└─────────────────────────────┘
```

Position Description

The Sound Technician working on the road has a good deal of responsibility. The main area he or she must be concerned with is good quality sound during a show.

The Sound Technician usually arrives at a concert hall earlier than the performers. Along with the rest of the road crew, he or she unloads, sets up and positions the equipment and the instruments. (In certain union situations, such as union halls, union employees must unload the equipment. In cases like this, the Sound Technician will supervise placement of equipment.)

The equipment and the instruments must be placed on the stage in such a way that the sounds of the instruments and the vocals will blend well. In addition, everything must be situated so that the sound is good and those on stage can both see and hear what goes on during the show.

After everything is set up, the musicians and the vocalists will arrive. The Sound Technician must then prepare for the all-important sound check. During this time the Sound Technician works with the talent. Each person will play his or her instrument or sing, and the Technician must listen to determine whether the sound is coming through properly. Sometimes this takes a great deal of time because acoustics are different in every hall. During this period as many adjustments as possible are taken care of. Minor adjustments will take place just before the show when the hall fills up.

During the show the Sound Technician works the sound board. He or she can adjust the volume of voices while changing the volume of instruments. Instruments can be made to sound more bass, treble, etc. The sound must constantly be balanced so that all the instruments and vocals blend together. The Sound Technician is usually situated somewhere in front of the stage during the performance. This is where the true sound can be heard the best.

After the show, the Sound Technician may be responsible for watching the loading and packing of the sound equipment. Big tours sometimes have an entire truck designated to haul only the sound equipment.

The Sound Technician might also be responsible for checking out the equipment after a show to see what needs repair or replacement. Many Sound Technicians know how to fix much of the equipment they work with. This is a plus, especially if the equipment breaks down just before or during a show.

Sound Technicians are responsible to the head road manager or tour coordinator. It depends on the acts they work with.

Sound Technicians do not work on a constant basis. They might work a six week tour with one act and have a month off before the next tour starts with another group. There are instances where the Sound Technician might go on a reduced salary while not on tour in order to make sure that he or she is available to a particular group.

Sound Technicians who work on the road must have the freedom to travel. In addition, they must be able to deal with long periods on the road and living out of a suitcase.

Salaries

Salaries for Sound Technicians vary greatly. Sound people working for a local band on its way up may make minimum wage or less. They may get the same percentage of the pot as each of the band members.

As Sound Technicians move up and work for better-known acts, their income increases. Salaries run from $7,500 to around $30,000+ yearly. The higher salary would, of course, go to a Sound Technician on the road with a very well-known act.

Sound Technicians working on the road usually receive a per diem to pay for living expenses while traveling.

It is important to note that if the Sound Technician freelances, he or she will probably not work fifty two weeks a year.

Employment Prospects

A Sound Technician has a fair chance of finding employment with a local or well-known regional band. Possibilities of finding work decrease as the popularity of the group with which one aspires to work increases.

Advancement Prospects

Advancement is difficult for Sound Technicians. They may find work with a more popular band or act, but this is not easy.

Sound Technicians may also advance to the position of road manager or tour coordinator if they exhibit sufficient drive, responsibility, and competence.

Education and Training

No formal education is required for the position of Sound Technician. Many individuals in this job picked up the basics by watching someone else work the board.

Other people do have some training in electronics or sound, possibly from attending a recording or broadcasting school.

Experience/Skills/Personality Traits

As noted above, many Sound Technicians pick up the basics of the work from watching someone else do it. They might occasionally assist or ask questions of a working Sound Technician.

Talented Sound Technicians usually have gathered a lot of experience. The more they work on the sound board, the better they get at balancing the sound.

As individuals in this field usually have to travel extensively, it is a must for the person to have the flexibility to travel and to enjoy it. Not everyone likes living out of a suitcase for weeks on end.

Certain Sound Technicians start out as roadies, helping or filling in with sound work along the way. Eventually they either fill an opening or apply for a job as a Sound Technician with another group.

Unions/Associations

Touring Sound Technicians do not usually belong to any union, although they could be members of the International Alliance of Theatrical State Employees (IATSE). Touring Sound People might belong to the Touring Entertainment Industry Association (TEIA). This organization provides a forum for people who work as or with touring talent.

Tips for Entry

1. If you are interested in working in this field, hang around clubs and bars that provide live entertainment. Most of the Sound Technicians working in this type of atmosphere will answer any questions you have. You might even offer to work for nothing. The experience you gain may pay you back with a job.
2. Working as a roadie for a short stint might not only train you, but also land you a job when the Sound Technician leaves.

3. You might consider taking out an advertisement (classified or display) in a trade magazine or a newspaper read by acts or managers requiring sound services. (*The Village Voice* in New York City frequently runs such ads.)

ADVANCE PERSON

CAREER PROFILE

Duties: Arriving ahead of the act to prepare for a concert; assisting tour coordinator or road manager with details prior to show

Alternate Title(s): Advance Agent; Advance Man; Advance Woman

Salary Range: $10,000 to $20,000

Employment Prospects: Poor

Advancement Prospects: Poor

Best Geographical Location(s) for Position: Positions are located in cities where major management and booking agencies are, such as New York City, Nashville, and Los Angeles.

Prerequisites:

Education or Training—No formal education required

Experience—Nonmusic Advance Person; roadie experience helpful

Special Skills and Personality Traits—Freedom to travel; enjoyment of traveling alone; organization; dependability

CAREER LADDER

```
┌─────────────────────────────────┐
│                                 │
│          Road Manager           │
│                                 │
└─────────────────────────────────┘

┌─────────────────────────────────┐
│                                 │
│          Advance Person         │
│                                 │
└─────────────────────────────────┘

┌─────────────────────────────────┐
│                                 │
│   Nonmusic-Oriented Advance Person;   │
│              Roadie             │
└─────────────────────────────────┘
```

Position Description

The Advance Person goes out on the road before a tour. He or she leaves the home base before any of the entourage does and always arrives before the rest of the group. Usually the Advance Person is gone by the time the act or group arrives at the destination.

When an Advance Person gets to a city in which an act is booked to perform, he or she will make sure that everything is set up as planned. He or she will check to see that posters and billboards are up. If they aren't, he or she might put them up or hire a crew to do it.

The Advance Person may bring in concert tickets. This happens rarely, though, because most concert halls utilize the services of a ticket service agency, such as Ticketron. The Advance Person might bring in and hand-deliver any press passes issued by the publicist and/or management team.

The Advance Person will also hand-deliver press packages, photos, and promotional copies of records to press and promoters in each city.

Often the Advance Person checks out the acoustics of the hall or auditorium where the concert is to be held. He or she checks to see the location of electric outlets and types of electrical service available. This information is relayed back to the tour manager or coordinator. The Advance Person might also check out seating and exits and entrances of halls, making diagrams for the road personnel to use later.

Depending on the position, the Advance Person might measure mileage and check routes between concert cities. He or she might see what options are available for transportation in each city. All this information is relayed back to the tour manager, coordinator, or management office.

Certain groups have tremendous fan clubs that organize events in honor of the act's arrival in town. The Advance Person might contact the fan club president and deliver press passes or group memorabilia.

To be an Advance Person, an individual must be very dependable and responsible. No one is looking over the individual's shoulder. He or she must be able to structure his or her own day in order to get everything accomplished.

He or she must also be personable and articulate. Much of the job involves talking to people about the concert tour. As an Advance Person, an individual represents the group or act he or she is working for. The Advance Person must also like to travel and not mind being alone most of the time.

The Advance Person is responsible to the management, booking agency, or act that retained his or her services.

Salaries

Salaries vary depending on the group or management team that the Advance Person is working with.

Salaries usually start at about $200 per week and go up to $400 weekly. Advance People always receive either a per diem or reimbursement for their traveling expenses.

Advance people are usually paid by the week for the time that they work. Weeks that they are not on the road, they might have a reduction in salary, no salary, or might be kept on a retainer.

Employment Prospects

Employment prospects for this position are poor. With the new overnight delivery systems, many management firms just mail what they need delivered and make phone calls for any information. Furthermore, not every act uses an Advance Person.

Advancement Prospects

If a person does obtain a position as an Advance Person, he or she might eventually become a road manager or even a tour manager. It all depends on the type of organization the individual works with.

The Advance Person also has the option of working for bigger acts and better, more prestigious tours.

Education and Training

There is no formal educational requirement for this position. The individual might, however, be required to have a driver's license.

Experience/Skills/Personality Traits

The Advance Person must like to travel and must not mind traveling alone. Advance People in the music business often have held positions as Advance People in other parts of the entertainment industry or for convention management.

The individual in this job must be extremely organized. He or she should be responsible and dependable. The Advance Person should also be personable and articulate.

Unions/Associations

The Advance Person may belong to the Touring Entertainment Industry Association (TEIA). This association holds conferences, conventions, etc. for people working in the touring industry.

Tips for Entry

1. This is a position either you get by contacts or by being in the right place at the right time. Pass along the word to musicians, groups, management, and booking agencies that you're looking for this type of job.
2. Advertise your availability in a small display or classified ad in one of the music trades.
3. Experience helps, whether it be experience as a nonmusic-oriented Advance Person or a travel agent, roadie, etc. Put in your resumé everything that might be of value to a potential employer.

MUSIC RETAILING
AND WHOLESALING

MUSIC SHOP MANAGER

CAREER PROFILE

Duties: Managing and running a music shop; buying and/or ordering instruments, sheet music, equipment, etc.

Alternate Title(s): Music Store Manager; Music Department Manager; Instrument Store Manager

Salary Range: $12,500 to $36,000+

Employment Prospects: Good

Advancement Prospects: Fair

Best Geographical Location(s) for Position: Any city or community that has a music shop

Prerequisites:

Education or Training—High school diploma minimum; college degree or background often required

Experience—Retail sales experience; music shop salesperson

Special Skills and Personality Traits—Understanding of business management; knowledge of wide variety of instruments; ability to manage

CAREER LADDER

```
┌─────────────────────────────────┐
│                                 │
│        Music Shop Owner         │
│                                 │
└─────────────────────────────────┘

┌─────────────────────────────────┐
│                                 │
│       Music Shop Manager        │
│                                 │
└─────────────────────────────────┘

┌─────────────────────────────────┐
│  Music Shop Assistant Manager;  │
│    Music Shop Salesperson       │
│                                 │
└─────────────────────────────────┘
```

Position Description

The position of Music Shop Manager can be an exciting one for a person who likes to be around musical instruments. The main function of the individual in this job is to manage and run a retail music shop. There are many duties within the job classification.

Naturally, the manager must oversee the day-to-day activities of the music shop. He or she is responsible for hiring and supervising employees. The manager is in charge of putting together a work schedule for those who are employed by the shop. The individual assigns staff to perform specific duties and trains them, if necessary.

The Music Shop Manager works closely with the store owner (or he or she may be the store owner). Together, they decide what policies will be used for the store regarding payment, layaway, instrument returns, special orders, music lessons, etc. They may work out a marketing, advertising, or promotional campaign together, too.

The Music Shop Manager is in charge of seeing that instruments are ordered and purchased. The individual will select the equipment, supplies, and/or sheet music the store will stock. He or she is responsible for making sure that orders come in, bills are paid on time, and internal problems with distributors or sales representatives are minimized.

If there is a problem with an instrument or piece of equipment that a customer has purchased in the music store, it is up to the manager to resolve the difficulty. The manager must try to keep customers happy and uphold the reputation of the store.

The Music Shop Manager may act as a salesperson, selling instruments, equipment, or other supplies to customers. The individual may be called on to explain in detail differences in quality or variations among instruments.

He or she assumes the responsibility for maintaining operating records of all daily transactions. Cash income must be reconciled with the day's receipts.

This type of position usually has fairly regular hours. The manager is responsible to the store owner or department store manager. If the Music

Shop Manager owns the store, as is often the case, the person is, of course, responsible to him or herself.

Salaries

Those who manage music shops or departments may expect salaries ranging from $12,500 to $36,000+ yearly. Salaries may consist of weekly salaries, bonuses, commissions, etc. The larger earnings go to individuals who are very experienced in managing music shops. The salary of a Music Shop Manager is also dependent on the location and size of the store.

Employment Prospects

Employment prospects for people seeking to be Music Shop or Department Managers are good. There are many opportunities for individuals in all sections of the country. People may find work in large stores, small shops, music store chains, or the instrument/sheet music department of a variety store.

Advancement Prospects

Music Shop or Department Managers move up the career ladder in a number of ways. They may advance by obtaining a job in a music store instead of a music department. An individual might move to a position in a larger, more prestigious store as a means of advancement. The other opportunity for a music department manager is to open his or her own music shop.

Education and Training

Music shops often prefer their managers to hold bachelor's degrees or at least have some type of college background. The exception would be an owner of a music shop who is also managing it. Even in such a situation, however, people find it helpful to have an education.

Music Shop Managers often hold degrees in business, liberal arts, music, retailing, music education, or music performance. A music background is necessary to successfully run a music store. This background may be obtained through the standard educational process, such as college or conservatory training, or might come from experiences dealing in music.

Experience/Skills/Personality Traits

The Music Shop Manager needs to have an understanding of retail business management. He or she must possess the ability to hire, fire, and train personnel. The manager will have to supervise the shop and the staff on a day-to-day basis.

The individual in this position needs knowledge of a wide variety of musical instruments. The person should be capable of playing or demonstrating most instruments in the store, or should find someone else who can handle this part of the enterprise.

Unions/Associations

Music Shop Managers may belong to the National Association of Music Merchants (NAMM). The individual might additionally be a member of the National Association of School Music Dealers.

Tips for Entry

1. Jobs for Music Shop Managers are advertised in the classified sections of newspapers.
2. Job openings may also be posted on the shop window.
3. People working in music shops are often promoted. Many Music Shop Managers started working as salespeople in the shop they currently manage.
4. Send resumés and cover letters to music shops and request that they keep them on file.

MUSIC SHOP SALESPERSON

CAREER PROFILE

Duties: Selling instruments, musical accessories, equipment, supplies, and sheet music to customers in a retail store

Alternate Title(s): Music Shop Clerk; Instrument Shop Clerk

Salary Range: $9,000 to $20,000+

Employment Prospects: Good

Advancement Prospects: Fair

Best Geographical Location(s) for Position: Any city or area with music shops

Prerequisites:

Education or Training—High school diploma minimum; some positions require college background or degree; musical training

Experience—Retail sales experience helpful

Special Skills and Personality Traits—Knowledge of musical instruments; ability to play instruments; ability to work well with people; salesmanship

CAREER LADDER

```
┌─────────────────────────────┐
│                             │
│     Music Shop Manager      │
│                             │
└─────────────────────────────┘

┌─────────────────────────────┐
│                             │
│    Music Shop Salesperson   │
│                             │
└─────────────────────────────┘

┌─────────────────────────────┐
│         Musician;           │
│         Student;            │
│     Retail Salesperson      │
└─────────────────────────────┘
```

Position Description

A Music Shop Salesperson sells instruments, musical accessories, equipment, supplies, and/or sheet music to customers in a retail store. The individual may specialize in selling brass, percussion, stringed, or woodwind instruments.

The Salesperson might act as a cashier, making a sale, totalling up the customer's purchases, arranging for layaways, taking money, and giving change.

The Music Shop Salesperson may perform a wide spectrum of other duties, depending on the job. A specific duty might be to assist customers in choosing the correct instruments for their needs. For example, someone may come into the store to buy a guitar. The Salesperson must find out a few things about the individual: Is the guitar going to be used for pleasure or to play in a band? Is the band a school group or a famous recording act? Does the customer want an electgric guitar or an accoustic instrument? What size guitar: standard, three quarters or child's size? What price range and brand is the customer considering? These are some of the questions the Salesperson needs answered in order to help a customer choose an instrument.

In this sales position, the individual might demonstrate a few different instruments to help a customer decide which has a better tone, sound, etc. The Salesperson talks to the potential buyer about the variables in the instruments versus the prices.

Salespeople or clerks in music shops may clean or repair instruments in addition to their sales duties. Depending on a person's talent, he or she might tune pianos, too.

The Salesperson in a music shop will take special orders for instruments not in stock. The individual often talks to schools in the area about their musical requirements and may try to solicit an order.

Salespeople in music shops frequently receive commissions on instrument sales as well as salaries. This gives them extra incentive to try to make additional sales.

Depending on the range of duties, the Salesperson may take inventory of existing merchandise and keep a list of what has been sold. He or she might send or call orders in to instrument sales representatives or companies.

In certain stores, the Salesperson also gives music lessons on various instruments. This depends on the competence of the individual teaching. The person is usually paid extra for this duty.

In a music shop, the Salesperson either works regular store hours or a particular shift. The job can be full- or part-time. The individual in this position is responsible directly to the store owner or manager.

Salaries

Salespeople working in music shops may be paid in a number of ways. The Salesperson may receive a straight salary, a commission on instruments sold, or a combination of the two. The salary range for music shop salespeople is approximately $9,000 to $20,000+ yearly. The lower figure represents the earnings of an individual working in a small shop with little or no experience. The higher figure is for a person who is working in a large music store in a city. That person probably has quite a bit of experience in the field.

Music Shop Salespeople who have the ability to play certain instruments well and can teach may make extra money by giving lessons.

Employment Prospects

Employment prospects for Music Shop Salespeople are good. Those who have the ability to play more than one instrument and can demonstrate to prospective customers may have even better prospects. Opportunities for work exist in major cities, smaller cities, and large towns. Individuals may find work in large stores, small shops, or in the music sections of department stores.

Advancement Prospects

Individuals might find openings as Salespeople in larger stores. Working in a larger shop could mean that the Music Shop Salesperson would be earning a higher salary and/or commissions.

Those working as Music Shop Salespeople might climb the career ladder by advancing to music shop managers or music department managers.

The Music Shop Salesperson may get experience, learn the business, and then open his or her own store.

Education and Training

Those working as Salespeople in music shops must usually hold at least a high school diploma. In larger, more prestigious music stores, manage-

ment and/or owners may require that their staff have college degrees or backgrounds. Individuals who hold music degrees are often hired in these shops.

It is helpful for the Salesperson to be trained to play at least one instrument, perferably more than one. It is also useful for the person to have a knowledge of music theory and be able to read music. This training may be obtained in school, conservatories, colleges, through private study, or be self-taught.

Experience/Skills/Personality Traits

The Music Shop Salesperson generally has had some type of retail sales experience prior to obtaining the music shop position. He or she must work well with people, making them feel comfortable purchasing in the store. The Salesperson must not pressure customers, but should be helpful and give honest, concise information about the instrument and accessories.

The Music Shop Salesperson who can play and/or demonstrate various instruments is a valuable commodity in a music shop. The individual may also teach students who have purchased instruments from the store. Therefore, an ability to teach is a plus.

The individual must understand how the instruments work and be able to identify their various parts.

Unions/Associations

Depending on the store where an individual works, a Music Shop Salesperson may or may not belong to a bargaining union. The union might be an in-house union or may be a union that encompasses the job classification.

Music Shop Salespeople might also belong to the National Association of Music Merchants (NAMM). This trade organization provides educational materials, training sessions, conferences, etc. for its members.

Tips for Entry

1. Jobs for Music Shop Salespeople are advertised in help wanted sections. Keep an eye on such headings as "Salesperson Wanted," "Instrument Sales," "Music Shop Clerk," etc.
2. Jobs are often posted in the shop's window.
3. You might consider sending resumés with cover letters to a number of stores. Follow up with a phone call.
4. Ask to see the store owner or manager and ask to fill out an application to be kept on file.

RECORD SHOP
(OR DEPARTMENT) MANAGER

CAREER PROFILE

Duties: Managing and running a record shop or department on a day-to-day basis

Alternate Title(s): Record Store Manager

Salary Range: $12,500 to $35,000

Employment Prospects: Excellent

Advancement Prospects: Good

Best Geographical Location(s) for Position: All locations have possible positions available

Prerequisites:

Education or Training—High school diploma minimum; some positions require or prefer college degree or background

Experience—Retail sales experience, preferably in record store or department

Special Skills and Personality Traits—Salesmanship; good administration; knowledge of retail record business; cognizance of customers' musical tastes

CAREER LADDER

```
┌─────────────────────────────┐
│     Record Shop Owner;       │
│  Record Shop Chain Manager   │
└─────────────────────────────┘

┌─────────────────────────────┐
│ Record Shop/Department Manager │
└─────────────────────────────┘

┌─────────────────────────────┐
│      Record Shop Clerk       │
└─────────────────────────────┘
```

Position Description

Record Shop Managers work in record shops or in department stores in the record department. Their basic function is to manage and run the record shop or department on a day-to-day basis. The manager may work for a private store owner, a record chain, a department store, or may be the actual shop owner.

Daily duties for the Record Shop Manager include the supervision of other employees in the store or department, development of work schedules, and assignment of employees to specific duties. He or she may be responsible for the hiring and firing of personnel.

The Record Shop Manager works in close contact with other employees, pitching in where needed. He or she may perform sales duties on a regular basis or assign these duties to clerks. The individual is responsible for taking care of any problems that arise with customers. These might include faulty merchandise, questions about orders, or difficulties with store personnel. It is up to the manager to deal with problems and complaints in a fair manner but according to store policy. At times, the manager may feel the need to go against store policy in order to keep a customer or to maintain good store relations. This is the individual's prerogative.

As the Record Shop Manager, the person is in charge of ordering merchandise. To do this, he or she must know what is hot. Managers of record shops must keep up with the current musical trends and customers' musical tastes.

The Record Shop Manager must take and/or supervise inventories of stock on hand. Certain records and tapes sell out as soon as they come in. Requisitions must be prepared to replenish the stock of records and tapes. Records and tapes that do not sell can often be returned to the distributor. Data must be kept on what records come in, from what distributor, and on what date.

A variety of other merchandise and products may be ordered in addition to records and tapes. These might include music videos, blank cassettes, stereo needles, music magazines, posters, etc.

It is the responsibility of the Record Shop Manager to make sure that operating data are kept, daily postings of transactions are prepared, and cash is reconciled with sales receipts.

Depending on the store, the manager may have to coordinate sales promotion activities and prepare advertisements and merchandising displays. The Record Shop Manager may perform any of these functions or supervise or direct other employees to do so.

The Record Shop Manager's hours vary, but are usually fairly regular. The manager is responsible to the storeowner, record chain supervisor, or department store manager. If the manager owns the store, he or she is responsible only to him or herself and to any investors.

Salaries

Salaries for Record Shop Managers fluctuate, depending on the size of the store, the location, and the experience of the individual.

Starting salaries are usually around $12,500 per year. Earnings for more experienced record shop managers may range from $20,000 to $35,000 yearly. Monies can come in the form of salaries, commissions, and/or bonuses.

Many Record Shop Managers own the shop they run and receive a percentage of the profits.

Employment Prospects

There are openings for Record Shop and Record Department Managers across the country. Individuals who have had sales experience in record shops and know how a store works are qualified for the many positions available.

With the great demand for records, there are more and more record shops opening. There is hardly a city or town in the country that does not have at least one store, and most have more than one.

Advancement Prospects

Advancement prospects for Record Shop Managers are good. Individuals may upgrade their careers in a number of ways.

One method is to obtain a position at a larger store with additional responsibilities and greater earnings. Others advance their career by moving from a job at a department store as a manager of the record department to a job as manager of a record shop. There are individuals who begin as Record Shop Managers and go on to manage whole chains of record stores. Of course, there are those people who promote themselves by buying their own record shops.

Education and Training

Record Shop Managers must usually have a minimum of a high school diploma. Some positions require or prefer a college degree or background. There are degree programs available in retailing, business administration, and music merchandising that can prove useful.

Experience/Skills/Personality Traits

Record Shop Managers generally have worked in a retail sales position previous to their appointment. Usually, they have worked in a record store as a clerk for a period of time. The duration of this experience varies from person to person. However, managers generally have worked long enough in a clerical position to learn how the retail record business is run. Depending on the geographical area of the record shop, managers must know the type of customers they will be servicing and what their musical tastes are. The Record Shop Manager must be reliable, honest, and hardworking. Besides this, he or she must be a good administrator, capable of hiring and firing employees.

Unions/Associations

Record Shop Managers may be members of the National Association of Recording Merchandisers (NARM). This organization is a trade association for people in the recording business.

Tips for Entry

1. These positions are often advertised in the help wanted sections of newspapers.
2. There are employment agencies that occasionally look for people to fill jobs as managers of record shops. Depending on the agency and the job, you might have to pay a fee if you obtain a position. Check it out first.
3. Many record stores like to promote from within. If you are working as a clerk in a store and impress the owner, you may be able to advance your career.
4. Record shops often advertise openings on their front window. Keep a lookout for these signs.

RECORD SHOP CLERK

CAREER PROFILE

Duties: Selling records and tapes in record shop or department; assisting customers

Alternate Title(s): Record Store Clerk; Record Shop Salesperson

Salary Range: $7,400 to $16,000

Employment Prospects: Excellent

Advancement Prospects: Good

Best Geographical Location(s) for Position: Any location nationwide may have positions

Prerequisites:

Education or Training—High school diploma (or high school student)

Experience—Retail sales experience helpful, but not required

Special Skills and Personality Traits—Sales ability; ability to work well with others; dependability; enjoyment of records and music

CAREER LADDER

```
┌─────────────────────────────┐
│                             │
│    Record Shop Manager      │
│                             │
└─────────────────────────────┘

┌─────────────────────────────┐
│                             │
│     Record Shop Clerk       │
│                             │
└─────────────────────────────┘

┌─────────────────────────────┐
│         Student;            │
│   Other Retail Sales Job    │
│                             │
└─────────────────────────────┘
```

Position Description

Record Shop Clerks work in record stores or departments selling records, tapes, and assorted music-oriented merchandise to customers. Other goods might include blank cassettes, cassette cases, stereo needles, recording maintenance equipment and supplies, music videos, posters, and music magazines.

The Record Shop Clerk or salesperson may perform a variety of functions. One of these is to assist customers. Patrons may need help locating records, deciding what tape would be suitable for a gift, or deciphering price codes on records.

The Clerk may be responsible for totaling a customer's purchases, taking money, giving change, and packaging or wrapping the merchandise. The salesperson will take down information for special orders for records or tapes that are not in stock. The Clerk will pass the information on to the store manager to order.

Under the supervision of the record shop manager, the Clerk may receive new records, tapes, etc. into the store from distributors. He or she may count and sort the merchandise and verify receipt of items on invoices. The individual will check that the items arriving are indeed the merchandise that was ordered.

The Clerk may take inventory of existing merchandise, maintaining lists and informing the manager of those records selling well and those that have not moved. He or she may pack up records that are being sent back to the distributor.

The Clerk might stamp, mark, or attach price tags to goods in the store. At times, he or she may stock record bins, shelves, etc. Depending on the situation, the individual may help the manager set up advertising displays or arrange merchandise in a manner that will promote sales.

Record Sales Clerks work different shifts. They may work full or part-time. Individuals in this position are responsible to the shop manager.

Salaries

Earnings for record shop clerks vary depending on the experience of the person, the size of the store, and the geographical location. Salaries begin at or slightly above the minimum wage. Clerks working in record shops can expect to earn $7,400 to $16,000 yearly. Sales Clerks may earn straight salaries or salaries plus commissions on each sale made. Sales Clerks might also receive bonuses.

Employment Prospects

Employment prospects are excellent. This particular job is one in which almost anyone can enter the music business. There are virtually thousands upon thousands of positions open in record shops, record chains, and department stores in every section of the country.

This is an entry level position. Young people still in high school or college often apply for jobs in record shops to learn about the record business.

Advancement Prospects

Those who wish to advance have good prospects. Record Shop Clerks are often promoted to record department managers, record shop managers, or other management positions in the store or chain.

As noted above, many individuals begin working in a record shop as a way of entering the music field. Learning about record sales helps prepare those aspiring to enter the recording industry. It affords them a positive means of entry.

Education and Training

Those working in record shops as clerks are usually required to hold at least a high school diploma. However, most stores will hire young people who are high school students as part-time workers or for summer jobs.

Experience/Skills/Personality Traits

Although some retail sales experience is helpful, it is often not required. What is required is that the Record Shop Clerk be pleasant and helpful to customers. A knowledge of the current records and trends is useful.

Record Shop Clerks must work well with others and be dependable and reliable.

Unions/Associations

In very small record shops, Clerks usually do not belong to unions. Record Shop Clerks often belong to unions in larger record shops or while working in the record department of a department store. The union may be an in-house union or a local union that encompasses the job classification.

Tips for Entry

1. Positions for Record Shop Clerks are often advertised in the classified sections of newspapers.
2. Openings are also often noted on the shop window or bulletin board.
3. You may consider going into a record shop and asking to see the manager. This individual will usually let you fill out an application and keep it on file for future reference.

INSTRUMENT SALES REPRESENTATIVE

CAREER PROFILE

Duties: Selling musical instruments to dealers

Alternate Title(s): Sales Rep; Rep; Manufacturer's Representative

Salary Range: $7,500 to $65,000+

Employment Prospects: Good

Advancement Prospects: Good

Best Geographical Location(s) for Position: Instrument manufacturers are located in various areas of the country

Prerequisites:

Education or Training—High school diploma minimum; some positions require college background or degree

Experience—Somes sales experience (either wholesale or retail) helpful

Special Skills and Personality Traits—Sales ability; communication skills; knowledge of music and instruments; ability to play instrument helpful

CAREER LADDER

```
┌─────────────────────────────────┐
│         Sales Manager           │
└─────────────────────────────────┘

┌─────────────────────────────────┐
│  Instrument Sales Representative │
└─────────────────────────────────┘

┌─────────────────────────────────┐
│       Nonmusic Sales Job        │
└─────────────────────────────────┘
```

Position Description

An Instrument Sales Representative sells musical instruments to shops, dealerships, and schools. Usually a Sales Rep has a specific territory. This area (sometimes called a region or district) may consist of a few cities, counties, or states, or an entire section of the country.

As a Sales Rep, the individual must know as much as possible about the instrument(s) and the manufacturer. Additionally, it is important for the person to know about instruments manufactured by competing companies. With this information, the individual can speak knowledgeably to dealers about comparisons. Actually, the more knowledge the Sales Rep has, the better qualified that person is to come up with a good sales pitch. Knowing about the weaknesses of a particular instrument (even if it's made by one's own company) helps prepare the individual to field questions on the subject.

In this position, a person may make sales calls either in person or on the phone or combine the two methods. The individual is responsible for visiting established accounts, seeing what they require and what has been sold since the last visit. The

Sales Representative will probably talk to the dealer for a short while, discussing any problems with instruments sold and under warranty. He or she may review new instruments, products, trends, etc. By the time the Sales Representative is ready to leave, he or she should have developed a large order for the company.

The Rep may also seek out new accounts (places to sell the instruments). To do this, the individual may call in advance to try to set up an appointment, send a letter and some product brochures, or just drop in. The dealer may not buy from the Sales Representative the first time, but possibly will after a relationship has been established.

As an Instrument Representative, the individual may call or visit schools to find out about their band and orchestra instrument needs. Making a sale in this area could mean a big order. Schools, both public and private, may create a new market for the Sales Rep.

The Instrument Sales Representative has duties other than selling. He or she must telephone established and new accounts, send letters and brochures, keep up on all the newest instrument technology, and maintain good records. Losing an order or forgetting to call back a potential buyer may mean not only a lost sale, but possibly a lost job.

The Sales Representative is usually directly responsible to the sales manager of the organization. Hours for this type of position vary. Some jobs offer more flexibility in working hours than others.

Salaries

Remuneration for Sales Representatives may be made in a variety of ways. Reps may be paid a straight salary, a commission, or a combination of the two. Instrument Sales Representatives additionally may receive bonuses and fringe benefits, including cars, traveling expenses, etc.

Earnings for Sales Representatives in the musical instrument field range from $7,500 to $65,000+. Individuals working on a commission basis can do quite well financially. The sky is the limit as far as earnings are concerned.

Employment Prospects

Employment prospects for this field are good. There are many openings for aggressive, talented Sales Representatives. Those who have a background in music and have the ability to play an instrument or group of instruments are in a better position.

Many positions require the individual to sell in large geographic areas. Those who don't mind traveling will find even greater opportunities.

Advancement Prospects

Advancement prospects for an Instrument Sales Representative are generally good. If the individual has done a good job, met sales quotas, maintained good relationships with shop owners and dealers, and opened new accounts, he or she may be promoted to a sales manager position. This position may be on a local, regional, national, or possibly even international level.

Education and Training

Educational requirements differ with each position. Many companies just require their Sales Reps to have high school diplomas. Others prefer that their sales staff have college backgrounds or degrees.

Some type of music or instrument training is useful for a better understanding of the product being sold.

Experience/Skills/Personality Traits

A person who works for a major music manufacturer as a Sales Representative will usually have had some type of retail or wholesale sales experience. The individual might have had other types of selling jobs unrelated to the music business.

The ability to come up with a good sales pitch is essential. The rep must be aggressive without being annoying. It helps immensely if the individual has the ability to be articulate both on the phone and in person. It is also useful for the Sales Representative to be knowledgeable about music and about the instrument being sold. The ability to play one or more instruments can also be helpful.

Unions/Associations

Instrument Sales Representatives may belong to the National Association of Music Merchants (NAMM). Depending on the type of instruments the individual sells, he or she may also belong to National Piano Manufacturers Association (NPMA) or the Guitar and Accessories Music Marketing Association (GAMMA).

Tips for Entry

1. Get some experience selling before you apply for a job as a Sales Rep. You might consider finding a job in a music instrument shop. This will give you an opportunity to talk to Sales Representatives to find out more about the job.
2. When you do apply for a job with a company, know as much about the company, their instruments, etc. as possible. This will help to impress the interviewer with your capabilities.
3. If you do play an instrument, try to find some manufacturers in that family of instruments. The ability to play that instrument is a plus when looking for a job of this type.

RACK JOBBER

Duties: Supplying records and tapes to shops whose main business is not the sale of records

Alternate Title(s): Subdistributor

Salary Range: $18,000 to $30,000+

Employment Prospects: Fair

Advancement Prospects: Fair

Best Geographical Location(s) for Position: Positions may be found in most cities across the country

Prerequisites:

Education or Training—High school diploma

Experience—Selling experience (both wholesale and retail) helpful

Special Skills and Personality Traits—Good business skills; knowledge of music market; good salesmanship; ability to work with figures and calculations

```
┌─────────────────────────────────────────┐
│            Owner of Record Shop;         │
│ Record Company Distribution Representative│
└─────────────────────────────────────────┘

┌─────────────────────────────────────────┐
│                                          │
│              Rack Jobber                 │
│                                          │
└─────────────────────────────────────────┘

┌─────────────────────────────────────────┐
│       Rack Jobber Field Representative   │
└─────────────────────────────────────────┘
```

Position Description

A Rack Jobber supplies records and tapes to shops that are not primarily in the record/tape business. Many of the record displays that are seen in supermarkets, department stores, automotive shops, discount stores, book stores, and drug stores are put together by Rack Jobbers. A Rack Jobber, incidentally, may have a number of people working in the business or may work alone.

As a Rack Jobber, the individual selects records and tapes to display and sell in a section of someone else's store or market. He or she receives space and in return either pays a rental fee, a leasing fee, a percentage of record sales, or a combination of these.

The job of a Rack Jobber is much like that of owning a retail record store. However, in this instance, the merchandise is in a space that already draws a stream of customer traffic. The Rack Jobber may have space in more than one store.

The Rack Jobber buys records from a distributor. Since he or she has limited space, it is impossible to stock every record, as a conventional record shop does. The most important records are those that have a high rating on the charts. The charts, in turn, are compiled in part by reports from Rack Jobbers on sales of specific records.

Rack Jobbers offer the store a record department. If a record doesn't sell, the Rack Jobber takes it back. This is a no-risk situation for the store's management.

It is the Rack Jobber's responsibility to select the records and place those that he or she feels will sell. After making sure that they get to the store, the individual must also make sure that they are displayed properly. This display should be pleasing to the eye and make people want to look at and purchase records. The Rack Jobber periodically comes into the store and takes inventory. He or she takes back merchandise that isn't moving and brings in better sellers.

Depending on the situation, the Rack Jobber must either hire a staff of salespeople (if it is a lease situation) or train and supervise members of the store's existing staff who will be working in the record department. In this instance, a rental fee or percentage may be paid to the store by the Rack Jobber.

In addition, the Rack Jobber supplies the store with advertising and promotional material to help sell the records. The Rack Jobber is in charge of keeping inventory and accounting records for his or her space.

As a Rack Jobber, the individual will get to know the distributors from many of the major record companies. This will enable the Rack Jobber to develop contacts within the recording industry.

The Rack Jobber must keep the stores happy and satisfied or they will not renew their contracts.

Salaries

Salaries for Rack Jobbers vary, depending on the company, its location, how many records are sold, and the type of salary received.

Earnings may be in the form of a straight commission or may be a guaranteed salary against a commission.

Salaries range from $18,000 to $30,000+.

Employment Prospects

There are many stores and shops that have record displays and/or record departments serviced by Rack Jobbers. The prospects are fair to good for people who want to find jobs in this field. A person may take over an entire rack jobbing operation or be a field representative. The field representative, incidentally, acts under the instructions of the main Rack Jobber, performing most of the same functions.

Advancement Prospects

Individuals who work as Rack Jobbers or Rack Jobber field representatives have a fair chance of moving ahead in their careers. If they decide that they like the business, they might open up their own record shops. A Rack Jobber may increase the size of his or her business immensely by broadening the base of operation.

As Rack Jobbers meet and work closely with distributors of major recording companies, they frequently make good contacts in the record industry. As a result, many of these individuals obtain jobs in the distribution department of large labels.

Education and Training

No educational background is required to be a Rack Jobber or to work for one, except possibly having a high school diploma. Individuals who do prefer to go to college, will find that courses in business, marketing, merchandising, and related fields will be useful. There are also music merchandising and music business majors available in many schools; these can be useful for individuals desiring to work in this field.

Experience/Skills/Personality Traits

A Rack Jobber needs a good business head. He or she must have the ability to sell and to be aggressive in a nice way. Knowledge of the current music market, trends, and the record business is essential to success. Being organized is also helpful.

Unions/Associations

Rack Jobbers may belong to a number of associations. These include the National Association of Music Merchants (NAMM) and the National Association of Recording Merchandisers (NARM). Both these organizations sponsor conventions, meetings, seminars, and conferences for their members. The associations also offer books, pamphlets, and other information useful to those selling or distributing records and tapes.

Tips for Entry

1. If you're looking for a job as a Rack Jobber/field representative, visit various drug stores, department stores, supermarkets, etc. Find out who their Rack Jobbers are. Get addresses and phone numbers and set up interviews.

2. Many of the major department stores around the country have record departments serviced by Rack Jobbers. To begin with, get a job as a clerk. Move up from there.

3. Call the distributor department of a major record company. Try to find out names and addresses of Rack Jobbers in your area. Send them your resumé and a cover letter. Try to arrange an interview.

The Business End
of the Industry

PERSONAL MANAGER

CAREER PROFILE

Duties: Representing act; overseeing and guiding all aspects of an artist's career

Alternate Title(s): Artist's Representative; Manager

Salary Range: 10% to 50% of artist's earnings

Employment Prospects: Good

Advancement Prospects: Poor

Best Geographical Location(s) for Position: Managers for major acts are usually located in New York City, Los Angeles, or Nashville; managers for lesser known acts may be located anywhere in the country.

Prerequisites:

Education or Training—No educational requirement; college background helpful; courses or seminars in business and music industry useful

Experience—Any type of experience in any phase of the music business is valuable

Special Skills and Personality Traits—Music industry contacts; aggressiveness; knowledge of music industry; ability to see raw talent; ability to work under pressure

CAREER LADDER

```
┌─────────────────────────────────────────┐
│  Personal Manager for Top Recording Act  │
└─────────────────────────────────────────┘

┌─────────────────────────────────────────┐
│            Personal Manager              │
└─────────────────────────────────────────┘

┌─────────────────────────────────────────┐
│ This position can be entry level or      │
│ individual can come from other facets of │
│ the music industry                       │
└─────────────────────────────────────────┘
```

Position Description

The main job of the Personal Manager is to represent one or more musical groups or artists. In doing this, the Manager oversees all aspects of an act's career.

The Personal Manager, in essence, deals with and advises the act on all business decisions and many of the creative decisions artists must make. In this manner, the Manager attempts to guide an artist's rise to the top.

The Manager begins by hearing and/or seeing an artist he or she feels has talent. After discussions with the act, a Manager may feel he or she has something to offer the act. The Manager should have the knowhow to direct a musical career. If a bargain is struck, the two parties usually sign a contract. It is then the Manager's job to begin to plan for stardom.

In this position, the Manager is the single most important person (talent notwithstanding) helping the act attain stardom or success. Soon after signing the contract, the Manager will begin looking for a record label that is interested in the group. This is accomplished in a variety of ways, including talking to the Manager's personal contacts, showcasing the act, and/or providing demo tapes and videos.

When the Manager finds a label interested in the act, he or she may negotiate a recording deal or recommend a music industry attorney to negotiate on behalf of the group.

The Manager seeks out booking agents to find engagements for the act. If the act is just starting out, the Manager may book it him or herself. However, it is illegal in a number of states for an individual to act as both a Manager and a booking agent. In other words, the Manager cannot usually take both a percentage of the artist's earnings for managing and an additional percentage for booking the act.

The Manager might help the artists polish their act by reviewing tunes, choreography, costumes, and backup musicians. He or she might also help choose musical personnel, producers, engineers, etc. for a recording date.

Representing the artist at all times, the Manager advises the act about other personnel to hire and/or fire. Personnel might include both business and talent people. Some examples of support personnel are: public relations firms, publicists, road personnel, producers, musicians, accountants, security people, and merchandisers.

As the Manager, the individual is responsible for advancing the act's career as much as possible. He or she must oversee all the personnel and their jobs in relation to the act. At times, the Manager might have to audit books or act as a road manager or even as the heavy in a dispute with a promoter.

A Manager must be willing to work hard for the success of the client. Working hard, however, doesn't always mean the artist will be successful. It is helpful for the Manager to have industry contacts. These contacts sometimes help the artist get to the top.

Managers are often given power of attorney for their clients. In some cases, the power of attorney is complete; in others, it is limited. Whatever the case, the Manager usually is given authority to approve concert dates and places, monies for concerts, publicity materials, etc.

The individual an act chooses to be its Manager must be compatible with the act. He or she must be available on a day-to-day basis to discuss any problems the artist has. In addition, the two parties must meet on a regular basis to discuss new ways to advance the career of the act.

In many cases, the Manager puts up money to finance the group or artist hoping to make the money back later. In other cases, the Manager might find a financial backer for the group.

The Personal Manager works closely with all members of the act's team. He or she may spend a great deal of time with the act's publicity or public relations firm working on building the image of the act.

The Manager will also be in constant communication with the act's booking agent or agency. The Manager must make sure that the act is always well represented by others.

The Manager is responsible directly to the act. Although the terms of each artist-manager contract are different, most run for a specified number of years. Some have option clauses that the Manager can pick up if he or she desires.

The lifestyle of a Personal Manager in the music business is a busy one. Long hours are spent with the act. More hours are used up dealing on the group's behalf. If a Manager is with an artist who makes it financially, he or she usually enjoy the success, too. Since Managers can handle more than one client (although they don't usually handle vast numbers at any one time), they can make out quite well financially.

Salaries

Personal Managers receive a percentage of artists' earnings. This percentage varies with the individual and the manager. It can range from 10% to 50%. The usual amount is 15% to 20% of artist earnings. In certain situations, the percentage goes up as an artist makes more money. For example, the Manager may make 10% of all earnings up to $100,000 and 15% on all monies after that.

Managers receive these fees off the top. Fees are received on monies from personal appearances, concerts, television, recording, etc. In some cases, the Manager also takes a percentage of merchandising paraphernalia sold (T-shirts, posters, bumper stickers, pins, etc.)

A Manager working with a band just starting out may earn the same amount of money as the band members until they get on their feet financially. The Manager may opt to take nothing until the group starts doing reasonably well.

The Manager often puts up money for the act in excess of his or her salary temporarily losing money. The Manager hopes that the money will be recouped later when the band is successful. (On the other hand, the band may break up or never get anywhere, and the Manager may incur a loss.)

A Manager working with a top recording group can make $500,000+. Managers often handle more than one act at a time.

Employment Prospects

Employment prospects are good for Personal Managers. As almost anyone can become a Manager, all one has to do is find acts to sign up. This is not to say that everyone can be a *good* Manager. In order to be successful, the Personal Manager must have contacts and guide the act's career.

There are many groups that are not yet signed with anyone. An individual with an eye for raw talent can certainly enter this field.

Advancement Prospects

There are many Managers around the country and the world. Most of them, however, do not handle major acts. In order to attract a top recording act, a Manager must have proven him or herself in the past. This usually means having a top act or an up-and-coming act signed. One other excellent method is for the Personal Manager to start with a new act and work with them, guiding their career until stardom. Unfortunately, though, as groups begin to attain success they often try to get out of their contracts with smaller Managers and sign with better known Managers.

Education and Training

There is no formal educational requirement to qualify one for a position as a manager. A college background is helpful, however. There are currently degrees and courses offered in the music business and music merchandising. Other useful majors and/or courses are business, law, communications, journalism, and marketing.

Experience/Skills/Personality Traits

A very broad knowledge of the entire music business is necessary for success as a Manager. Many new managers (those starting out with local acts, for instance) learn the ropes as they go. It is important for the individual to acquire as many useful music contacts as possible. This helps the Manager to help an act.

Successful Managers are hard-working individuals, always making efforts on their group's behalf. A Personal Manager should have the ability to see raw talent and work with it until it is polished to perfection.

Many Managers begin their careers as musicians and find they enjoy the business end of the industry more. Personal Managers should be adept at all the business facets of an entertainer's career. The ability to give positive, constructive advice on the creative end is a plus.

Unions/Associations

There is no bargaining union for Personal Managers. There is an association called the Conference of Personal Managers. This organization sets standards for the conduct of Personal Managers.

Tips for Entry

1. Try to break into management on a local level. There are many acts waiting for someone to help them.
2. You might consider working for a management agency as a secretary or assistant to learn the ropes.
3. There are often ads placed in the classified sections of newspapers and trades by groups seeking management. Some of these acts need management to find a backer. Some will want the Manager to be the backer, while others may just need to have someone notice their talent. Check it out.

BOOKING AGENT

CAREER PROFILE

Duties: Securing engagements for musical artists and groups

Alternate Title(s): Booking Manager; Theatrical Agent; Booker; Agent; Booking Representative

Salary Range: $12,500 to $500,000+

Employment Prospects: Fair

Advancement Prospects: Fair

Best Geographical Location(s) for Position: New York City, Los Angeles, and Nashville for major agencies; other cities may have opportunities

Prerequisites:

Education or Training—No educational requirement

Experience—Experience in various facets of music business; sales jobs; buying talent for college concerts

Special Skills and Personality Traits—Ability to communicate; knowledge of music business; knowledge of routing; ability to talk on phone for great lengths of time; good salesmanship

CAREER LADDER

```
┌─────────────────────────────────────┐
│      Booking Agency Owner;           │
│   Booking Agent for Major Talent     │
└─────────────────────────────────────┘

┌─────────────────────────────────────┐
│                                     │
│           Booking Agent             │
│                                     │
└─────────────────────────────────────┘

┌─────────────────────────────────────┐
│       Agent for Local Bands;        │
│             Musician                │
└─────────────────────────────────────┘
```

Position Description

Booking Agents are also known as booking managers, theatrical agents, bookers, agents, and booking representatives. Whatever name the individual goes by, he or she performs one main job: securing engagements for musical artists and groups.

The Booking Agent works in a number of ways. To start with, an Agent needs the talen to book. He or she may send out literature, brochures, pictures, etc. to a variety of clubs and concert halls to obtain bookings for a client. The Booking Agent usually follows up with many phone calls to these places.

If an Agent is dealing with a recognized talent (for example, a group with a Top 40 record on the charts) things are different. Under these circumstances, the Agent is usually called by clubs and promoters who want the act to appear in their venues. The Booking Agent works very closely with the act's manager and knows what fee to charge. The Agent will often negotiate with a promoter or club who wants the act for a lower price.

After a deal has been struck on the phone, the Agent sends out copies of contracts to be signed by the promoter or club owner. These contracts include all the information required by the promoter for the show or concert. Included is the name of the group, the date of the concert, the times of the shows, how many performances are required, how much money will be paid for the performance, and in what manner it will be paid. Agents, as a rule, require a percentage of the money up front. This amount varies, but is usually about 50%. The money is due when the contract is signed. The Agent collects the money, takes his or her percentage, and pays the group. The rest of the money is usually paid at the performance.

The contracts Agents send to people employing their acts may also have a rider attached that stipulates any extras the group is to receive. These extras might include expense money, hotel rooms, food, limousines, or instrumental augmentation, among other things.

In large agencies, Agents are often separated into categories. For instance, one Agent may handle classical acts, another rock acts, still another R & B acts. Other agencies may handle just one variety of artist.

Agents representing top groups may set up complete concert tours for the acts and deal with promoters all over the country. During these tours, the Agent works with the artist's manager and record company, deciding where concerts will be most effective.

In many states, booking agencies and Agents must be licensed. These licenses, like those of other employment agencies, are usually obtained through state agencies.

Agents often audition new talent that comes to them seeking representation. In addition, many Agents attend showcases, local clubs, etc. looking for talent to book.

Agents may represent a client exclusively or nonexclusively, depending on the circumstances. The Agent may also represent a client exclusively in one field (e.g., concerts) and nonexclusively in another (e.g., personal appearances).

Agents can represent as many clients as they can handle. They often book artists who compete with one another in the marketplace. Agents strive to build up a roster of clients. In addition, Agents aspire to have clients who command large fees.

The Agent is responsible to the artist and his or her manager. An agent may sign an artist for a specified number of years.

Most of the working day of an Agent is spent on the phone trying to sell the acts, talking about the acts, negotiating for the acts, etc. Most Agents spend 7 to 8 hours a day on the phone and use the phone as the vehicle to success.

Salaries

Booking Agents are paid a commission. They receive a percentage off the top of the artist's fee. Commissions vary, but usually range from 10% to 20% of the act's gross income per show.

Agents working in agencies may be paid a salary plus a percentage of the monies they bring into the agency. Agents who make the most money usually handle more than one act. The most successful Agents may earn $200,000 to $500,000+ per year. Individuals just starting out in the industry make much less. The variables are too great to estimate the average salary.

Employment Prospects

It is extremely difficult to break into booking on a major scale. Entering on a local level, however, prospects are much brighter. Many aspiring agents begin by booking local talent (or possibly even their own band) in local clubs and bars.

There are also agencies located in most cities. These agencies do not usually book major talent. Instead, they book regional talent. Entry into such an agency is another possibility for the individual looking for a job as an agent.

Most booking agencies that book major talent are located in New York City, Los Angeles, and Nashville. Many of these agencies have offices in other cities around the country.

Advancement Prospects

Agents may advance in a number of ways. They may begin booking a local band that gains some notoriety and go up the success ladder with them.

Another way an Agent may advance his or her career is to gain entry into a regional agency. After obtaining experience, the Agent might be able to move into a major agency.

Agents frequently become talent buyers for concert halls, clubs, arenas, etc. Other Agents build up enough of a client roster to start their own talent agency. There is no one way to advance a career like this. There are a number of Booking Agents and agencies around the country who are making a fortune booking acts on a regional level. Some of these people earn more than agents who work in a major agency in a music capital.

Education and Training

There is no educational requirement to work as a Booking Agent. There are seminars, workshops, and courses available in booking entertainment. Courses in business may be useful. There are also classes and seminars in contracts and/or contract law offered in many colleges.

Experience/Skills/Personality Traits

A Booking Agent, in effect, sells a group or an artist. Therefore, first and foremost an Agent must possess sales ability.

In order to be a successful Agent, one must be aggressive. Much of the selling of acts is done on the telephone. Agents of major groups may stay on the phone pushing their acts for 7 to 8 hours a day or even more.

As in most jobs in the music industry, Agents must be able to work under extreme pressure. Acts constantly call to see if they have new jobs. Managers call to tell the Agent they want more money for their acts. Clubs call to negotiate for an act for less money. Even after everything is set up, the group might cancel. The Agent must be able to keep his or her cool under these conditions.

Unions/Associations

Major Booking Agents usually work under a union contract, such as that of the American Federation of Musicians (AFM), the American Federation of Television and Radio Artists (AFTRA), the American Guild of Variety Artists (AGVA), the Screen Actors Guild (SAG), or the American Guild of Musical Artists (AGMA). These unions specify what percentage an agent can get from an act, how long contracts can run, etc.

Tips for Entry

1. Start booking groups in your area. All groups need work and most can never find enough jobs. Make sure the groups you book know that you will be taking a percentage. This money won't make you rich, but it will give you an opportunity to gain valuable experience in this type of position.
2. You might consider calling clubs in your area, too. Try to set up a meeting with the owner or club manager to see if they need entertainment for their clubs. Indicate that you will hire the entertainment under their direction, taking into account their budget, style of music, etc. Then place an ad for bands looking for work. Always keep a list of possibles in case an act cancels out.
3. In both of the above instances, try to use some form of contract as protection for yourself so that you get your commission.
4. If you want to work in a major agency, you might have to accept an entry level position as a secretary, receptionist, or mailroom clerk. Once you get in, ask questions and be interested.
5. If you are familiar with the business and have some experience, keep knocking on doors and calling major agencies. They often feel that if you can sell yourself to them, you can certainly sell the acts.
6. Look into the training programs some of the bigger agencies have established. There is a list of major agencies in the appendix.

CONCERT PROMOTER

CAREER PROFILE

Duties: Presenting talent in concert, club, or festival settings; overseeing every aspect of putting on a show

Alternate Title(s): Talent Promoter

Salary Range: $0 to $1,000,000+

Employment Prospects: Poor

Advancement Prospects: Poor

Best Geographical Location(s) for Position: Large cities for major concerts; smaller cities for other types of shows

Prerequisites:

Education or Training—No educational requirement

Experience—Music business background helpful; booking acts on any level; working as an assistant to a concert promoter or in a promotional company helpful

Special Skills and Personality Traits—Ability to finance shows; knowledge of music business; knowledge of area where concert is being promoted; stamina; contacts within the industry

CAREER LADDER

```
┌─────────────────────────────────┐
│  Concert Promoter of Major Talent │
└─────────────────────────────────┘

┌─────────────────────────────────┐
│       Concert Promoter          │
└─────────────────────────────────┘

┌─────────────────────────────────┐
│   Assistant to Concert Promoter  │
└─────────────────────────────────┘
```

Position Description

The Concert Promoter is responsible for putting concerts together. As a Promoter, the individual has many duties.

The first thing a Promoter needs to do is secure the money required for the venture. In some cases, the Promoter raises and invests the money and is the backer him or herself. In other situations, the Promoter finds others who share the expenses and profits.

The Promoter must have a definite plan of action. In what city will the concert take place? Which hall (or club, arena, etc.) will be used? When will the show be? How many shows will be promoted? Who will headline?

Creation of a preliminary budget is one of the most important tasks the Promoter will undertake. Underbudgeted, the Promoter will lose money; overbudgeted, he or she is in a better position. The extra budget funds will often take care of situations that don't go according to plan. The preliminary budget will be reworked after negotiations for the main act have taken place.

Once the Promoter has completed the negotiations, signed the headliner and a supporting act, and rented a venue, he or she must go to work to sell tickets.

The Promoter generally must advertise. He or she will decide where the advertising dollar buys most—on radio or TV, or in the print media. The Promoter will buy advertising space, keeping in mind the money allocated for advertising in the budget. If, near the show date, ticket sales are low, the Promoter might put extra money into advertising.

The Promoter will have posters, flyers, etc. printed and put up around the area. He or she will also need a place for tickets to be sold. This might be the box office of the concert hall, a ticket selling agency, or record stores in the area.

The Promoter may work with the act's record company or the act themselves putting together interviews, publicity stunts, press conferences, etc. in order to build momentum before the concert. The Promoter may hire a publicist or public relations firm to help orchestrate these things or may do them him or herself. The Promoter or the publicist also sees that the press releases, press kits, and free tickets are delivered to media people prior to the event.

The Promoter is in charge of supervising any workers, specialists, etc. who have been hired. Depending on the circumstances under which the hall is rented, the Promoter may be responsible, additionally, for hiring and/or supervising stage managers, ushers, security guards, lighting technicians, sound technicians, and people to move equipment.

The night of the concert the Promoter will go over the final box office receipts, often with the act's manager or road manager in attendance. At this time, the act is usually paid the monies that were not advanced to them on signing the contract.

After the show, the Promoter will make sure that the hall is in proper order. At this point, many Promoters throw parties, either for the act or for the people who helped pull the event together.

After checking the expenses and the box office receipts, the Promoter can tell whether he or she lost money, made money, or broke even. The Promoter, incidentally, may promote an act's entire tour or just one concert. This individual may also promote in more than one area.

This career is best suited to those in a position to take financial risks. The Promoter must also have the stamina and enthusiasm of ten people in order to pull off a successful event or try another promotion after one has failed.

Salaries

There are a great many variables that influence the earnings of Promoters. These include the area where they promote shows, the kind of talent used, how successful the talent is, and plain luck.

If the show is successful, Promoters wind up with a percentage of the profits. More often than not, Promoters lose money on shows they put together. Breaking even is sometimes thought of as a blessing by those in the business.

Promoters who are successful in the business can earn a great deal of money. This sometimes goes into the hundreds of thousands of dollars a year.

Employment Prospects

It is very difficult to break into the world of concert promotion. Most areas are locked up by Promoters who have a proven track record in the business. Turnover of these Promoters is very slow.

Many agents do not want to take chances and work with new Promoters, especially with their major acts.

It is sometimes easier, though, to break into the smaller promotional field of halls and clubs with up-and-coming acts.

Advancement Prospects

It is difficult to advance in the concert promotion field. As noted above, there is not a high turnover of successful Promoters in an area, and in order to promote, agents prefer those with a proven track record. It turns into a "Catch 22" situation.

Advancing by promoting an up-and-coming act which does rise to the top, is one method of moving upward in this profession. If one has a great deal of money to promote shows and a lot of good contacts in the industry willing to take a chance, possibilities for success increase.

Education and Training

There is no educational requirement for a Promoter. There are those in the business who have no education whatsoever, and those who hold graduate degrees from leading colleges and universities.

It does help to have some type of business background, either from formal education or from practical experience. Learning the basics of music promotion from a college course or music seminar might help, too.

Experience/Skills/Personality Traits

The successful Concert Promoters—those who make money most of the time—often have a background in the music business. They have built up a list of contacts and friends in the business with whom they can work.

The most important thing a Concert Promoter needs to get any show off the ground is money. Sufficient funds are required that if the show loses money or breaks even, the Promoter can learn from the experience and try again.

Unions/Associations

Concert Promoters do not belong to any union, although they probably work with a few unions when putting together a concert.

Many Concert Promoters are associate members of the National Academy of Recording Arts and Sciences (NARAS), the organization that gives out the Grammy awards.

Promoters may also belong to the Country Music Association (CMA), the Black Music Association (BMA), and the Gospel Music Association (GMA).

Tips for Entry
1. Try finding a position with an established concert promotion company as an assistant, receptionist, secretary, gofer, etc. Watch what is going on in the company and learn the ropes.
2. If you decide to promote on your own, start small. Promote a concert with a small outlay of money instead of an enormous one.
3. Try promoting on someone else's money. Donate your services to a school, church, or organization that will put up the money and give you help. You book the show and take care of the details. You might not make any money (you won't lose any either), but you will gain invaluable experience.
4. Get on your college's entertainment or concert committee. This is a great way to learn about concert promotion.
5. There are organizations and associations dealing with concert promotion in colleges. They sometimes offer apprenticeships, workshops, or conferences on concert promotion.

MUSIC PUBLISHER

CAREER PROFILE

Duties: Publishing music; negotiating royalty agreements with composers; screening songs; printing music; acquiring copyrights; distributing music; finding material

Alternate Title(s): None

Salary Range: $0 to $1,000,000+

Employment Prospects: Fair

Advancement Prospects: Fair

Best Geographical Location(s) for Position: New York City, Los Angeles, Nashville

Prerequisites:

Education or Training—Educational requirements vary according to position; some jobs require bachelor's degree

Experience—Working in all facets of music business useful

Special Skills and Personality Traits—Understanding of music industry; ability to hear hit tunes; knowledge of copyright laws; business orientation; contacts in music business

CAREER LADDER

```
┌─────────────────────────────────────┐
│                                     │
│          Music Publisher            │
│                                     │
└─────────────────────────────────────┘

┌─────────────────────────────────────┐
│  Song Plugger/Professional Manager; │
│            Songwriter;              │
│             Musician                │
└─────────────────────────────────────┘
```

Position Description

Individuals working as Music Publishers are responsible for acquiring the copyrights to songs and publishing them. People in this profession may work in a variety of job situations. They might work for a very large music publishing company and perform one or two specific duties of a Music Publisher. They may work for a relatively small firm and fulfill a variety of functions. Another option for an individual in music publishing is to become an independent Music Publisher, with one's own music publishing firm.

The Music Publisher has many responsibilities. The first is to obtain music to be published. In order to do this, a Music Publisher must listen to demos that are sent or brought into the office. The Music Publisher may also visit clubs, cabarets, showcases, and concerts to locate new material. The purpose is to find potential hit songs. This function may be accomplished by or with a song plugger or professional manager.

In this position, the individual must decide which materials are good and which ones are not. Bad songs must be rejected. Writers of good songs are offered contracts. If the songwriter (or owner of the song) has had prior hits, the Publisher may negotiate until the contract is acceptable to both parties. Once the contract is signed, the publisher has the rights to the song. His or her main concern then is to sell it in as many ways as possible. This may mean getting a group to record it, having it used for motion picture music, sheet music, etc. Every time that musical piece is used in any way, the Music Publisher will make money. This process is called "exploiting the work (or copyright)".

In order to sell the song, the Music Publisher must have a demo to bring or send to potential buyers. The Publisher should have contacts in the business. These might include recording groups, record producers, managers, agents, etc. The Music Publisher tries to get as many people as possible to listen to the demo in the hope that he or she will find someone to record it. If a Music Publisher has a song in the catalog that has been recorded previously, that individual will try to get it recorded again and again, in an attempt to turn it into a standard that everyone will want to record.

The Music Publisher will prepare printed music (sheet music, songbooks, etc.) and have it distributed. Before this occurs, the Publisher must make sure that the music is technically correct, proofed, and printed. This is another method by which the Music Publisher can collect fees. Before the record industry became as large as it is today, Music Publishers made most of their earnings publishing printed editions.

An important function of the Music Publisher is to file copyright forms on behalf of the song. As the Publisher, he or she is responsible for making sure that there is no copyright infringement and/or unauthorized use of the material.

In the position of Music Publisher, the individual may also seek to subpublish any of the music from his or her catalog out of the country. This may be done through a subsidiary of the Music Publisher in a different nation or through a different publishing company in the other country.

Publishing companies make money by exploiting songs. The more the song is recorded, played, distributed as sheet music, etc., the more income the Music Publisher earns. As a Music Publisher, the individual is in charge of collecting fees for the use of the songs. Publishers may collect fees or royalties from a variety of sources. These include performance fees (fees for each time a song is played on the radio, TV, etc.), mechanical royalties (from the sale of each record or tape), printed edition royalties (from songbooks, sheet music, etc.), synchronization fees (from the use of a Publisher's song in a movie), and ancillary income (from commercials, advertisements, music boxes, and on such merchandising paraphernalia as toys, clothes, greeting cards, T-shirts, bumper stickers, etc.).

People in this field work under a great deal of pressure, constantly trying to sell songs from their catalog. Hours depend on the work situation but are often flexible.

Salaries

It is difficult to estimate the earnings of a Music Publisher. Incomes vary widely, depending on the songs the Publisher has in his or her catalog; how often they are recorded; the size of the catalog; etc. A Music Publisher who has just one song that hits the top of the charts can make a fortune. Conversely, there are Music Publishers who never have a hit tune in their catalog. One of the exciting things about music publishing, though, is that a good song can become a hit anytime. This means that a Music Publisher can bring in thousands of dollars anytime. It does take luck, perseverance and, of course, a good song.

Music Publishers' earnings can range from almost nothing to a million or more dollars a year.

Employment Prospects

Employment prospects for Music Publishers are fair. If an individual cannot find a job, it is not uncommon for him or her to become an independent Music Publisher. Entering this field without experience or knowledge may not be the best idea in the world, but it sometimes works.

Those seeking employment in established firms must have extensive knowledge and experience in the business. Individuals with a good working knowledge of the copyright laws may have a better chance of getting in the door.

Advancement Prospects

The more background in the business one has, as noted above, the better the chances of not only getting into music publishing, but moving up.

The individual who has a proven track record in music publishing will probably have no trouble finding a job. Many people advance their careers in this field by becoming independent Publishers or owners of large music publishing companies.

The difficulty in moving ahead in this field, however, is that it is hard to know what will turn into a hit song. Locating these hits and acquiring the copyrights on them is the real key to advancement.

Education and Training

There are many different sizes and kinds of publishing companies. Education for this career varies. There seems to be a correlation between the size of the firm and the educational requirements. The bigger the company, the more education usually required. This stems from the fact that in smaller companies, an individual may perform a variety of functions, while in larger firms, individuals usually perform one or two tasks.

Some publishing companies require their people to hold bachelor's degrees. Others don't care much about the education an individual has as long as he or she has had experience in the music industry and/or music publishing.

There are some schools that offer a major in the music business or music merchandising. These schools usually have courses in music publishing. There are also a number of seminars given on the subject. All these information resources will prove helpful to the aspiring Music Publisher.

Experience/Skills/Personality Traits

A total understanding of the music industry is needed by a Music Publisher. Contacts in the business are vital, too. The individual must have extensive knowledge of copyright laws and business in general.

As a Music Publisher, one of the most important qualifications is the ability to hear a hit song before it is a hit. The individual must be aggressive enough to sell a song and/or get appointments for it to be listened to. The Music Publisher must also be organized in business. Records must be kept accurately in order for songwriters to be paid properly.

Unions/Associations

Music Publishers may belong to the Music Publishers' Association of the U.S. (MPA) and/or the National Music Publishers' Association. Individuals in this field might also be associate members of the National Academy of Recording Arts and Sciences (NARAS). This is the organization that gives out Grammy awards each year.

Tips for Entry

1. Positions in this field are not usually advertised. If you want to get into this type of work, put together a good resumé, including all experience in the music field. Send it with a cover letter to a number of the larger music publishing companies. These firms are more apt to have openings.

2. You can open your own music publishing firm. However, try to get some experience beforehand. Knowing the ropes can not only make you money, but also save you money.

3. There are a number of music publishing companies owned by record companies. As indicated throughout this book, many of these record companies have internships and minority training programs.

4. Try to be as knowledgeable about the subject as possible. If you can find a course or seminar in music publishing, take it.

PROFESSIONAL MANAGER

CAREER PROFILE

Duties: Persuading acts to record other writers' tunes; acquiring songs to plug

Alternate Title(s): Song Plugger

Salary Range: $7,500 to $100,000+

Employment Prospects: Fair

Advancement Prospects: Fair

Best Geographical Location(s) for Position: New York City, Los Angeles, Nashville

Prerequisites:

Education or Training—No educational requirement

Experience—Working in music industry in any capacity helpful

Special Skills and Personality Traits—Perseverance; a feel for the right song and act; knowledge of music business; contacts in the industry; salesmanship

CAREER LADDER

```
┌─────────────────────────────────────┐
│  Major Buyer of Tunes for Music      │
│  Publishers;                         │
│  Professional Manager                │
└─────────────────────────────────────┘

┌─────────────────────────────────────┐
│                                      │
│      Professional Manager            │
│                                      │
└─────────────────────────────────────┘

┌─────────────────────────────────────┐
│      Entry Level Position;           │
│      Musician;                       │
│      Songwriter                      │
└─────────────────────────────────────┘
```

Position Description

A Professional Manager or song plugger works for a music publisher. Depending on the size of the publishing company, the publisher might also act as the song plugger. This happens most frequently in one-man operations.

In the Professional Manager capacity, an individual has a number of duties. One of these is to perform the administrative functions of the publishing office.

In this role, the Professional Manager must find possible hits to add to the publisher's catalog. Naturally, in order to be good at the job, the individual must have a feel for a good song. The Professional Manager may look for material by attending concerts, clubs, showcases, etc. The Professional Manager also goes through material sent to the publishing company, listening to a piece of each song until one clicks.

The individual also is responsible for finding acts to record songs from the publisher's catalog. The catalog contains all tunes to which the publisher has the rights. Each time the song plugger gets a singer or group to record a tune from the catalog, money is made for the publishing company.

After songs are recorded by one group, the Professional Manager will often try to get the tune covered by another. A tune that is covered enough becomes a standard. Standards make publishers wealthy. A Professional Manager who is good at his or her job is in great demand.

The method most song pluggers use to get songs recorded and/or rerecorded is calling personal contacts. These contacts can make or break a Professional Manager and/or publisher. By contacting people in the industry (such as recording acts, record producers, A&R personnel, personal managers, etc.), the Professional Manager often can get his or her song listened to. A good tune is useless to a Professional Manager or a publisher if it sits idly in the catalog.

The Professional Manager often assists artists with tunes he or she believes in by helping them make professional-sounding demos. These demos help the individual sell the tune. The demos are either brought in person or mailed to the key people noted above. As a rule, if the Professional Manager is not mailing or dropping off the demo to someone he or she knows, the individual will make a phone call and write a brief note to accompany the tape. It is very rare for a Professional Manager to send a demo tape completely unsolicited.

Salaries

Salaries for Professional Managers vary widely according to a number of factors. These include the size of the music publishing company, the number of songs recorded, and the songs' popularity.

Professional Managers usually receive a weekly salary. When they are successful in getting tunes recorded by known acts, they may also receive a bonus. Individuals in this field earn between $7,500 and $100,000+ annually.

Employment Prospects

There are innumerable groups looking for material to record and many songs that need to be published. Technically, an individual has a fair chance of becoming a Professional Manager.

The hard part is getting a foot in the door. If one can find the way in, there are quite a few jobs in this field.

Advancement Prospects

Advancement for a Professional Manager comes only when the individual has attained some success. Success means that the Professional Manager or song plugger has picked up one or more tunes that have become hits or that the person has matched a tune in the publisher's catalog with an act that has turned it into a hit. After this happens, the Professional Manager is in a very good position.

Many Professional Managers become the major buyers of songs for prestigious music publishers. Other individuals strike out on their own and form new publishing companies. Individuals who have been acting as Professional Managers in their own companies find success through increased earnings.

Education and Training

Professional Managers are not required to have any specific education. Many people in the profession are former musicians. Other individuals have degrees in areas ranging from business to music to broadcasting.

Professional Managers who desire to move into other phases of the industry would be wise to have some business background. Any seminar or course on music publishing would also prove useful.

Experience/Skills/Personality Traits

The most successful Professional Managers have had experience in many different phases of the music industry. Over time, they have made innumerable personal contacts. These contacts are what help the Professional Manager attain success.

The individual must have a feel for the right song and the ability to put songs and artists together in an effort to get the song recorded. If a person has a good song and believes in it, he or she must have the perseverance to work with it until someone else believes in it, too.

Unions/Associations

Professional Managers may belong to the Music Publishers' Association of the United States (MPA) and the National Music Publishers' Association (NMPA). These organizations provide programs, conferences, seminars, etc. on all aspects of music publishing. The Professional Manager may be an associate member of the National Academy of Arts and Sciences (NARAS).

Tips for Entry

1. Music publishing companies can be small or very large. Send your resumé to some of the larger companies. Make sure you include all your experience in the music business, from writing tunes to working in a record store.
2. Some individuals form their own publishing companies. As indicated above, you can act as a Professional Manager while being a music publisher. Remember, just forming a company does not make money. Acquiring songs and getting them recorded does.
3. Learn which organizations, associations, and schools are putting on seminars or giving courses in music publishing. You should know as much as possible about the entire business, especially if you do not have a lot of experience in the music industry.

BUSINESS MANAGER

CAREER PROFILE	CAREER LADDER

Duties: Managing the financial affairs of musicians and entertainers

Alternate Title(s): Business Agent

Salary Range: $15,000 to $250,000+

Employment Prospects: Fair

Advancement Prospects: Fair

Best Geographical Location(s) for Position: New York City, Los Angeles, Nashville; other cities may have positions

Prerequisites:

Education or Training—No educational requirement; most individuals have degrees in business administration with concentration in accounting or management

Experience—Accounting experience helpful; dealings in entertainment or music industry useful

Special Skills and Personality Traits—Knowledge of negotiating, accounting skills, cognizance of investments, thorough knowledge of tax laws

CAREER LADDER

```
┌─────────────────────────────┐
│                             │
│    Top Business Manager     │
│                             │
└─────────────────────────────┘

┌─────────────────────────────┐
│                             │
│      Business Manager       │
│                             │
└─────────────────────────────┘

┌─────────────────────────────┐
│         C.P.A.;             │
│ Assistant to Business Manager│
│                             │
└─────────────────────────────┘
```

Position Description

A Business Manager handles financial affairs for singers, musicians, and other entertainers. A person in this position may have one or more clients. Acts that hire Business Managers are usually doing quite well financially.

The Business Manager (or agent, as the person is sometimes called) must oversee the finances of an act or individual in order to maximize the earning potential. The individual is responsible for collecting all monies due and paying all the bills.

The Business Manager performs a number of duties as part of the job. The Business Manager may negotiate with agents and/or representatives for contracts and appearances. He or she might negotiate with union officials, motion picture studios, television producers, concert halls, record companies, merchandising firms, or publishing companies. The Business Manager may seek out firms, companies, and corporations that will pay the artist for endorsements or sponsor a large con-

cert tour. After the act has performed a service, the individual will make sure they are paid in a timely fashion.

The individual is in charge of checking all bills for accuracy. If bills are in order, the Business Manager pays them. The person may be responsible for paying employees of the act, such as road personnel, secretaries, musicians, vocalists, publicists, public relations firms, lawyers, etc. The Business Manager may also pay the artist's personal bills. He or she must keep records of all monies taken in and paid out.

Depending on the requirements of the act, the Business Manager may plan budgets for the group or for individual members. The individual may work with the record company or the booking agent and personal manager in designing budgets for various projects.

The Business Manager might act as a financial or business advisor, counseling the act and its members on good investments, taxes, legal matters, or other income interests.

If the act is experiencing differences concerning contractual rights and obligations with their representatives, the Business Manager may act as a liaison during these difficulties. The Business Manager may also request audits of firms with which the act is or has been doing business. The individual might hire a C.P.A. to conduct these audits.

The person hired as a group's or individual's Business Manager will regularly summarize and send statements of investments, property, and financial status to the client. He or she will also be available for meetings with the act or their representatives to discuss investments, problems, audits, etc.

Salaries

The salary of a Business Manager varies from individual to individual and from year to year. Individuals just starting out may earn only $15,000. Persons doing well can earn $250,000+. Variables include the number of clients one has, how well each of them is doing financially, geographical location of the Business Manager, and his or her experience and expertise.

The Business Manager makes money by charging clients fees. Fees can be obtained in a variety of ways. The most common is to charge a percentage of the act's total gross income. This percentage varies from 3% to 10%. The individual can also charge a flat retainer or an hourly fee. Some Business Managers charge a combination of a minimum fee against a commission on total monies earned by the client.

It is important to remember that a Business Manager may (and usually does) service more than one client.

Employment Prospects

A qualified individual has a fair chance of becoming a successful Business Manager. The person seeking this type of job will probably have to work in or near one of the music capitals to obtain clients. There are frequently offices in which a person can work as an administrative assistant to a Business Manager and learn the ropes. Once again, these are usually located in one of the music cities—New York City, Los Angeles, or Nashville.

An individual might also work as a Business Manager or accountant for nonmusic-oriented clients and then actively seek music clients. Most of the time, this must be accomplished through contacts in the music business, although there are Business Managers who advertise in the music trades.

Advancement Prospects

The way a Business Manager advances his or her career is by obtaining more clients. Conversely, the Business Manager can take fewer clients, if they are large ones.

More prestigious clients are obtained by word of mouth. If a Business Manager can advise well and help the act save and make money, that individual will probably become successful.

Education and Training

Although there is no educational requirement for a person in this field, most individuals do have college degrees in business administration, finance, or accounting. Persons who are very successful as Business Managers usually have gone through a graduate program in one of the above fields.

There are some business managers who are C.P.A.'s and others who are not. Business Managers might retain the services of a C.P.A. when needed.

Experience/Skills/Personality Traits

Business Managers should be cognizant of all types of investments. The individual may advise the client on investments outside of the music industry. These are often thought to be safer. The Business Manager must have the ability to negotiate with people in all phases of business. He or she should have a total understanding of the music business in order to negotiate efficiently.

The individual in this position must also have a good knowledge of tax laws. It is beneficial to be able to advise the act how to save money on taxes. The ability to help the artist make money through investments, endorsements, etc. is another valuable commodity.

Unions/Organizations

Business Managers may belong to a number of associations. If they are accountants, they might belong to the American Institute of Certified Public Accountants (AICPA), the National Association of Accountants (NAA), or the National Society of Public Accountants (NSPA).

Individuals might also be members of the International Association For Financial Planning (IAFP) or the Institute of Certified Financial Planners (ICFP).

If the individual is also a personal manager, he or she could belong to the Conference of Personal Managers (COPM).

Tips for Entry

1. Try to locate some successful Business Managers and apply for a position as an administrative assistant.

2. Make sure you are qualified for a position like this. Big acts will not go near a person who has not yet proven him or herself. Smaller, lesser-known acts might.

3. This is a position in which contacts in the music business help. Let people know what you are doing (or trying to do).

4. Take seminars on business management, investments, tax shelters, etc. These courses need not be specific to the music business. Many of the investments you advise your clients to make will not be music-oriented. You need to be well versed in a full range of investments.

INSTRUMENT REPAIR,
RESTORATION
AND DESIGN

MUSICAL INSTRUMENT BUILDER/DESIGNER

CAREER PROFILE

Duties: Building and/or custom designing instruments for sale privately or through a shop or factory

Alternate Title(s): Musical Instrument Master Craftsman (or Woman); Custom Instrument Builder

Salary Range: $8,000 to $35,000+

Employment Prospects: Good

Advancement Prospects: Poor

Best Geographical Location(s) for Position: Larger cities may have more positions in factories and shops; many custom Instrument Builders/Designers work from their homes in any town or city

Prerequisites:

Education or Training—Training or an apprenticeship in instrument building and designing

Experience—Working with wood and metal (depending on family of instruments the individual designs and/or builds)

Special Skills and Personality Traits—Knowledge of instruments; woodworking; metal working; good musical "ear"; mechanical ability

CAREER LADDER

```
┌─────────────────────────────────────────┐
│      Master Craftsman (or Woman);        │
│ Self-Employed Instrument Builder/Designer │
└─────────────────────────────────────────┘

┌─────────────────────────────────────────┐
│     Musical Instrument Builder/Designer   │
└─────────────────────────────────────────┘

┌─────────────────────────────────────────┐
│        Musical Instrument Builder/        │
│            Designer Apprentice            │
└─────────────────────────────────────────┘
```

Position Description

The Instrument Builder/Designer is a creative person. He or she not only loves instruments, but loves to touch them and find new ways they can be shaped or built.

The individual's main function is to take materials and turn them into functioning instruments. He or she does this by watching other Instrument Builders work, examining other instruments, reading books on the subject, and visiting museums that have collections of instruments from other eras. By noting how these instruments are constructed, the Builder/Designer can often develop interesting, usable ideas for instruments of today.

The Instrument Builder/Designer usually knows how to play at least one instrument. Sometimes he or she knows how to play almost an entire family of instruments. It is usually that family of instruments that the individual artisan yearns to build and/or design.

The Builder/Designer has a number of options as to where he or she can work. He or she might choose a position on staff in a music factory or store or the individual might design and build instruments on speculation or from custom orders in his or her workshop.

Instrument Builders/Designers are usually handy people. They have an interest in handcrafts as well as in musical instruments. The ability to work with hands is essential. They are not only creative, but usually extremely inventive as well.

Although almost any instrument can be built and designed, there is a great market for violins, guitars, dulcimers, harpsichords, banjos and flutes that are finely crafted and have excellent tones. Many self-employed Instrument Builders/Designers find that not only can they sell as many instruments as they can make, but often they cannot keep up with their orders.

Once Instrument Builders/Designers have been trained as master craftspeople in their field, they are also qualified to teach others who aspire to learn the art.

Salaries

Salaries vary according to the instruments built or designed. Highest salaries go to Builders/Designers of rarer instruments. Salaries run from $8,000 for a beginner to $35,000+ yearly for Builders/Designers in large musical instrument companies. Individuals can also custom design and build instruments for skilled classical musicians and pop/rock stars. Skilled craftsmen may sell their works of art for $2,500—$25,000+ per instrument. Yearly salaries depend upon the number of custom instruments an individual completes and sells.

Employment Prospects

There are always openings for qualified Instrument Builders/Designers. These individuals can work in factories, shops, or companies or on their own.

Once a Builder/Designer is qualified, he or she can usually find work and make a good living.

It should be noted that with the current influx of electronic instruments, there is a budding new field that is waiting to be tapped.

Advancement Prospects

As indicated above, qualified individuals can usually find work in the field. However, depending upon the individual, it may take years to become a skilled master craftsman (or woman).

Education and Training

There are courses and technical schools around the country that teach the fine art of building and designing musical instruments. However, they are often difficult to locate.

The best training might be available through working for a qualified Builder/Designer as an apprentice. To enter into an apprenticeship, one needs a degree of knowledge in woodworking skills. This can often be picked up in high school through industrial arts programs or at an extension course from a community college or other institution. Some knowledge of instrument technology is also useful.

Experience/Skills/Personality Traits

Instrument Builders/Designers must usually go through an apprenticeship. This apprenticeship helps hone the skills needed for this type of career. The Instrument Builder/Designer needs to know all there is to know about the type and family of instruments he or she is working with.

The individual must also be creative enough to come up with unique ways to put instruments together. A good musical "ear" is necessary. Knowledge of woodworking and/or metalworking is also required.

Unions/Associations

There are no unions for Instrument Builders/Designers. Depending on the types of instruments the individual works with, he or she might belong to the Acoustical Society of America, the National Council of Acoustical Consultants, The Piano Technicians' Guild, or the Electronic Industry Association.

Tips for Entry

1. To find a person with whom to apprentice, contact a manufacturer of the type of instrument you would like to work with. Tell them what you are looking for and ask for their help.
2. There are a number of associations dealing with specific families of instruments. These associations—the Acoustical Society of America, the National Council of Acoustical Consultants, the Piano Technicians' Guild, and the Electronic Industry Association—might also be able to help you find training in your area. In addition, they may know of any seminars or training programs scheduled around the country.
3. Go into your local instrument shop and see if you can get a job for the summer. Try to learn as much as possible about instruments.

INSTRUMENT REPAIR & RESTORATION SPECIALIST

CAREER PROFILE

Duties: Repairing and restoring instruments that are damaged, broken, or not in correct working order

Alternate Title(s): Instrument Repair & Restoration Expert

Salary Range: $8,000 to $35,000+

Employment Prospects: Good

Advancement Prospects: Fair

Best Geographical Location(s) for Position: Large cities have many opportunities

Prerequisites:

Education and Training—Training in instrument technology

Experience—An apprenticeship in instrument repair and restoration lasting from two to five years is usually necessary

Special Skills and Personality Traits—Interest in instruments; good musical "ear"; knowledge of woodworking and/or metalworking; mechanical ability

CAREER LADDER

```
┌─────────────────────────────────────────────┐
│           Private or Self-Employed          │
│  Instrument Repair and Restoration Specialist │
└─────────────────────────────────────────────┘

┌─────────────────────────────────────────────┐
│  Instrument Repair and Restoration Specialist │
└─────────────────────────────────────────────┘

┌─────────────────────────────────────────────┐
│  Instrument Repair and Restoration Specialist │
│                  Apprentice                 │
└─────────────────────────────────────────────┘
```

Position Description

An Instrument Repair and Restoration Specialist usually loves instruments. He or she likes to hear them, play them, and work with them. His or her main function is to take instruments that are damaged, broken, or not in correct working order and repair and/or restore them.

The Instrument Repair and Restoration Specialist can specialize in string and fretted instruments, pianos, organs, brass instruments, percussion instruments, or a combination of the above.

The individual must be familiar with the various parts of many different instruments. In addition, he or she must know where they belong in the instrument and how to get them there. Many parts for older instruments are not even made today. In cases such as this, the Repair and Restoration Specialist must often create and build new parts.

Repair and Restoration Specialists usually enjoy music and instruments during their school years. Most like woodworking and other industrial arts subjects in high school.

Many Repair and Restoration Specialists know how to play a variety of instruments. This musical knowledge is helpful in repairing or restoring an instrument to its original state.

The Repair and Restoration Specialist can work on staff in a music store, factory, or school. He or she might also work for a museum, restoring instruments from earlier time periods. If on staff, the Specialist may be paid a weekly salary, a commission, or a combination of the two.

As the individual becomes more proficient, he or she might decide to work as a self-employed Instrument Repair and Restoration Specialist. Eventually, he or she might also take on an apprentice and help that individual hone his or her skills.

In areas where the Instrument Repair and Restoration Specialist does not have sufficient work to make a full-time living, the individual might also build, design, or supervise the production of instruments for manufacturers, shops, or individuals.

Salaries

As there is a tremendous shortage of Instrument Repair and Restoration Specialists, salaries can get quite high. Salaries depend on the experience level of the Repair and Restoration Specialist and where he or she works.

Depending on whether the Specialist works for him or herself or is on staff at a music store or factory, the individual may earn between $8,000 and $35,000+ annually.

Those who work on instruments that are more difficult to repair and for which there are fewer trained specialists command higher wages, some earning up to $100 per hour.

Employment Prospects

As noted above, there is a shortage of qualified Instrument Repair and Restoration Specialists. The prospects of finding a job in this field after apprenticeship are good. The individual would probably have to live in a culturally active location, however, or he or she would not be able to locate work.

Advancement Prospects

After training in the craft of instrument repair and restoration, the individual must find a skilled craftsman (or woman) to work with as an apprentice. Depending on how quick he or she learns, the individual might apprentice for two to five years.

Usually, the Repair and Restoration Specialist works in a shop or factory for a few years after the apprenticeship. After this, he or she may stay in a shop or factory setting or move on the a self-employed situation.

Education and Training

A successful Specialist needs the appropriate training in instrument technology and repair. These courses are given in schools and colleges or through private instruction.

The position also requires a knowledge of woodworking and/or metalworking, depending on the type of instrument in which one specializes. This is often acquired in high school courses. Additional training is available at many technical schools and colleges.

A good Instrument Repair and Restoration Specialist needs to know how to play a variety of instruments. The more instruments with which he or she is musically adept, the more flexible he or she can be.

Experience/Skills/Personality Traits

To become an Instrument Repair and Restoration Specialist, one must go through an apprenticeship with a talented individual in the field. The apprenticeship can last anywhere from two to five years, depending on the individual. This on-the-job training is often picked up by working in instrument repair shops and factories.

The Instrument Repair and Restoration Specialist needs a good musical "ear". He or she must have a total dedication to learning the craft. The individual must also have a great deal of patience and good mechanical ability.

Unions/Associations

There are no unions for Instrument Repair and Restoration Specialists. Depending on the type of instruments that they work on, they can belong to the Acoustical Society of America, the National Council of Acoustical Consultants, the Piano Technicians' Guild, or the Electronic Industry Association.

Tips for Entry

1. Try to find an instrument repair and restoration shop and get a job there part-time doing anything. Watch, learn, and gain experience. If you can apprentice in a shop such as this, do so.
2. Learn to do minor repairs, such as changing or replacing strings on stringed instruments, becoming skilled in as many repairs as possible.

PIANO TUNER-TECHNICIAN

CAREER PROFILE

Duties: Tuning and repairing pianos

Alternate Title(s): None

Salary Range: $8,000 to $27,000+

Employment Prospects: Fair

Advancement Prospects: Fair

Best Geographical Location(s) for Position: Large cities offer the most opportunities

Prerequisites:

Education or Training—Training in piano technology and/or an apprenticeship

Experience—Apprenticeship with Tuner-Technician or in shop or factor

Special Skills and Personality Traits—Interest in piano; knowledge of instrument; mechanical ability; good musical "ear"; patience

CAREER LADDER

```
┌─────────────────────────────────────┐
│                                     │
│  Independent Piano Tuner-Technician │
│                                     │
└─────────────────────────────────────┘

┌─────────────────────────────────────┐
│                                     │
│       Piano Tuner-Technician        │
│                                     │
└─────────────────────────────────────┘

┌─────────────────────────────────────┐
│                                     │
│   Piano Tuner-Technician Apprentice │
│                                     │
└─────────────────────────────────────┘
```

Position Description

A Piano Tuner-Technician's main job is to tune pianos and keep them in tune. After deciding to become a Piano Tuner-Technician and getting the proper training, an individual must usually apprentice in order to hone his or her skills to perfection.

The Piano Tuner-Technician must know the piano inside and out. He or she must recognize the 6,000 to 8,000 different pieces of each instrument. The Tuner-Technician must know what each of these parts is, where it belongs in the instrument, and what it does.

The individual adjusts the piano strings so that they will be in proper pitch and sound musically correct. There are approximately 220 strings in a standard eighty-eight key piano. After muting the strings on either side, the Tuner-Technician uses a tuning hammer to tighten or loosen the string being tested until its frequency matches that of a standard tuning fork. The Piano Tuner-Technician tunes the other strings in relation to the starting string. A good musical "ear" is essential in order to attain a perfect pitch, tone, and sound.

The Piano Tuner-Technician often works with electronic tuning devices. These devices are relatively new in the field. Old-time master craftsmen usually do not use these aids and don't encourage their apprentices to use them, either. With these electronic devices, however, Piano Tuner-Technicians can usually take care of more pianos in a shorter period of time. This is important if the individual is being paid per instrument tuned.

The tuner may make minor repairs, such as replacing worn or broken hammers in the piano. He or she may also detect and correct other problems in the instrument that affect its sound. More serious problems that the Piano Tuner-Technician may take care of include realigning hammers that do not strike the strings just right and replacing the felt on hammers. The Piano Tuner-Technician may have to dismantle the piano to find out what is wrong with it and fix the problem.

The Tuner-Technician may also teach piano to add to his or her income.

Salaries

Salaries for Piano Tuner-Technician vary according to the types of jobs they hold. A Piano

Tuner-Technician working in a piano factory can earn between $8,000 and $25,000 per year. Tuners working for music dealers can average between $10,000 and $27,000 annually.

Tuner-Technicians are often self-employed or independent. These individuals charge fees for each piano they work on. Fees vary according to whether or not the individual is a member of the Piano Technicians' Guild.

A Tuner can obtain contracts with music conservatories, universities, studios, and/or music groups. Independent Piano Tuner-Technicians, working full time, can earn $25,000+ annually. Tuner-Technicians who are self-employed must pay their own expenses. These might include tools, travel expenses, etc.

Employment Prospects

Piano Tuner-Technicians have the opportunity to work full-time or part-time, for themselves or on staff for dealers, factories, music schools, conservatories, universities, colleges, music shops, or music groups.

Clients can be obtained by advertising or word of mouth. Satisfied clients can make a successful independent Piano Tuner-Technician.

Large cities with many stores, factories, dealers, etc. offer the best opportunities for Tuner-Technicians. In smaller communities with limited music outlets, Piano Tuner-Technicians often do other piano-related work, including teaching.

Advancement Prospects

Piano Tuner-Technicians who have been trained well and have apprenticed with skilled Tuner-Technicians can usually get a position as a staff tuner. After a few years, many individuals find that they prefer to work on their own as self-employed or private Piano Tuner-Technicians. They then have the opportunity to build as large a business as they can handle.

Education and Training

A training program and/or an apprenticeship is required to become a Piano Tuner-Technician. The best type of course to take is one endorsed by the Piano Technicians' Guild. Check the appendix for a list. A good course of study will usually take two to three years to complete.

The individual might opt to take an apprenticeship with a skilled Piano Tuner-Technician. These opportunities are often difficult to locate for those without experience. After completing a training program, however, the individual will probably need to apprentice with an individual or a shop or in a factory.

Experience/Skills/Personality Traits

To become a Piano Tuner-Technician, an individual must have experience as an apprentice. The Tuner must have a good musical "ear". He or she should have a great interest in the piano, a knowledge of the instrument, and the ability to play it.

The Piano Tuner-Technician must have a mechanical ability and dexterity. In addition, he or she must have an enormous amount of patience.

Unions/Associations

A Piano Tuner-Technician may belong to the Piano Technicians' Guild. This association is open to Tuner-Technicians who pass an exam given by the guild. After becoming a member, the Piano Tuner-Technician's fees are set by the guild. Nonmembers are free to charge lower fees.

Tips for Entry

1. Prepare well by obtaining good training. Your best bet is to go to a school the Piano Technicians' Guild endorses.
2. Try to find the most skilled person possible to apprentice with. It is during this apprenticeship that you pick up much of the craft.
3. If you are trained in the profession, put your business card up in music stores, record shops, and supermarket bulletin boards.

BOW REHAIRER AND RESTORER

CAREER PROFILE

Duties: Rehairing stringed instrument bows and restoring old or damaged bows

Alternate Title(s): Bow Restorer; Craftsman

Salary Range: $20.00 to $40.00 per bow

Employment Prospects: Fair

Advancement Prospects: Poor

Best Geographical Location(s) for Position: Major cultural centers such as New York City, Boston, Cleveland, Philadelphia, Chicago, Los Angeles, etc.

Prerequisites:

Education or Training—Training at workshops or seminars on subject; apprenticeship

Experience—Hands-on experience in craft is necessary

Special Skills and Personality Traits—Fine craftsmanship; dexterity; ability to work with detail; patience; desire to develop the craft

CAREER LADDER

```
┌─────────────────────────────────┐
│                                 │
│     Bow Rehairer and Restorer   │
│                                 │
└─────────────────────────────────┘

┌─────────────────────────────────┐
│                                 │
│          Apprentice;            │
│        Workshop Student         │
│                                 │
└─────────────────────────────────┘
```

Position Description

Bow Rehairers and Restorers replace the bow hair of stringed instrument bows. They also restore old and/or damaged bows and put them back in working condition.

The work is done using such hand tools as small knives, chisels, short- and long-nose pliers, scissors, and a comb. The individual must disassemble the bow and remove the spent or used hair. (Most bows are made of the hair of horses' tails.) The person then examines the bow to see what condition it is in, check for damage, etc. The Rehairer also cleans the various bow parts.

If the bow is old and/or damaged, the individual may restore it. The Bow Rehairer and Restorer may concentrate on a broken bow tip, a cracked frog, or the timber. This restoration, too, is done with hand tools.

People in this line of work require a great deal of manual dexterity. They may have to hand-carve replacement wedges and/or plugs to fit the bow. These parts must fit exactly or it will affect the quality of the sound produced by the bow.

The Bow Rehairer must select new hairs for the bow. Once this is done, the individual will bind one end with special threads. This bound end will be secured into one end of the bow with the hand-carved wedges.

The Bow Rehairer will comb the hair neatly and bind the remaining loose ends with the special thread. This end will then be secured with wedges.

The quality of construction and rehairing of the bow affects the quality of tone and sound of the stringed instrument. The Rehairer is totally responsible for this task. There are Rehairers who are famous for their craft and skill.

The Rehairer may work full- or part-time at this job, depending on how many customers he or she can obtain. Many people in this position contact schools, colleges, conservatories, and orchestras to obtain contracts to perform all the rehairing required for the group's stringed instruments.

Hours are flexible. Many rehairers are working or aspiring musicians, usually with an ability to play a stringed instrument.

Salaries

It is impossible to estimate the yearly salary of a Bow Rehairer and Restorer. Individuals who perform this work often do so on a part-time basis while pursuing performance or teaching careers, or careers in instrument building or instrument repairing and/or restoring.

People who rehair and restore may get contracts to take care of all the stringed instruments in a school, college, conservatory, or orchestra. The normal charge for bow rehairing ranges from $20.00 to $40.00 per bow. Fees for restoring bows depend on the amount and type of damage done to the bow. Restoration fees range from $20.00 to $75.00 per item.

Employment Prospects

As there are not many people who know how to correctly rehair and/or restore bows, individuals who do have fair chance of locating work. There are opportunities in the major cultural cities, such as New York City, Boston, Cleveland, Philadelphia, Chicago, and Los Angeles. These locations have symphony orchestras, chamber music groups, etc. that use a large number of stringed instruments. Individuals looking for work in the Bow Rehairing field might have to relocate to one of these major cities.

Advancement Prospects

Advancement as a Bow Rehairer and Restorer is difficult to achieve. The best way to do it is to obtain a lot of clients. People in this field may open their own music or repair shop.

Education and Training

There is no specific educational requirement for a Bow Rehairer and Restorer, but people must be trained in the craft. This may be accomplished in workshops or seminars given on the subject or through an apprenticeship with a master craftsman.

Experience/Skills/Personality Traits

To perfect this craft, a person needs hands-on experience in bow rehairing. This may be acquired through an apprenticeship.

The individual doing this type of work needs manual dexterity. The person must also be extremely patient and capable of working on details.

Many who perform this job are aspiring or working musicians who love the sound of good music.

Unions/Associations

Bow Rehairers and Restorers have no union. If they are performing musicians as well as Rehairers and Restorers, they might belong to the American Federation of Musicians (AFM). Individuals may also belong to the Accoustical Society of America and/or the National Council of Accoustical Consultants.

Tips for Entry

1. Teachers of violin often know of workshops in the art of rehairing bows.
2. Violin or other string players usually know of people in this field. Talk to a Bow Rehairer and inquire about an apprenticeship.
3. If you already know how to rehair bows, go to schools, colleges, and orchestras to obtain clients.
4. Put up a sign, poster, or business card on the bulletin boards in music stores.

PUBLICITY

PUBLIC RELATIONS COUNSELOR

CAREER PROFILE

Duties: Creating an image for a musical group, artist, product, place, or company; writing press releases; compiling press kits; arranging press conferences

Alternate Title(s): Publicist, P.R. Counselor

Salary Range: $8,500 to $75,000+

Employment Prospects: Fair

Advancement Prospects: Fair

Best Geographical Location(s) for Position: New York City, Los Angeles, Nashville, Philadelphia, Chicago, etc.

Prerequisites:

Education or Training—College degree in communications, journalism, English, advertising, marketing, or public relations

Experience—Some type of music or nonmusic-oriented publicity position; journalism experience

Special Skills and Personality Traits—Good writing skills; knowledge of music business; creativity; agressiveness; ability to work under pressure

CAREER LADDER

```
┌─────────────────────────────────┐
│     Public Relations Director;   │
│   Public Relations Agency Owner  │
└─────────────────────────────────┘

┌─────────────────────────────────┐
│                                 │
│    Public Relations Counselor    │
│                                 │
└─────────────────────────────────┘

┌─────────────────────────────────┐
│                                 │
│      Public Relations Trainee    │
│                                 │
└─────────────────────────────────┘
```

Position Description

The main function of P.R. Counselors in the field of music-oriented public relations is to create an image for a group or artist. If the counselor is working in a radio station or concert hall, his or her function is to create a good image of and for the business.

The Public Relations Counselor must begin by evaluating the public's perception or image of the client. Sometimes the client is well-known but has a poor image. In this case, the Public Relations Counselor is often retained to help change this public perception. Sometimes the client is an act or a club that is just starting out and is not known. In this case, the Public Relations Counselor must start from scratch, building the client's image.

The counselor might begin by outlining a campaign for the client. This campaign will vary according to any image problems and to the budget available to accomplish the task.

The P.R. Counselor must know how to write press releases, compile press kits, arrange press con-ferences and parties, etc. In addition, the counselor must know how to find an angle to arouse media interest.

P.R. Counselors usually spend a great deal of time with a client getting pertinent information. During this period, he or she usually learns some interesting facts about a client that may be unrelated to the music business. For example, a club might have been the place a famous president stayed during a war. This theme might be the basis of a feature article about the club. Another example is a singer whose hobby is cooking. The counselor could expand the client's image from singer (in music magazines) to singer who likes to cook (gourmet cooking magazines). This gives the singer a more rounded personality. In essence, the P.R. Counselor works on creating a fuller image for clients.

P.R. Counselors usually have a large list of media contacts to call upon and use when they require press for their clients. When calling on this press, the counselor must always try to remain as credible as possible; otherwise, he or she won't be able to use the press effectively.

As with all positions in promotion and publicity, public relations people must be able to work under a great deal of pressure. There are constant demands by clients, deadlines to meet, things to accomplish, and parties to attend.

As a rule, the Public Relations Counselor working in a P.R. firm is directly responsible to his or her supervisor. On occasion, he or she might be responsible to the client. A counselor working in a radio station is usually responsible to the general manager of that station. P.R. Counselors or directors working in concert halls or arenas are generally responsible to the concert hall director or manager.

The Public Relations Counselor must be willing to work behind the scenes and not expect any public recognition. A successful campaign for a client will yield only personal satisfaction. An unsuccessful campaign will often yield an unhappy client who blames the Public Relations Counselor.

Salaries
Salaries for Public Relations Counselors vary depending on the firm or company, geographical location, and type of job held.

A Public Relations Counselor in a music industry firm can earn anywhere from $12,500 to $75,000+. In addition, P.R. Counselors often earn 10% to 15% of all income from clients they bring to the firm. This can add up to thousands of dollars.

A radio station Public Relations Counselor or director might make from $8,500 at a small station to $37,000+ at a larger station.

A Public Relations Counselor or director working at a concert hall or auditorium would be at the same income level as the P.R. person working at a radio station. Once again, salaries vary according to the size of the business and the location of the company.

Employment Prospects
There are only a limited number of music-oriented public relations firms. Competition for jobs in the field is very heavy.

There are, however, a fair number of positions as Public Relations Counselors and directors at firms that are music-oriented. Some of these include radio stations, night clubs, concert halls and arenas, music stores, etc.

Advancement Prospects
A Public Relations Counselor working in a P.R. firm specializing in music will usually get more res-

ponsibility and more challenging clients as he or she gains experience. Experienced P.R. people sometimes strike out on their own and open firms.

There is usually very little advancement opportunity in a radio station or concert hall P.R. department. In smaller radio stations there is usually only one person in the P.R. department. The job, however, is often classified as P.R. director. The individual always has the option of moving on to a bigger station or concert hall with the job of P.R. director on his or her resume. Having worked in radio stations, concert halls, record stores, etc., the individual has the opportunity to gain experience in the music business and move into a position in a P.R. firm.

Education and Training
A college degree in communications, public relations, journalism, English, advertising, marketing, or music merchandising is preferable. Depending on the firm the individual wants to work with, some positions require a masters degree.

There are numerous public relations seminars given around the country by colleges, universities, and the Public Relations Society of America. These are very useful to one aspiring to be in the public relations field or one who has already landed a P.R. position.

Experience/Skills/Personality Traits
A good P.R. Counselor must have excellent writing skills. The counselor must also be creative enough to come up with a really special campaign so the act or product will be a hit.

A good knowledge of the music business is essential to the P.R. Counselor in the music industry. He or she must understand the complexities of the industry in order to be effective in his or her client's campaign.

Many P.R. Counselors in the music industry work in nonmusic-oriented public relations or publicity positions prior to entering the music business. Other aspiring P.R. people work for newspapers or magazines as reporters, critics or reviewers.

Unions/Associations
Public Relations Counselors can belong to the Public Relations Society of America (PRSA). The association is run by and for public relations people and works to keep ethics in public relations high. The assocation also prints a magazine and runs seminars throughout the year.

Public Relations Counselors may also belong to the Association of Theatrical Press Agents and Managers (ATPAM).

Tips for Entry
1. If you can't get the position you want, try to get some experience in the public relations department of a record store, radio station, or concert hall.
2. Attend seminars such as those given by the Public Relations Society of America. You might make some contacts with people who know of openings.
3. Attend a music industry convention. There are a number of conventions around the country throughout the year. These conventions also offer great potential for making contacts. It could be worth the price of attending.
4. If you can't locate a position in a music-oriented field, see if you can find a job in nonmusic-oriented public relations (there are many more of these). The experience might be all you need.

PUBLIC RELATIONS TRAINEE

CAREER PROFILE

Duties: Assisting public relations counselor in servicing clients; learning basic public relations techniques

Alternate Title(s): Public Relations Assistant; P.R. Trainee

Salary Range: $8,500 to $15,000

Employment Prospects: Fair

Advancement Prospects: Fair

Best Geographical Location(s) for Position: New York City, Los Angeles, Nashville, Chicago, Philadelphia, and other large cities

Prerequisites:

Education or Training—College degree in public relations, journalism, marketing, English, communications, advertising, or music merchandising preferable

Experience—Writing experience; attending seminars on music business or public relations helpful

Special Skills and Personality Traits—Good writing skills; knowledge of music business; outgoing personality; creativity

CAREER LADDER

```
┌─────────────────────────────────┐
│                                 │
│   Public Relations Counselor    │
│                                 │
└─────────────────────────────────┘

┌─────────────────────────────────┐
│                                 │
│    Public Relations Trainee     │
│                                 │
└─────────────────────────────────┘

┌─────────────────────────────────┐
│       College Student;          │
│ Nonmusic Oriented Publicity Position; │
│     Print Media Journalist      │
└─────────────────────────────────┘
```

Position Description

A Public Relations Trainee or Assistant usually has little or no experience in public relations. In the music business, however, Public Relations Trainees often have had experience working at nonmusic-oriented publicity firms. People in music business P.R. like to train their people with the music business as a focal point.

The P.R. Trainee learns how to develop a campaign for a musical act or product. He or she learns to talk to a client, gather information, and put together press releases. Once the press release is written, it must usually be approved by the Trainee or Assistant's supervisor.

The Trainee makes the many contacts he or she needs by calling people, following up on press releases or client activities. He or she might also meet media people at a press conference or press party for a client's campaign.

The Public Relations Trainee learns how to put together these important press functions. The individual does this by handling details for the P.R. supervisor.

The Public Relations Trainee often studies previous campaigns put together and implemented by other counselors. Using these programs, he or she learns how to create an angle or "hook" for a campaign.

The P.R. Trainee sits in on many meetings with clients and throws out his or her ideas for the campaign. As the Trainee gains experience, he or she might begin to implement certain facets of the actual campaign.

The Trainee responds to many of the calls from clients dealing with details such as dates and times. The Assistant/Trainee often accompanies the client to interviews or public appearances that have been scheduled. In addition, the Trainee accompanies the client to television or radio spots that have been arranged.

As a Public Relations Assistant, he or she attends many social functions on behalf of his or her firm or company or its clients. It is at these luncheons, dinners, cocktail parties, etc. that the P.R. Trainee has opportunities to make new contacts and meet new people in the industry.

A P.R. Trainee/Assistant working for a concert hall or auditorium might be responsible for showing the press around the facility. At a radio station, he or she might be responsible for introducing media or recording acts to the staff.

Unless the company has a clipping service, the P.R. Trainee/Assistant might also be responsible for clipping press releases, articles, feature stories, and photographs of the client from magazines, newspapers, trades, etc. These clippings are put together in a client's portfolio with tapes of interviews, advertisements, etc.

The P.R. Trainee is responsible directly to his or her supervisor who checks most work done by the Trainee.

Salaries

Salaries for Public Relations Trainees/Assistants in the music field start low. A beginning salary might be around $8,500 for a trainee who has no public relations experience at all. The salary is usually higher for people who have previously worked in the public relations industry. A top P.R. Trainee's salary in the music field would not be over $15,000 per year.

Employment Prospects

The job market for music-oriented public relations is competitive. Music-oriented firms are limited. There are positions for trainees in concert halls, auditoriums, radio stations, etc.

Advancement Prospects

If the trainee shows promise and talent, he or she will have the opportunity to move up the career ladder. P.R. Trainees must work very hard to move up. Often there are no positions in the company open as a public relations counselor. With the experience as a P.R. Trainee in the music field, however, the individual has the opportunity to go to other firms that have openings. Many of these companies might want the person to stay in the position of P.R. Trainee for a short time to train him or her their way.

Education and Training

The best education for a Public Relations Trainee is a college degree with a major in public relations, journalism, English, or communications. Courses in music merchandising are useful. As creative writing is one of the important skills required of a Public Relations Trainee, a variety of writing courses should be included in the curriculum.

Experience/Skills/Personality Traits

A Public Relations Trainee needs many of the same skills as a public relations counselor or publicist. He or she must be a good writer. That skill might come from writing for a college newspaper or reviewing concerts for a local magazine or newspaper.

The trainee must be creative and have an outgoing personality. Many P.R. Trainees in the music field work in nonmusic-oriented positions prior to obtaining their positions in music public relations.

A summer internship is a useful, fun way of learning the different skills needed in a music-oriented P.R. firm as well as an opportunity to make contacts.

Unions/Associations

Public Relations Trainees may belong to the Public Relations Society of America (PRSA). This organization puts out many useful booklets and a magazine and presents communications seminars throughout the country.

Tips for Entry

1. Try to get into a summer internship position in one of the music-oriented public relations firms. Although they usually are not paid, interns might get positions as Trainees after the summer.
2. Write for a local or college paper reviewing concerts and records. Make copies of the clippings and send them with your resume. This helps prove that you have talent. (Always keep copies of *everything* you have written that has been printed.)
3. On occasion, openings for P.R. Trainees in music-oriented P.R. firms are advertised in the classified sections of newspapers.

PUBLICIST

CAREER PROFILE

Duties: Getting a musical act's name better known; compiling press kits; writing press releases; arranging press conferences

Alternate Title(s): Press Agent

Salary Range: $12,500 to $75,000

Employment Prospects: Fair

Advancement Prospects: Fair

Best Geographical Location(s) for Position: New York City, Los Angeles, Nashville, Philadelphia, Chicago, and other cities that are music centers

Prerequisites:

Education or Training—College degree in communications, journalism, English, advertising, marketing, public relations, or music merchandising preferred

Experience—Prior position in music or nonmusic-oriented publicity; newspaper reporter, journalist, or critic experience helpful

Special Skills and Personality Traits—Creative writing skills; persuasiveness; ability to work under pressure; knowledge of music business; love of music

CAREER LADDER

```
┌─────────────────────────────┐
│                             │
│    Independent Publicist    │
│                             │
└─────────────────────────────┘

┌─────────────────────────────┐
│                             │
│         Publicist           │
│                             │
└─────────────────────────────┘

┌─────────────────────────────┐
│                             │
│     Assistant Publicist     │
│                             │
└─────────────────────────────┘
```

Position Description

The basic duty of a music-oriented Publicist or press agent is to create ways to make a musical act's name, record, and video better known. The best way to get a group's or artist's name or product in the spotlight is to keep it in the public eye as much as possible. The better the act and the product are known, the more records, tapes, videos, and concert seats will sell.

The Publicist must know how to write creative press releases that the press will use. Press kits consisting of press releases, biographies, pictures, and reprints of reviews and articles must be compiled. The Publicist must then see that the press kits are given or sent to music editors, disc jockeys, TV producers, etc. around the country.

The Publicist must know what type of event is important enough to call a press conference for, how to put one together, and how to get the right people to attend.

The Publicist must know how to get through to music editors, disc jockeys, TV producers, etc. in order to place the client on a television or radio show or have a feature story written on the act.

Many times, the press isn't interested in an act until it is so well known that publicity self-generates. In such a case, the Publicist must be creative enough to come up with a unique angle to get attention for the act from the press and/or radio and television.

There are some acts, on the other hand, that are so well known that every editor and disc jockey wants an interview. In this case, the Publicist must be selective and decide which interviews are in the best interest of the client. The Publicist has to act as the bad guy and keep the press away from a client if he or she feels it would harm a client's image to give interviews. The Publicist must say no in such a way as to save the media contact without blaming the act.

Publicists are famous for creating hype. Hype is the practice of taking a group or record and super-selling it with media saturation and (sometimes exaggeration).

Part of the Publicist's job is attending a lot of parties, luncheons, and dinners on a client's behalf or to make important contacts. The Publicist's social life and business life are frequently rolled into one.

Contacts are important for the Publicist, especially if he or she is working as an independent. One of the ways new clients are obtained is through these musical cocktail parties that "everyone" attends.

The Publicist employed by a record company generally works to help the artists sell their records, videos, and concert seats. He or she is usually responsible to a supervisor. Independent Publicists are usually responsible directly to the client and the client's management team.

A Publicist must have the ability to work under the constant pressure of deadlines. He or she must also be willing to accept the fact that if a publicity campaign is successful, the act will get the credit, while if it fails, the Publicist will most likely get the blame.

Salaries

Salaries vary according to the type of firm or company the Publicist works for and the geographical location of that firm. Firms or companies in New York City, Los Angeles, Nashville, and Chicago tend to pay more. Some Publicists start out at $12,500 per year. Others at more prestigious firms have a starting salary of $18,000. As the Publicist gains more experience and recognition in the field, he or she can make $35,000 to $45,000 per year. In addition, Publicists who attract new clients to their firms are often given 10% to 15% of all monies brought in by the new clients. Depending on what the clients pay the firm, this can add up to a great deal of money.

Independent Publicists are paid directly by their clients. Fees range from $850 per month per client to $1,500+ per week per client. The fees depend on the status of the musical act or artist being publicized. In addition, the Publicist often earns a percentage of any monies brought in from commercials, endorsements, TV or movies that he or she obtains for the client. Independent Publicists are usually paid their fees as a monthly retainer. They are often reimbursed for out-of-pocket expenses as well.

Employment Prospects

Music-oriented Publicists may work for record companies to promote their acts or any upcoming promotional tours. Record companies generally have a number of Publicists on staff. Although there were once many positions in this field, economic problems at record companies have resulted in the elimination of a number of these positions.

Music-oriented Publicists can also find work in firms that specialize in publicity or public relations for the music business. These positions are limited but more available than those in record companies.

Publicists may also work as independents, which means that they must get their own clients and are paid a fee instead of a salary. Independent Publicists and press agents have to be very good or they won't get clients. They must have a proven track record with clients in order to be successful on their own.

Advancement Prospects

A good Publicist will usually be promoted to better clients, more interesting projects, and less tedious work in a firm or record company. If the Publicist can deliver a good campaign, a lot of TV and radio talk shows, good placement of press releases, and a happy client, he or she will move up. Good Publicists are sought after by other companies, firms, and clients. Although the public doesn't usually know who "made" a star, group, or artist, the insiders usually find out. Competition is keen in publicity positions, so the Publicist must be the best.

Education and Training

Different positions in publicity require different amounts of education. The most qualified person has a better chance of getting the job. A college degree in communications, journalism, public relations, advertising, marketing, English, or music merchandising is helpful in honing the skills needed for a position as a music business Publicist. Courses or seminars in publicity and the music business are also useful.

Experience/Skills/Personality Traits

A music industry Publicist must be able to work under pressure. The constant stress of deadlines and clients changing their minds about what image they want to project can take its toll.

Publicists must be creative enough to come up with an angle for a client and then be persuasive enough to make the client and his advisors like it, too. He or she must have the ability to make a news release about an ordinary subject into an exciting story the press will pick up. Many Publicists have worked with the press as reporters, reviewers, or talent coordinators. Contacts picked up from other positions are valuable. The Publicist must have a reputation for credibility, however, or all contacts will prove useless.

Unions/Associations

The best-known organization that Publicists can belong to is the Public Relations Society of America (PRSA). This organization offers seminars, booklets, a magazine, and other helpful information.

Publicists might additionally belong to the Association of Theatrical Press Agents and Managers (ATPAM).

Tips for Entry

1. Find out if the record company or public relations firm has an internship program for Publicists. Most internships are unpaid.

2. Prepare your resumé and a few samples of your writing style and write to the record company or publicity firm where you want a job, call for an appointment, or go knock on doors.

3. Work with a local music group as an independent Publicist to get some experience for yourself and for your resumé. (You frequently have to work for a nominal fee.)

ASSISTANT PUBLICIST

CAREER PROFILE

Duties: Assisting the publicist; compiling press kits; writing press releases; double-checking information for accuracy

Alternate Title(s): Publicist Trainee; Press Agent Trainee; Assistant Press Agent

Salary Range: $8,500 to $18,000

Employment Prospects: Fair

Advancement Prospects: Fair

Best Geographical Location(s) for Position: New York City, Los Angeles, Nashville, Philadelphia, Chicago, and other cities that are music centers

Prerequisites:

Education or Training—College degree in communications, journalism, English, advertising, marketing, public relations, or music merchandising preferred

Experience—Working in music or nonmusic publicity; attending seminars on publicity and the music business

Special Skills and Personality Traits—Good writing skills; knowledge of music business; outgoing personality; aggressiveness; typing ability

CAREER LADDER

```
┌─────────────────────────────────┐
│                                 │
│          Publicist              │
│                                 │
└─────────────────────────────────┘

┌─────────────────────────────────┐
│                                 │
│      Assistant Publicist        │
│                                 │
└─────────────────────────────────┘

┌─────────────────────────────────┐
│   Nonmusic-oriented Publicist;  │
│     Secretary to Publicist;     │
│        Student; Intern          │
└─────────────────────────────────┘
```

Position Description

The main function of an Assistant Publicist is to help the head publicists in a company sell an act's name, records, and videos. The Assistant Publicist learns from watching and doing. He or she writes press releases and helps compile press kits. It is usual for all of the Assistant Publicist's work to be reviewed and checked for accuracy and content by the individual's superior.

Many Assistant Publicists sit in on meetings with clients, joining the publicist assigned to that client. They often throw in ideas for the act's publicity campaign. However, as a rule, they are never totally responsible for originating and implementing an entire campaign.

At times, the Assistant Publicist will accompany an act to radio, television, or public appearances. He or she will also be asked to go with the act for interviews or photography sessions set up by the head publicist.

The Assistant Publicist will handle many of the details of press parties the head publicist arranges. He or she may also be responsible for extending invitations to the media and other guests who will be invited.

The Assistant Publicist might also go to dinners, luncheons, and/or cocktail parties on behalf of a client or his or her company.

Responding to a client's calls and answering questions about schedules, dates, etc. is one of the responsibilities of the Assistant Publicist. He or she also will have to do what appears to be secretarial work, such as typing press releases, making phone calls, confirming appointments, checking out information, etc.

The individual might also be responsible for clipping press releases from magazines and newspapers. These clippings are put together in the client's portfolio, along with copies of advertisements, photos, and tapes of interviews.

The Assistant Publicist must be ready and willing to work overtime. Deadlines must be met, after-hours functions must be attended, and calls must be made.

Salaries

Assistant Publicist's salaries are rather low, usually ranging from $8,500 to $13,500 yearly. Salaries depend on the type of firm or company at which the Assistant Publicist is employed. Salaries also vary by geographical location. Highest salaries are usually found in Los Angeles and New York City. As the Assistant Publicist gets more experience, he or she begins to make more money. Assistant Publicists who work for public relations firms specializing in music acts usually earn more than Assistant Publicists who begin at record companies. The record companies, as a rule, have better benefits.

Employment Prospects

The job market is tight for Assistant Publicists, but there are openings. Many firms hire only full-fledged publicists who have experience. Record companies have limited their publicity departments and hire somewhat fewer Assistant Publicists than they did in previous years.

Advancement Prospects

A talented Assistant Publicist will move into the position of publicist. Assistant Publicists must show a lot of promise and be willing to put in extra effort to get promoted. Once an Assistant Publicist has some experience under his or her belt, he or she can apply for a position in another record company or P.R. firm. However, companies often promote from within in these position categories.

Education and Training

An Assistant Publicist needs a background in writing. A college degree in communications, journalism, English, advertising, marketing, public relations, or music merchandising is preferred. Courses in the music business or seminars on the subject are also useful. To achieve the position of Assistant Publicist, one may start out as a secretary to a publicist. When this is the case, the individual must also have training in secretarial skills. A good course in typing is always useful in the event the office is backed up and the Assistant Publicist must type a story or press release.

Experience/Skills/Personality Traits

An Assistant Publicist needs most of the same skills as a publicist. He or she must be able to work under pressure. The individual must be able to foresee what both the head publicist and the client want.

He or she must be creative enough to write press releases and stories that will grab the attention not only of the press, but of his or her superiors, too.

Experience working in a publicity office or the publicity department of a record company helps the aspiring Assistant Publicist understand the activities of the publicity office. If a summer internship opens up, it is worth investigating. The internship is a useful tool in helping to learn different techniques and skills and in making contacts.

Unions/Associations

There are no unions representing publicists in the music field. There are a number of organizations and associations an Assistant Publicist may belong to. The best known is the Public Relations Society of America (PRSA). The organization offers many seminars throughout the year on public relations and publicity subjects.

Tips for Entry

1. Find out if the record company or public relations firm for whom you would like to work has an internship program for publicists. (Most intern programs are unpaid positions.)
2. Certain record companies and music organizations have minority training programs. Check with the companies you would like to work with.
3. Prove yourself by presenting reviews you have written on concerts or records for local, school, or college newspapers. Send copies of the clippings to the act's record label's publicity department. Make sure you include a short letter telling them your name, address, phone number, qualifications, and the type of position you're interested in. Persistence and perseverance sometimes land a job.

SYMPHONIES, ORCHESTRAS, ETC.

CONDUCTOR

CAREER PROFILE

Duties: Preparing the orchestra for the performance; conducting the orchestra

Alternate Title(s): Musical Director

Salary Range: $12,000 to $250,000+; individuals working in small orchestras may earn $50 to $200 per service

Employment Prospects: Poor

Advancement Prospects: Poor

Best Geographical Location(s) for Position: Major cultural centers and other large cities which house orchestras

Prerequisites:

Education or Training—Training in conducting; musical study

Experience—Practical experience conducting different types of orchestras and/or chamber ensembles is useful

Special Skills and Personality Traits—Ability to communicate musical thoughts; proficiency at piano and at least one other instrument; thorough knowledge of symphonic repertoire

CAREER LADDER

```
┌─────────────────────────────────┐
│   Conductor of Major Orchestra   │
└─────────────────────────────────┘

┌─────────────────────────────────┐
│           Conductor             │
└─────────────────────────────────┘

┌─────────────────────────────────┐
│       Assistant Conductor        │
└─────────────────────────────────┘
```

Position Description

The Conductor holds the top musical job in the orchestra. His or her main duty is preparing the orchestra for the finest performance they are capable of presenting. The job is stressful as well as demanding. Hours are long. The Conductor must often put many hours into rehearsals before a performance. When the orchestra is on tour in cities throughout the country or the world, he or she must travel, too.

Top Conductors possess dynamic, charismatic stage personalities. This, plus immense talent, is what makes the difference between a good Conductor and a great Conductor.

As a Conductor, an individual must be proficient in at least one instrument in addition to the piano. He or she must have the ability to sight-read. Most important, the Conductor must know how to communicate musical thoughts and ideas not only verbally during rehearsals, but also through his or her body movements while involved in a performance.

The Conductor is responsible for choosing the orchestra's repertoire. He or she studies the orchestral scores and decides how the works will be played. The same piece of music might sound different depending on which individual conducted it. Each Conductor possesses his or her own style.

A good Conductor with a unique technique is often sought out to make appearances as a guest Conductor with other orchestras. As a guest Conductor, the individual's only responsibility is to prepare for the particular performance.

While with his or her own orchestra, the Conductor has many other responsibilities. In addition to preparing the orchestra for individual performances with numerous rehearsals, the Conductor must plan an entire musical season. He or she is responsible for choosing guest soloists, artists, and other conductors to guest or fill in with the orchestra.

The Conductor's job includes advising various section leaders and assisting them when auditions are held for section members. The Conductor of an orchestra is also called on for public and private appearances at fund-raising events on behalf of the orchestra. During summers, many leading Conductors teach at seminars, assisting aspiring Conductors to reach their goals.

The Conductor of an orchestra is usually responsible to the board of directors of that orchestra.

Salaries

Conductors' salaries vary widely. In major orchestras the Conductor may earn up to $250,000+. In smaller orchestras, the individual may earn between $50 and $200 per service. In between there are orchestras where Conductors' salaries range from $12,000 to $60,000+. As a rule, Conductors negotiate their salaries with individual orchestras.

Employment Prospects

Jobs are not plentiful for Conductors. The field is very limited. To get a job as a Conductor or even as an assistant Conductor one must have the opportunity to audition. Competition is fierce. Most Conductors work for years as musicians while studying to become Conductors.

Possibilities for work as a Conductor include all varieties of orchestras. Not all positions are full-time jobs. Many successful Conductors have agents and/or managers who seek positions for them.

Advancement Prospects

The Conductor has the top position in an orchestra. Conductors can, however, advance from one type of orchestra to another. For instance, one might obtain a job as a Conductor in a community orchestra and eventually move up to the position of assistant conductor in an urban orchestra. In this profession, advancement occurs as a result of both great talent and a degree of luck.

Education and Training

An individual might have a doctoral degree in conducting and still not land a job as a Conductor. A conservatory or college degree in conducting is not usually required, but may be helpful. Training similar to that received in an educational setting is required, whether it be through seminars or private study.

Summer seminars in conducting are extremely useful to an individual aspiring to be a Conductor. Through these seminars, one can find out if he or she has the talent to be in this field. The best seminars are led by world-renowned Conductors. A seminar given by a skilled Conductor can help an individual bring out his or her own personal style of conducting.

Experience/Skills/Personality Traits

Any practical experience is useful in becoming a Conductor. Conducting chamber ensembles, small community orchestras, youth orchestras, etc. gives the individual needed experience. Most conservatories and music-oriented schools also offer assistant programs where the student is given an opportunity to conduct.

Summer seminars, such as those held at Tanglewood in Massachusetts, also offer individuals a chance for conducting experience.

Unions/Associations

Conductors may belong to the American Federation of Musicians (AFM) or the American Guild of Musical Artists (AGMA), depending on their situation. For example, if the conductor plays or played an instrument, he or she probably belongs to the AFM. If the individual was a soloist, he or she might also belong to AGMA. However, many Conductors do not belong to either union.

Tips for Entry

1. Try to attend a summer seminar that has world-renowned conductors associated with it. Aside from the excellent experience gained at these seminars, you can often make important contacts. If you show exceptional talent in the art of conducting, a well-known Conductor may help you and guide you up the ladder to success.

2. There are a number of orchestras that offer internships and fellowships in conducting. Check with orchestras to see what programs they offer and whether you qualify.

3. Positions are advertised in many music-oriented publications, including *The International Musician*.

SECTION LEADER

Duties: Leading a section of the orchestra; supervising any rehearsals with the section; assigning parts to players in the section

Alternate Title(s): Principal

Salary Range: $11,000 to $75,000+ in major orchestras; part-time or per service wages in smaller orchestras

Employment Prospects: Poor

Advancement Prospects: Poor

Best Geographical Location(s) for Position: Major cultural centers and other large cities

Prerequisites:

Education or Training—Extensive musical training

Experience—Performing as a section member; acting as section leader in youth or college orchestra

Special Skills and Personality Traits—Leadership skills; exceptional musical talent

```
┌─────────────────────────────────┐
│                                 │
│   Concertmaster (if violin)     │
│                                 │
└─────────────────────────────────┘

┌─────────────────────────────────┐
│                                 │
│        Section Leader           │
│                                 │
└─────────────────────────────────┘

┌─────────────────────────────────┐
│                                 │
│        Section Player           │
│                                 │
└─────────────────────────────────┘
```

Position Description

Each section of an orchestra has a leader called the Section Leader or the principal player. The Section Leader is responsible to the concertmaster. The main duty of the Leader is to lead the section so that the sound is the best that can be produced. It is important that the leader communicate what he or she expects of the section. This is a job that has to be done subtly. It must be obvious only to the section and never the audience.

The string Section Leader, for example, must decide where the bowing should be inserted. The individual must make a decision on the correct phrasing and on who in the section should play the individual parts.

In the wind section, the Section Leader emphasizes such techniques as correct breathing. In certain sections, like that of the oboe, the Section Leader has different responsibilities because there are so few members of that section. Those sections function much more as a personal team than the larger sections do.

To obtain a position as a Section Leader, an individual must audition. Committees are usually set up to listen to these auditions and select the best candidate.

A good stage presence and creative musical ability help place one musician above the rest. A thorough knowledge of the symphonic repertoire is essential. The Section Leader must know how to sight-read and be ready to do so at any time.

At times, the Section Leader has to be able to recognize talent. This individual is on the selection committee during auditions for the section. The Section Leader, additionally, must supervise any rehearsals within his or her section.

Certain orchestras require their Section Leaders to participate in the orchestra's chamber music group. This is usually specified in the job description.

Salaries

Salaries for Section Leaders in orchestras depend on a number of variables. These include the type of orchestra (major, metropolitan, urban, etc.), its location, the number of weeks the orchestra is in session, and the seniority of the player.

Minimum earnings are negotiated by the American Federation of Musicians (AFM) local unions. In some orchestras, the Section Leaders receive the same amount of money as other section players. In other orchestras, Section Leaders receive a specific amount of money over the scale set for the section members. This may be from $15 to $55. In other cases, the Section Leader's salary will be from 10% to 35% over those of section members. Certain Section Leaders negotiate their contracts directly with the orchestra.

Section Leaders in major orchestras earn from $11,000 to $75,000+. Section Leaders in smaller orchestras earn considerably less. As many of the smaller orchestras offer only part-time work, Section Members may be paid on a per service basis.

Section Leaders may earn additional income by teaching or by participating in recording sessions.

Employment Prospects

To become a Section Leader, one must first be a section member of an orchestra. In the ladder of experience, therefore, it is usually the older players with experience in a few different orchestras who obtain these positions. The opportunity does exist, however, to become a Section Leader of a community orchestra or an urban orchestra.

Advancement Prospects

The Section Leader of the violin section can move up to the concertmaster/concertmistress position. However, these positions do not often open up.

The Section Leader of the flute or any of the wind instruments, on the other hand, cannot move up to a concertmaster/concertmistress position. They have the opportunity, though, to train to be conductors or to obtain jobs as a Section Leader or section members in more prestigious orchestras.

Education and Training

As with most symphonic positions, a college degree is not required. Conservatory training or a degree in music performance may help the musician in his or her journey toward becoming a great musician and Section Leader. Years of intensive training and study in the instrument of choice are essential.

Seminars in section leading are also available and often prove to be useful.

Experience/Skills/Personality Traits

Section Leaders must have experience as section members. Many also play in chamber music ensembles.

Section Leaders often begin playing in youth orchestras. There they gain the experience of acting as Section Leaders. Of course, a Section Leader must be an exceptional musician on his or her instrument.

The Section Leader must be a good leader, able to communicate to the section without being obvious to the audience.

Unions/Associations

Section Leaders must belong to a musician's union. Most belong to the American Federation of Musicians (AFM). This union sets the minimum pay scale for musicians.

Tips for Entry

1. This position is obtained through application and auditions.
2. Prior to applying, take part in as many different orchestral situations as possible.
3. The National Orchestral Association holds training programs for individuals entering the orchestral music field.
4. Take part in seminars and internships offered by orchestras, organizations, colleges, and associations.
5. Positions are listed in music-oriented journals and newsletters such as *The International Musician.*

SECTION MEMBER

CAREER PROFILE

Duties: Playing an instrument in an orchestra

Alternate Title(s): Classical Musician; Artist; Section Player

Salary Range: $11,000 to $41,000+ in major orchestras; part-time or per servce pay in smaller orchestras

Employment Prospects: Poor

Advancement Prospects: Poor

Best Geographical Location(s) for Position: Major cultural centers and other large cities

Prerequisites:

Education or Training—Extensive musical training

Experience—Performance in chamber music ensembles, youth, college, urban, and/or metropolitan orchestras useful.

Special Skills and Personality Traits—Exceptional musical talent; dedication to music; perseverance

CAREER LADDER

```
┌─────────────────────────────┐
│                             │
│      Section Leader         │
│                             │
└─────────────────────────────┘

┌─────────────────────────────┐
│                             │
│      Section Member         │
│                             │
└─────────────────────────────┘

┌─────────────────────────────┐
│   Freelance Performer;      │
│   Conservatory Student      │
│                             │
└─────────────────────────────┘
```

Position Description

The Section Members of the orchestra are the people who make up the musical portion of the orchestra. There are different numbers of Section Members in each orchestra.

To be a Section Member, an individual must have exceptional talent with his or her instrument. In addition, the individual must like to perform on stage.

The Section Member must have a full knowledge of the orchestral repertoire. He or she must know the music before going into rehearsal. Rehearsals are mainly for putting together all the parts played by the orchestra.

An important part of the Section Member's responsibility is to play with a group. This is what makes an orchestra sound the way it does.

The Section Member is responsible to his or her section leader. The musician must take cues such as where the correct bowings or phrasing should be (in the string section), correct breathing (in the brass sections), who will play what part, etc.

Section Members must continually practice their instruments and rehearse musical pieces. As a Section Member, an individual must always keep trying to better his or her musical skill.

The Section Member is under contract to perform a specific number of concerts and rehearsals per week. Any rehearsal or concert over that number (the number differs with various orchestras) and any recording the Section Member participates in qualifies the individual for additional monies.

The Section Member must be available to travel, as orchestras often tour other cities and countries. Travel expenses are paid by the orchestra management.

Section Members who work full-time in major or regional orchestras generally receive at least four weeks vacation, usually when the orchestra takes its break.

Section Members often earn additional income teaching privately. If the individual is a noted member of the orchestra, he or she may also become a speaker on the lecture circuit.

Salaries

Salaries for Section Members depend on a number of factors. These include the type of orchestra (major, metropolitan, urban, etc.), its location, the number of weeks the orchestra is in session, and, in some cases, the seniority of the player.

Minimum earnings are negotiated by the American Federation of Musicians (AFM) local unions. Depending on the location, Section Members working in a major orchestra may earn between $330 and $780 per week (1983-84 rate). Annual salaries depend on how many weeks per year the orchestra is in session. Major orchestras run from thirty to fifty-two weeks a year. In addition to salaries, Section Members receive vacation pay and other benefits.

Section Members working in smaller orchestras usually earn considerably less than those playing in major orchestras. Many of the smaller orchestras offer only part-time work. Members are paid on a per service basis. This means that they are paid for each concert in which they perform. In most cases, these individuals are also paid for each rehearsal they attend.

Section Members in youth and college orchestras generally do not get paid and play for the experience.

Section Members might earn additional income by teaching or by participating in recording sessions.

Employment Prospects

The chances of obtaining a position as a Section Member in a major orchestra are limited. There are many talented, qualified musicians vying for few positions. There is intense competition.

Prospects in the smaller and less prestigious orchestras are slightly better.

Many orchestras now audition people in back of a screen. Using this technique, there can be no racial or sexual discrimination in the selection process. This technique came about after many years of orchestras that were dominated by white males.

Advancement Prospects

Once a Section Member obtains a position in an orchestra, the individual has a chance of advancing to a section leader position. The Section Member must be very talented to advance in this manner. Section Members also have the opportunity to advance their careers by trying to land positions as Section Members in more prestigious orchestras.

Education and Training

No college degree is required for a position as a Section Member. However, extensive musical training is essential. This training might be acquired at a conservatory or college, or through intensive private study.

Experience/Skills/Personality Traits

Any type of performance experience is helpful to an aspiring Section Member. Performing in youth or college orchestras or chamber music ensembles is most useful. Auditioning is useful for the experience.

Section Members must be very dedicated to their music. They must also have the perseverance to keep trying to land a position in an orchestra.

Unions/Associations

Section Members may belong to the American Federation of Musicians (AFM). This union negotiates minimum wages for the musician, maximum number of rehearsals, etc.

Tips for Entry

1. This position is obtained through application and auditions.
2. Prior to applying, take part in as many different orchestral situations as possible.
3. The National Orchestral Association holds training programs for individuals entering the orchestral music field.
4. Take part in seminars and internships offered by orchestras, colleges, and associations.
5. Positions are listed in music-oriented journals and newsletters such as *The International Musician*.

MANAGING DIRECTOR

CAREER PROFILE

Duties: Overseeing the administrative functions of the orchestra

Alternate Title(s): Executive Director; Chief Administrator

Salary Range: $15,000 to $55,000+

Employment Prospects: Poor

Advancement Prospects: Poor

Best Geographical Location(s) for Position: Major cultural centers and other large cities that house orchestras

Prerequisites:

Education or Training—College background or degree with major in business, arts administration, or music management recommended

Experience—Positions in supervisory capacities; experience in public relations helpful; orchestra manager position useful

Special Skills and Personality Traits—Management skills; supervisory skills; personability; responsibility; business ability

CAREER LADDER

```
┌─────────────────────────────────────────┐
│  Managing Director of a Major Orchestra  │
└─────────────────────────────────────────┘

┌─────────────────────────────────────────┐
│            Managing Director             │
└─────────────────────────────────────────┘

┌─────────────────────────────────────────┐
│            Orchestra Manager             │
└─────────────────────────────────────────┘
```

Position Description

The Managing Director of the orchestra holds the top administrative position in an orchestra. It is his or her job to oversee all of the administrative functions of the orchestra and to supervise the administrative personnel.

The individual works closely with the orchestra manager. Together they work with and supervise the development, public relations, business, educational activities, and ticket subscriptions directors and their departments. Both the orchestra manager and the Managing Director must be knowledgeable about these departments, their internal problems, and their activities.

The Managing Director acts as a liaison between the orchestra's board of directors and the administrative departments. It is his or her responsibility to make sure that the policies set up for the orchestra are carried out. The individual attends most of the orchestra board's meetings, working with the board on many of the policies developed. He or she will also report on any administrative problems.

Through these meetings, the Managing Director keeps the board members aware of all that is happening within the orchestra.

The Managing Director, or executive director, as he or she is sometimes called, takes part in all labor negotiations involving the orchestra. The individual must have the ability and the knowledge to effectively negotiate with unions.

The Managing Director of an orchestra usually works in many of the other departments of the orchestra's administration before attaining the Directorship. This experience makes the Director better qualified to handle the details of managing the orchestra.

As the Managing Director, the person is responsible for insuring that the orchestra meets the needs of the community from a cultural standpoint. He or she might decide that the community needs more children's concerts or a summer concert series. In these cases, the individual will work with the orchestra board and the community to try to put these programs together.

At times, the Managing Director will work with the personnel director. He or she will ultimately be responsible not only for hiring administrative personnel, but also for firing individuals who don't work out.

The Managing Director must work with the development department and the business department, making up budgets and raising money for the orchestra. Some of this money is made available through foundations, corporations, and arts councils. The Managing Director is responsible for locating as much money as possible through this system and bringing it to the attention of the development department.

The Managing Director of the orchestra is responsible to the president of the board of directors and to the board members. His or her days are long, but they are challenging and exciting.

Salaries

Symphony orchestras are classified into different categories according to their size, budget, etc. Salaries will naturally depend on the size, budget, and location of the orchestra. Individuals working as Managing Directors in major orchestras earn more than those working in smaller organizations. Salaries range from $15,000 to $55,000+ per year.

Employment Prospects

There are a limited number of major and regional orchestras. Employment prospects at that level are limited, too. Positions are more frequently available at the metropolitan and urban levels of orchestras.

Advancement Prospects

The orchestra's Managing Director may advance by obtaining the job of Managing Director with a bigger, more prestigious orchestra. The Managing Director of the orchestra holds the top position in the administrative side of the organization.

Education and Training

A college degree is not always required for this position, although it is usually preferred. Courses in arts administration, music arrangement, business, publicity, and journalism are helpful in handling the job.

Seminars on arts and orchestral administration, given by various colleges and by associations such as the American Symphony Orchestra League (ASOL), are a bonus to the individual seeking or already holding a position as an orchestra Managing Director.

Experience/Skills/Personality Traits

The Managing Director must be an enthusiastic type of person. The individual must be personable and congenial, as he or she must deal not only with the orchestra but also with the entire orchestra administration and the board of directors.

The Managing Director must have the ability to supervise and must do so effectively. He or she must be sensitive and understanding toward both the musicians and the administration.

Unions/Associations

The Managing Director of an orchestra may belong to the American Symphony Orchestra League (ASOL). This association sponsors seminars and internship programs in addition to publishing a magazine/newsletter. Many individuals also belong to the Associated Council of the Arts and/or local arts councils.

Tips for Entry

1. Find an orchestra, school, or association that offers an internship program. Interns have a much better chance of obtaining a position.
2. Attend seminars on orchestral management. These seminars are given by colleges, orchestras, and associations such as the American Symphony Orchestra League (ASOL). These will train and educate you and help you develop important contacts.
3. Vacancies are listed in the ASOL newsletter, the Associated Council of the Arts newsletter, and many regional arts organizations' publications.
4. Take a chance and send your resumé with a cover letter to a number of orchestras. One might have an opening for an assistant.

ORCHESTRA MANAGER

CAREER PROFILE

Duties: Assisting managing director in various management duties; negotiating contracts for musical orchestral personnel

Alternate Title(s): Assistant Manager; Operations Manager

Salary Range: $13,000 to $48,000+

Employment Prospects: Poor

Advancement Prospects: Fair

Best Geographical Location(s) for Position: Positions may be available in cultural centers or other cities that house orchestras

Prerequisites:

Education or Training—College degree preferred or recommended for most positions

Experience—Positions in supervisory capacities helpful

Special Skills and Personality Traits—Management skills; supervisory skills; personability; ability to negotiate

CAREER LADDER

```
Managing Director
```

```
Orchestra Manager
```

```
Director of Development;
Publicity or Public Relations Position
```

Position Description

The Orchestra Manager is the assistant to the orchestra's managing director. A primary duty is negotiating with the musicians union on behalf of the orchestra. An Orchestra Manager must try to get the best deal for the orchestra management from the union while keeping the players happy.

The Orchestra Manager is also in charge of arranging any concert tours for the orchestra. He or she not only arranges the details of the tour, but also tries to make it easy for the orchestra members who will be traveling. The individual is responsible for any problems that are not directly music-related. These could include anything from a musician's instrument that arrives late to an auditorium with bad acoustics. A musician who becomes ill in the middle of the night in a strange town or a dispute caused by hot tempers that erupt on the road become the Orchestra Manager's responsibilities. The Orchestra Manager must deal with crises that occur while traveling. With the pressures of touring, many problems are magnified.

The Orchestra Manager also oversees the orchestra's administrative employees, including the director of development, director of public relations, music administrator, business manager, director of educational activities, and director of ticket subscriptions. He or she must be knowledgeable about these positions and the problems that might occur. The person must have a broad understanding of the needs of the community or area in which the orchestra is based. As Orchestra Manager, he or she must negotiate contracts for guest soloists and guest conductors.

The Orchestra Manager is responsible to the managing director of the orchestra. The position is not a nine to five job. The successful Orchestra Manager loves symphonic music. This makes the job—which involves long hours and hard work—worthwhile.

Salaries

Symphony orchestras are classified into different groups depending on size, budget, and other factors. There are major orchestras, such as the Boston

Symphony or the Cleveland Orchestra; there are regional orchestras, like the Birmingham Symphony Orchestra or the Memphis Symphony Orchestra; there are metropolitan, urban, community, college, and youth orchestras. Salaries of Orchestra Managers vary according to the classification and location of the orchestra. Salaries range from $13,000 to $48,000+ annually. Orchestra Managers of urban, community, college, or youth orchestras often work on an avocational or per service basis.

Employment Prospects

There is a limited number of major and even regional orchestras in the country. Therefore, employment prospects at this level are poor. Positions are sometimes available at the metropolitan, urban, and community levels. However, these jobs are not always full-time.

Advancement Prospects

The position of an Orchestra Manager is not an entry level job. Positions held prior to Orchestra Manager might include public relations director, fund-raising director, business manager, or assistant in one of these fields. Once an individual has proven him or herself in the position of Orchestra Manager, he or she is a valuable commodity to the orchestra and has the opportunity to move up to the position of managing director or to move to an open position in a better orchestra as Orchestra Manager.

Education and Training

A college degree is preferred or recommended for most positions as Orchestra Manager. Individuals may find a few positions without this requirement. These are usually in smaller orchestras.

Courses in music management, administration, and/or business are helpful. Classes in publicity, labor negotiations, fund-raising, and psychology are useful, too. There are also seminars given around the country in arts administration. These seminars put the individual in touch with others already in the field and help develop contacts.

Experience/Skills/Personality Traits

A good sense of business is important to an Orchestra Manager. An understanding of and sensitivity to musicians and their problems and pressures is almost equally important. To do the job well, one must be able to deal effectively with problems and people under pressure. Hands-on experience is always helpful. Many conservatories and universities have internship programs that provide practical experience. Enjoying music makes it all worthwhile.

Unions/Associations

The Orchestra Manager may belong to the American Symphony Orchestra League (ASOL). He or she might also belong to a local arts council.

Tips for Entry

1. Find an orchestra or school that has an internship in orchestral management. The American Symphony Orchestra League (ASOL) sponsors a variety of internship programs.
2. Attend seminars on orchestral management. Seminars are sponsored by various universities and orchestras in addition to the ASOL.
3. Vacancies are listed in the ASOL newsletter, the Associated Council of the Arts newsletter, and many regional arts organizations' publications.

BUSINESS MANAGER

CAREER PROFILE

Duties: Supervising the financial affairs of the orchestra; preparing and distributing payroll

Alternate Title(s): Controller

Salary Range: $15,000 to $45,000

Employment Prospects: Fair

Advancement Prospects: Poor

Best Geographical Location(s) for Position: Major cultural centers such as Boston, Philadelphia, New York City, Chicago, etc.

Prerequisites:

Education or Training—Educational requirements vary; all positions require at least a high school diploma; many require a college degree

Experience—Bookkeeping experience, accounting positions, etc.

Special Skills and Personality Traits—Skill with figures; accuracy; responsibility; accounting and/or bookkeeping skills; cognizance of orchestral procedures

CAREER LADDER

```
┌─────────────────────────────────────┐
│  Business Manager of Major Orchestra; │
│         Orchestra Manager            │
└─────────────────────────────────────┘

┌─────────────────────────────────────┐
│                                     │
│         Business Manager            │
│                                     │
└─────────────────────────────────────┘

┌─────────────────────────────────────┐
│            Bookkeeper;              │
│            Accountant               │
└─────────────────────────────────────┘
```

Position Description

The Business Manager of the orchestra is in charge of supervising all its financial affairs. Depending on the size and the budget of the organization, the Business Manager may work alone or have an assistant and a staff.

The individual in this position must check all bills the orchestra receives. If they are correct, he or she issues checks and pays them. If they are wrong or if there is a discrepancy, the Business Manager or controller attempts to rectify the problem. The individual is responsible for paying all bills on time. These may include rentals for music, transportation costs for out-of-town concerts, hotel bills, etc.

The Business Manager may look at comparative prices of various items to make sure that the organization is buying well. For example, the person may check the prices of music stands from four or five companies before purchasing to establish a good price. The individual may work out deals with hotel or motel chains for putting up the orchestra members while on tour. As most orchestras' budgets are extremely tight, the Business Manager will always try to save money for the group.

Accurate records must be kept on all expenditures paid out for the orchestra. Payment dates, check numbers, and lists of items purchased must be kept meticulously. If there are any guarantees or warranties on products purchased, it is usually up to the Business Manager to keep these on file.

The Business Manager is responsible for preparing the payroll and distributing it at the proper times. If a guest conductor or soloist has been employed by the orchestra, the individual must make sure that they are paid, too. These payments must be disbursed in accordance with union regulations. The individual must make sure that the proper deductions are taken from everyone's salary and that these monies are correctly deposited and reported to the government.

The person in this position works closely with the director of development. The Business Manager may be responsible for keeping a tally of money raised or for depositing donations. He or she might be in charge of the bookkeeping for the fund-raising department.

The Business Manager also works with the orchestra manager and the managing director in putting together a yearly budget for the organization. After the budget is approved by the board of directors, the business manager works to stay within its bounds.

The individual in this position works fairly regular hours. He or she may report to the orchestra's managing director or to the board of directors.

Salaries

The salary of a Business Manager working for an orchestra will vary depending on the classification, size and budget of the orchestra. Salaries might also vary due to an individual's qualifications and responsibilities. A Business Manager working full time may earn from $15,000-$45,000 yearly.

Employment Prospects

Employment prospects are fair for those wanting jobs as business managers in orchestras. Almost every orchestra in the country which has any type of income and/or expenses hires at least a part-time person to fill this position. Larger orchestras may hire a full-time Business Manager and one or more assistants.

Advancement Prospects

Advancement prospects for a Business Manager in an orchestra are poor. The individual may be promoted to orchestra manager, but this may take a long time.

A Business Manager working for a smaller orchestra may, however, advance his or her career by finding employment with a larger or more prestigious orchestra. This usually means more responsibility and an increase in salary.

Education and Training

Education requirements vary greatly according to the orchestra and the position. For example, a Business Manager working part-time in a small orchestra may only be required to have a high school diploma. A major orchestra might, however, require an individual to have a degree in accounting, business, finance, or a related area.

There are many people who work in all phases of the orchestral system who have music performance degrees but cannot get performance-related jobs. A good number of these individuals take jobs in non-performance areas such as Business Management just to be close to the orchestral setting.

Experience/Skills/Personality Traits

One of the primary skills a Business Manager needs is an ability with figures. Many people in these positions have bookkeeping experience or accounting skills. Accuracy is essential.

It is helpful, too, for the individual to have a basic knowledge of orchestra procedures.

Unions/Associations

The Business Manager in an orchestral situation does not usually belong to any union. He or she may belong to a number of orchestra-related associations. The most prominent in the field is the American Symphony Orchestra League (ASOL).

Tips for Entry

1. Jobs as Business Managers of orchestras are often listed in the classified sections of newspapers. Most often these jobs open up at the end of a season.
2. Openings are listed in the American Symphony Orchestra League (ASOL) newsletter and various other arts council newsletters.
3. Send a resumé and a cover letter to a few orchestras. They may have openings coming up.

DIRECTOR OF DEVELOPMENT

CAREER PROFILE

Duties: Coordinating annual giving activities, capital campaigns, and deferred giving opportunities for donors and potential donors to an orchestra

Alternate Title(s): Fund-Raising and Development Director

Salary Range: $10,000 to $55,000+

Employment Prospects: Fair

Advancement Prospects: Fair

Best Geographical Location(s) for Position: Any city that hosts an orchestra—New York City, Boston, Memphis, Phoenix, Syracuse, Pittsburgh, Philadelphia, etc.

Prerequisites:

Education or Training—College degree not required in all positions, but may be preferred

Experience—Fund-raising and development experience required in music or nonmusic-oriented positions

Special Skills and Personality Traits—Communication skills; creativity; enthusiasm; organization

CAREER LADDER

```
┌─────────────────────────────┐
│                             │
│     Orchestra Manager       │
│                             │
└─────────────────────────────┘

┌─────────────────────────────┐
│                             │
│   Director of Development    │
│                             │
└─────────────────────────────┘

┌─────────────────────────────┐
│      Assistant to the       │
│   Director of Development    │
│                             │
└─────────────────────────────┘
```

Position Description

Getting people to donate money isn't easy, especially when there are so many causes and organizations soliciting. The Director of Development of the orchestra has one job: to raise money for the orchestra.

He or she does this in a number of ways. The Director of Development will coordinate the annual giving activities, capital campaigns, and deferred giving opportunities for donors and potential donors.

As part of this project, he or she might develop special events and programs to support the orchestra financially. These programs may increase attendance or develop direct financial support.

Activities of a Director of Development might include direct mail campaigns, telephone and telethon fund-raisers, balls, dinners, or cocktail parties.

In order for the Director of Development to reach people who are interested in these fund-raisers, he or she must do a great deal of research. Questionnaires and surveys are used to locate potential supporters.

The Director of Development should have strong public contacts. Through these contacts the Director learns the needs of the community in relation to the orchestra. He or she works closely with both the director of public relations and the orchestra's manager.

The Director of Development usually reports to either the orchestra manager or the managing director, as well as to the orchestra's board of directors.

The Director of Development acts as a liaison between donors, potential donors, and the orchestra's management and board of directors. He or she informs the management and the board of any occurrences affecting donors. The Development Director also works with the board projecting support programs for fund-raising projects.

At times, the Director of Development may also work with volunteers, getting them involved in such orchestra fund-raising activities as auctions, dinner-dances, etc., to benefit the organization. He or she will reach out to the community for much-needed volunteer support.

The Director of Development creates fund-raising literature and audio-visual materials such as brochures, booklets, pamphlets, programs, volunteer training films, slide shows, and tapes.

A large amount of money for orchestras is raised through grants, foundations, corporations, and endowments for the arts. The Director of Development must keep up with the latest information on these. He or she must know how to apply for grants, how to write proposals, and how to follow up in order to receive the largest gifts possible.

He or she must be an enthusiastic individual. Believing in the cause (financial support of the orchestra) is crucial to the successful Director of Development. Days are long. In addition to regular work hours, he or she must attend community meetings, volunteer meetings, and special events.

Salaries

The Director of Development's salary is commensurate with the size of the orchestra and its fund-raising goals. Directors of Development for small orchestras start out at around $10,000 yearly. Individuals working with larger orchestras and with greater responsibility can earn up to $55,000+ annually.

Employment Prospects

Directors of Development who can produce results are always in demand. There is a turnover of people in this field. Much of the turnover is a result of an individual's failure to satisfy the board of directors of the orchestra in fund-raising. It takes a number of years to develop a producing program and many boards are impatient, demanding immediate results.

Advancement Prospects

As noted above, Directors of Development who can produce are in demand. An individual who is knowledgeable in coordinating fund-raising and can back up that knowledge with results can move on to a development position with a more prestigious orchestra. He or she may also try to advance his or her career by becoming an orchestra manager.

Education and Training

College degrees are not always required of Directors of Development. However, they are often preferred. There might be several applicants who are qualified, and the difference between them might be a college background or degree.

There are a number of colleges around the country that offer degrees in arts administration or management. If attending a school with such a major is impossible, the individual should take courses in marketing, public relations, and business. These courses will help lay a foundation for a job in the development field.

Experience/Skills/Personality Traits

Many people get into fund-raising by acting as chairperson for a club or organization. They find that it is a challenge to bring in money for a specific cause or organization. These individuals are enthusiastic about fund-raising and finding ways to get other people to give.

As a rule, Directors of Development are persuasive in an inoffensive way. They not only know the methods to use to bring in potential donations, they know how to get others to volunteer to help. This is important to an orchestra that depends on fund-raising to stay alive financially.

Unions/Associations

Many Directors of Development of orchestras belong to the American Symphony Orchestra League (ASOL), the Associated Council of the Arts, and/or local arts councils.

Tips for Entry

1. There are internship programs in the various positions of orchestral management, including development. These internships are made available through orchestras, colleges, or organizations.
2. There are also many seminars offered in both the development and fund-raising field and specialized orchestral development. These programs are sponsored by major orchestras, colleges, or other organizations. Look into them.
3. Vacancies are listed in the American Symphony Orchestra League (ASOL) newsletter, the Associated Council of the Arts newsletter, and many regional arts organization publications.
4. If you are interested in a position of this type, write to a number of orchestras and ask if you may submit an application to work as an assistant or trainee.

DIRECTOR OF PUBLIC RELATIONS

CAREER PROFILE

Duties: Handling press and promotion of the orchestra and its activities; possibly handling advertising (for small orchestra)

Alternate Title(s): P.R. Director; Director of Press Relations; Publicity Director

Salary Range: $12,500 to $45,000

Employment Prospects: Fair

Advancement Prospects: Poor

Best Geographical Location(s) for Position: Cultural centers that host major orchestras other cities that host smaller orchestras

Prerequisites:

Education or Training—College degree not always required, but sometimes preferred

Experience—Publicity and public relations experience in orchestral or nonorchestral situation

Special Skills and Personality Traits—Good writing skills; ability to work under pressure; creativity; knowledge of orchestras

CAREER LADDER

```
┌─────────────────────────────────────┐
│     Director of Public Relations     │
│      for Prestigious Orchestra;      │
│       Director of Development        │
└─────────────────────────────────────┘

┌─────────────────────────────────────┐
│                                     │
│     Director of Public Relations     │
│                                     │
└─────────────────────────────────────┘

┌─────────────────────────────────────┐
│   Assistant Public Relations Director; │
│              Publicist               │
└─────────────────────────────────────┘
```

Position Description

The Director of Public Relations for an orchestra is in charge of handling the press and promotion of that orchestra and its activities.

Throughout the season, the orchestra puts on a number of concerts. It is the job of the Director of Public Relations to see that the community and the press know of these concerts. Most orchestras also plan special activities, such as children's concerts, educational activities, holiday shows, etc. The P.R. Director must make sure that the community is aware of these events.

The way most Public Relations Directors alert the community to orchestra activities is through publicity. This is attained through press releases and advertising.

P.R. Directors must build up a media contact list to which to send out important news items. After writing a news release and sending it out, the P.R. Director's job is not complete. He or she must follow up on stories, calling the press to see if they need additional information, photos, interviews, etc.

The Public Relations Director works with the development department. When that department is trying to raise monies through an annual fund-raising drive, for example, the P.R. department will usually do a story on the activity.

The P.R. Director will also put together a number of press parties, press conferences, cocktail parties, and other functions. These affairs are used by the P.R. Director to help promote the orchestra.

The Director of P.R. might supervise the writing, layout, and printing of publications prepared for the orchestra, including those used for promotion, education, or fund-raising.

In his or her position, the Director of P.R. might also work with other organizations or corporations for tie-in possibilities. For instance, the orchestra might work with a shopping mall in a promotion for both the mall and the orchestra.

The Director of P.R. would also do publicity on the hiring of a new conductor. He or she might write press releases on new section members. The individual must put together press packages for the media to use routinely or for special events.

If the orchestra hires a guest conductor, the Director of Public Relations may do a special news release as well as setting up interviews between the conductor and media.

The Director of Public Relations is responsible to the orchestra manager or managing director, depending on the size and structure of the organization. He or she might also be responsible to the orchestra's board of directors.

The Director of Public Relations for an orchestra might supervise a number of people in the organization's P.R. department or might be the sole employee of that department. This depends, of course, on the size and budget of the orchestra.

Salaries
Salaries of Public Relations Directors for orchestras are usually commensurate with the size of the orchestra.

P.R. Directors working for small orchestras might have yearly salaries of $12,500. P.R. Directors for these smaller orchestras might also work part-time or on a per project basis. Fees for specific types of P.R. projects vary.

Public Relations Directors working in larger orchestras have yearly incomes ranging from $18,000 to $45,000 annually.

Employment Prospects
If an individual is interested in working in an orchestral setting and can write and communicate fairly well, this may be the type of position to seek.

Most orchestras employ at least a part-time person for the position of Public Relations Director or publicist.

Larger orchestras may have five or more people working in their P.R. departments.

Advancement Prospects
There are a number of ways for a Public Relations Director to advance. The individual may seek a position with a more prestigious orchestra. These are often hard to obtain, as people in these positions do not tend to float from job to job. The individual may also move into the development department, possibly as director of development. Financially, this does not represent that much of a promotion; however, since these two jobs are often interrelated, many people do advance to these positions.

Education and Training
Directors of Public Relations in orchestras are not always required to hold college degrees, although it is sometimes preferred.

Courses in journalism, communications, public relations, publicity, and marketing help. A knowledge of the activities of an orchestra is helpful, too.

There are seminars and programs given by schools, associations, and organizations on public relations and music. These might be useful.

Experience/Skills/Personality Traits
Any type of writing skill and experience is helpful to a Director of Public Relations. P.R. Directors often come from the ranks of newspaper and magazine journalists.

Other P.R. Directors work as assistants in the orchestra or with other companies. Still other individuals work as publicists in either music or nonmusic fields.

Whatever the experience, the P.R. Director needs sound, creative writing skills. The individual should also have built up or be able to build up a list of media contacts.

As in most jobs in P.R., the Director must have the ability to work under tremendous pressure.

Unions/Associations
The P.R. Director of an orchestra might belong to the Public Relations Society of America (PRSA). This organization works to uphold the ethics of P.R. people. In addition, the organization offers seminars, a magazine, pamphlets, and other useful information.

The individual might also belong to the American Symphony Orchestra League (ASOL). This organization, too, provides many useful seminars, workshops, and a newsletter.

Tips for Entry
1. There are numerous internship programs in various orchestral management positions, including the public relations department. These internships are made available directly through orchestras, colleges, and organizations.
2. There are vacancies listed for these positions in the ASOL (American Symphony Orchestra League) newsletter, the Associated Council of the Arts newsletter, and many regional arts organization publications.
3. Even if there is not an opening listed, you might want to contact a number of orchestras and send them your resumé plus a few samples of your writing style. Ask the personnel people to keep your resumé on file in case an opening develops.

SUBSCRIPTIONS AND TICKET SERVICE DIRECTOR

CAREER PROFILE

Duties: Obtaining new subscriptions for orchestra season; renewing current subscriptions; keeping records of ticket sales

Alternate Title(s): Head of Subscriptions; Ticket Service Director
Salary Range: $10,000 to $25,000

Employment Prospects: Poor

Advancement Prospects: Fair

Best Geographical Location(s) for Position: Any city that hosts an orchestra such as New York City, Boston, Memphis, Phoenix, Syracuse, Pittsburgh, Philadelphia, etc.

Prerequisites:

Education or Training—College degree not required for all positions, but may be preferred

Experience—Volunteer work with orchestras; fund-raising; prior promotional work helpful; working in box office

Special Skills and Personality Traits—Organization; ability to write; knowledge of orchestras; bookkeeping skills

CAREER LADDER

```
┌─────────────────────────────────┐
│                                 │
│     Director of Development      │
│                                 │
└─────────────────────────────────┘

┌─────────────────────────────────┐
│                                 │
│ Subscriptions and Ticket Service Director │
│                                 │
└─────────────────────────────────┘

┌─────────────────────────────────┐
│                                 │
│       Box Office Director;       │
│            Student               │
│                                 │
└─────────────────────────────────┘
```

Position Description

The Subscription Ticket Service Director is responsible for selling and keeping track of tickets and subscriptions for the orchestra season.

In this position, the individual must put together programs to obtain new subscribers for the upcoming season. Although part of the income of the orchestra is derived from grants and funding, much of it comes from subscriptions. In order to procure these new subscriptions, the director of this department often runs a variety of campaigns directed toward locating potential subscribers. These programs might include mass telephoning, mailings, or telethons. Additionally, the individual runs advertisements and sends out press releases on the subject. Some of these functions might be handled in conjunction with the public relations department.

Depending on the orchestra, the Subscriptions Director may work with a number of volunteers who help run the above events. In a major orchestra, the director of the department may have a paid staff.

The Subscription and Ticket Service Director must also keep track of current subscribers. Renewal forms have to be sent out at the appropriate time. In certain instances, these renewal forms must be followed up with phone calls, At times, the director of the department will ask a board member to make a follow-up phone call or visit a subscriber regarding a renewal.

The person in this position is in charge of coordinating the sales of individual concert tickets. Records must be kept on how many tickets are sold at each location. Tickets may be sold at the box office, schools, stores, or a ticket service. If a ticket service (such as Ticketron) is used, the Director must make sure they receive monies owed to them for ticket sales.

The individual in this job must keep precise records of everything in the department. He or she has to know at a glance who was sent what, when it was sent, when a follow-up call was made, etc. Records must also be maintained on monies arriving for subscriptions and tickets.

The Director of Subscriptions may be called upon to speak to groups or to attend functions on behalf of the orchestra. He or she usually works fairly regular hours. The director of this department is responsible to the orchestra manager and/or the board of directors.

Salaries

Salaries range widely for Subscriptions and Ticket Service Directors. In very small orchestras, the position may be a voluntary one. In large orchestras, an individual may earn from $10,000 to $25,000 yearly, depending on the size of the orchestra and its budget.

Employment Prospects

Employment opportunities in this type of position are not bountiful. There are only a limited number of orchestras employing a full-time paid person to do this job.

Individuals will find that only the larger orchestras, such as major and regional ones, have these jobs. Additionally, there is not a large turnover in this department.

Advancement Prospects

Advancement is difficult but possible. Individuals in this field may find employment in the same position in larger, more prestigious orchestras, or they may advance their careers by becoming Directors of Development.

In order to advance in the current organization, he or she may need additional training or education.

Education and Training

As in many positions in the music industry, educational requirements vary widely. In larger major orchestras, the position of Subscriptions and Ticket Service Director may require or prefer a college background or degree.

In a smaller orchestra the individual may need only bookkeeping experience and training.

Experience/Skills/Personality Traits

A Subscription and Ticket Service Director must be a totally organized individual. He or she needs the ability to keep accurate records. A good memory is a must.

Additionally, the person seeking this job should have the ability to write well and creatively. The individual must possess a talent for supervising both staff and volunteers. Knowledge of bookkeeping is essential. The Director of Subscriptions must be fully cognizant of the way an orchestra functions.

Unions/Associations

A Subscription and Ticket Service Director may belong to the American Symphony Orchestra League (ASOL), the Associated Council of the Arts, or any number of local arts councils.

Tips for Entry

1. If you think you might be interested in a position of this type, try volunteering. Go to an orchestra and ask if it would be possible to help out on a ticket subscription campaign.
2. Check with various orchestras and colleges to find out if they offer internships programs.
3. Openings are found in the American Symphony Orchestra League (ASOL) newsletter and various other arts council newsletters. On occasion, an orchestra may advertise an opening for a job of this type in the local newspaper.
4. Send a resumé and a cover letter to a few orchestras. They may find a position for you.

DIRECTOR OF EDUCATIONAL ACTIVITIES

CAREER PROFILE

Duties: Coordinating activities for students; designing young people's concert series; planning learning activities relating to orchestra

Alternate Title(s): Education Director

Salary Range: $10,000 to $25,000

Employment Prospects: Poor

Advancement Prospects: Poor

Best Geographical Location(s) for Position: Major cultural centers

Prerequisites:

Education or Training—Bachelors degree required or preferred for most positions

Experience—Experience in orchestra administration and business helpful

Special Skills and Personality Traits—Writing skills; knowledge of orchestra & music, public relations skills; communication skills

CAREER LADDER

```
Director of Educational Activities for Major
Orchestra; Director of Public Relations,
Fund-Raising, Development, Etc.
```

```
Director of Educational Activities
```

```
Assistant Director of Educational Activities;
Publicist;
Student
```

Position Description

The Director of Educational Activities in an orchestra is responsible for coordinating all orchestral activities for students and other young people in the community.

One of the main functions of this individual is to keep in close contact with the schools in the area surrounding the orchestra's base of operations. The Director may call or meet with school district music supervisors, music teachers, etc.

At times, the orchestra may offer concerts to the schools. They might bring the entire orchestra or just parts of it directly into the school to perform. Other educational activities might include offering the conductor or other orchestra members as speakers at school assemblies or at career days.

The individual in this position works closely with the music administrator, managing director, and/or orchestra manager designing young people's concerts. These concerts may be coordinated with school visits by members of the orchestra.

As the Director of this department, the individual may recommend reduced prices for student tickets. Additionally, the individual is responsible for making sure that students, parents, and administrators are aware of the special activities, ticket prices, etc. This may be accomplished by the Director designing and sending brochures or posters to the schools, placing them in the surrounding areas, sending out press releases to newspapers, and mailing notices to current subscribers. This function may be accomplished with the help of the public relations director.

The Director of Educational Activities may plan tours for students of the orchestra hall, backstage, rehearsals, and/or business offices. He or she may prepare booklets dealing with the different career opportunities in the orchestral field. This person might counsel or find appropriate people to counsel students on educational requirements and/or training needs of various positions in the field.

It should be noted that this position is not found in all orchestras. In smaller orchestras, responsibilities of this job overlap into other areas such as public relations or the ticket subscription department.

The Director of Educational Activities may be responsible to the orchestra manager, the managing director, or the organization's board of directors.

Salaries

The Director of Educational Activities in an orchestra may work on a part-time or full-time basis, depending on the size of the orchestra. Part-time workers work by the project or by the hour.

Full-time people in this position have salaries that range from $10,000 to $25,000 annually. Salaries vary according to the size and budget of the orchestra and the specific duties of the individual.

Employment Prospects

This is a hard position to locate. Jobs are very limited. In smaller orchestras, this job is often combined with the duties of other jobs. There are only a limited number of orchestras in the country in which to seek positions. Orchestra jobs in this specialty area are so hard to locate that there is not a high turnover rate.

Advancement Prospects

An individual in the position of Director of Educational Activities may advance his or her career in a number of ways. The person may seek a job in the same field with a more prestigious orchestra. The person man move up in the organization and become a director of public relations, development, fund-raising, etc.

Advancement opportunities are poor. There is not a high turnover rate in any of the jobs in the orchestra. This makes it difficult to advance to another position.

Education and Training

Educational requirements for the Director of Educational Activities in an orchestra vary. In some jobs—mainly in the larger major orchestras—individuals are either required or preferred to hold college degrees. Other positions—those in smaller orchestras—do not require anything over a high school diploma.

Experience/Skills/Personality Traits

People in this position must be knowledgeable about the working of the orchestra and music in general. They must have the ability to write clearly and creatively.

Individuals working in this job must be articulate, congenial, and able to relate well to young people.

Some individuals working as Directors of Educational Activities obtain the position soon after leaving college. Other individuals work in various capacities with the orchestra or at arts councils. There are other people who work as reporters, publicists, or musicians before entering the field.

Unions/Associations

The Director of Educational Activities of an orchestra may belong to the American Symphony Orchestra League (ASOL). This association offers seminars, information, and other help to people working with orchestras.

Tips for Entry

1. Look for seminars and courses on orchestral management and administration. These are given by colleges, universities, associations, organizations, and orchestras.
2. Internships—paid, unpaid, and credit-bearing—are sometimes available. Check with your college, various orchestras, and the American Symphony Orchestra League (ASOL).
3. Openings for these positions are often listed in the ASOL newsletter as well as in various arts council newsletters.
4. If you're still in school, you might volunteer your services or look for a summer job in this career area, either in an orchestra or in a similar position with arts council projects.

PERSONNEL DIRECTOR

CAREER PROFILE

Duties: Sending out notices for job openings in orchestra; screening applications; maintaining files of potential job candidates

Alternate Title(s): Personnel Manager

Salary Range: $12,500 to $39,000+

Employment Prospects: Poor

Advancement Prospects: Poor

Best Geographical Location(s) for Position: Major cultural centers and other cities that house orchestras

Prerequisites:

Education or Training—Educational requirements vary from orchestra to orchestra; some positions require college background or degree, others do not

Experience—Working in personnel positions

Special Skills and Personality Traits—Knowledge of music and positions in orchestra; communication skills; ability to write; organization

CAREER LADDER

```
┌─────────────────────────────┐
│   Personnel Director for    │
│ More Prestigious Orchestra; │
│    Possible Advancement     │
│    to Other Departments     │
└─────────────────────────────┘

┌─────────────────────────────┐
│                             │
│     Personnel Director      │
│                             │
└─────────────────────────────┘

┌─────────────────────────────┐
│                             │
│    Personnel Staff Member   │
│                             │
└─────────────────────────────┘
```

Position Description

The Personnel Manager of an orchestra is responsible for all the hirings and firings of personnel in that orchestra. He or she is in charge of sending out notices whenever openings occur in either the business end or the talent end of the operation. These notices are usually sent to schools, colleges, conservatories, newsletters, associations, and organizations. In addition to notices, the Personnel Manager writes ads and places them in newspapers or magazines to alert people to these openings.

The Personnel Manager screens all applications that come to the orchestra. In the case of talent positions (section members, leaders, etc.), he or she will usually work in conjunction with the conductor, the concertmaster, and the section leaders who will be doing the auditioning.

In cases where the position is on the business side, the Personnel Manager would not only screen the applications, but also give preliminary interviews. After the first interviews are held, the Personnel Manager calls back the best candidates for further interviews.

Substitute musicians are often required by orchestras. It is the duty of the Personnel Manager to hire these substitutes. As these individuals are often needed on the spur of the moment, the Personnel Manager must maintain a list of backups for each instrument in the orchestra.

Before an individual is hired, the Personnel Manager usually explains orchestra policies, rules, regulations, and salaries. He or she must see that all forms are filled out and all information needed by the orchestra is supplied.

In the event that an individual must be fired, this job usually falls to the Personnel Manager, too. The Personnel Manager keeps track of employee attendance and, in the case of musicians, punctuality.

This individual works with all the other departments of the orchestra. He or she must have the ability to put people into jobs for which they are best suited.

Salaries

Salaries for the Personnel Director of an orchestra vary according to the size of the orchestra, its budget, and its location. Earnings will also depend on the qualifications of the individual and his or her duties. The Personnel Director has a salary between $12,500 and $39,000+ annually.

Employment Prospects

There are only limited positions open for Personnel Directors in orchestras. Employment prospects for this job are not good. There are more and more people with personnel training that want to get into work involving music and/or orchestras, and there are not enough positions to go around. Additionally, there is not a high turnover of people in these positions.

Advancement Prospects

Advancement in this job is difficult. Finding a position as a Personnel Manager with a more prestigious organization is very hard. As competition is tough and people don't leave these jobs often, it is almost impossible.

Personnel Directors may, however, advance to other departments in the orchestra if they are qualified. Personnel Directors with the correct training may also go into labor relations and negotiating.

Education and Training

Educational requirements for the position of Personnel Director vary from orchestra to orchestra. Some do not require a college degree, while others do. Certain positions require at least some college background.

Major orchestras often require their Personnel Directors to have degrees in personnel administration.

There are colleges around the country that grant degrees in the field of personnel.

Experience/Skill/Personality Traits

Personnel Directors need the ability to put the right people in the right jobs. In the symphony orchestra, Personnel Directors must have at least a basic knowledge of music and of the other business positions in the organization.

The individual must be skilled at interviewing potential employees, screening applications, etc.

In addition, the Personnel Director must be extremely articulate, able to communicate ideas well, and organized.

Unions/Associations

The Personnel Director of an orchestra may be a member of the American Symphony Orchestra League (ASOL), the Associated Council of the Arts, or other arts councils in the area.

Tips for Entry

1. Try to find an internship program. Internships help you get a foot in the door.
2. Openings for these positions are sometimes listed in the American Symphony Orchestra League (ASOL) newsletter, the Associated Council of the Arts newsletter, regional arts organizations' publications, and local newspaper advertisements.
3. No matter what educational requirement an orchestra has for this position, it doesn't hurt to be overtrained. It makes it easier to get a job and easier to advance if you have the education beforehand.

ORCHESTRAL MUSIC LIBRARIAN

CAREER PROFILE

Duties: Cataloging and ordering music for orchestra; assisting conductor copying scores and parts

Alternate Title(s): None

Salary Range: $12,00 to $18,000+

Employment Prospects: Poor

Advancement Prospects: Poor

Best Geographical Location(s) for Position: Cities that host large orchestras, such as New York City, Boston, Memphis, Phoenix, Syracuse, Pittsburgh, Philadelphia, etc.

Prerequisites:

Education or Training—Bachelor's degree in music history or theory and library sciences; master's degree in music or library science often required

Experience—Position as music librarian assistant; library experience

Special Skills and Personality Traits—Interest in orchestral music; extensive knowledge of music; ability to copy musical notations; organization

CAREER LADDER

```
┌─────────────────────────────────────┐
│                                     │
│  Music Librarian for Major Orchestra │
│                                     │
└─────────────────────────────────────┘

┌─────────────────────────────────────┐
│                                     │
│          Music Librarian             │
│                                     │
└─────────────────────────────────────┘

┌─────────────────────────────────────┐
│                                     │
│      Music Librarian Assistant       │
│                                     │
└─────────────────────────────────────┘
```

Position Description

Orchestral Music Librarians combine their skills as librarians with their love for and comprehensive knowledge of music. An Orchestral Music Librarian has many duties. He or she catalogs the orchestra's printed music. The individual is also responsible for ordering new music. If the orchestra decides not to purchase certain pieces of music, the Music Librarian is in charge of locating the music, renting it, and seeing that it gets back when it is no longer needed.

The Orchestral Music Librarian must be competent in copying musical markings. The individual often assists the conductor after he or she has looked at a piece of music and made changes in it. The Music Librarian may copy parts for the different section members, making the necessary corrections and adding bowings and or phrasings where indicated.

During rehearsals or concerts, it is the Music Librarians's job to hand out the music to the section members. These are collected after the rehearsal or performance has concluded.

The Music Librarian travels with the orchestra when it goes on tour or performs special concerts. On the road, the individual is totally responsible for the sheet music. The Music Librarian also makes contact with any guest conductor the orchestra might be hosting. It is his or her duty to question the conductor about his or her music requirements.

The Orchestral Music Librarian has more contact with live music than a Music Librarian working at a school or a library. Although many of the responsibilities are the same, there are some differences. The Music Librarian must decide what type of setting he or she prefers.

The Orchestral Music Librarian does not work regular hours, as Music Librarians in other places of employment usually do. He or she is usually responsible to the orchestra conductor.

Salaries

As with all orchestral positions, salaries depend on the type of orchestra. A Music Librarian working for a major orchestra makes between $15,500 and $18,000 annually.

A Music Librarian working for a regional or metropolitan orchestra might make between $12,000 and $16,000 yearly. In local orchestras, the Music Librarian is often a section member who works gratis.

Employment Prospects

There are only a few major orchestras in the country. As noted above, not all orchestras employ paid Music Librarians. The employment prospects for a position such as this are limited.

Advancement Prospects

The possibility for advancement is poor as a result of the small number of Music Librarian positions available in orchestras. There are more candidates than there are jobs to fill.

An individual in an orchestral setting might find that he or she wants to move into another type of position, such as one in a library or educational setting. However, these, too, may be limited.

Education and Training

The education needed for a Music Librarian working in an orchestra is much the same as for any Music Librarian. All positions require at least an undergraduate degree in music theory or history. Some positions require a dual major in music and library sciences. Still others require a master's degree in either music or library sciences.

Additionally, the Music Librarian in this setting needs training in copying parts and scores.

Experience/Skills/Personality Traits

Orchestral Music Librarians often work as music librarian assistants prior to becoming full-fledged Music Librarians. These positions are usually available only in larger symphonies. However, there are internship programs to help the aspiring Music Librarian gain experience.

The Music Librarian must have neat handwriting. The individual must also be able to copy conductor's markings on scores.

In addition, the Orchestral Music Librarian must be extremely organized and very personable.

Unions/Associations

The Orchestral Music Librarian might belong to a number of associations. These include the American Library Association (ALA), the Special Libraries Association (SLA), or the American Symphony Orchestra League (ASOL). These organizations help the individual to maintain contacts and they provide seminars, newsletters, and other valuable information. The Orchestral Music Librarian might additionally belong to the American Federation of Musicians (AFM).

Tips on Entry

1. Try to find an internship as a Music Librarian in a major, regional, or metropolitan orchestra.
2. Act as the Music Librarian of your college or school orchestra or band for experience.
3. Find out what orchestras employ music librarian assistants and try to obtain a job.

ARENAS, FACILITIES, HALLS, AND CLUBS

CONCERT HALL MANAGER

CAREER PROFILE

Duties: Managing concert hall; overseeing all activities in venue; supervising employees

Alternate Title(s): Theater Manager; Arena Director; Facility Director; Director of Hall Operations

Salary Range: $12,500 to $38,000+

Employment Prospects: Fair

Advancement Prospects: Poor

Best Geographical Location(s) for Position: Most geographical locations have positions; cities tend to have more concert halls and/or arenas

Prerequisites:

Education or Training—High school diploma minimum; some jobs may require additional education

Experience—Working in concert halls, clubs, etc. in various positions; concert hall assistant manager experience useful

Special Skills and Personality Traits—Responsibility; ability to handle crises; knowledge of music business, contracts, etc.; cognizance of hall and theater business

CAREER LADDER

```
┌─────────────────────────────────┐
│     Manager of Large Facility    │
│   or Prestigious Concert Hall    │
└─────────────────────────────────┘

┌─────────────────────────────────┐
│       Concert Hall Manager       │
└─────────────────────────────────┘

┌─────────────────────────────────┐
│   Concert Hall Assistant Manager │
└─────────────────────────────────┘
```

Position Description

A Concert Hall Manager is in charge of managing the hall and overseeing all activities that occur in the facility. The individual has diverse duties to perform depending on the facility and the position.

One of the functions of the Hall Manager is to supervise all employees of the facility. These workers include electricians, sound people, lighting people, ticket sellers, ushers, security, clean-up people, and a host of others. In some situations, the person might also hire a publicist, public relations firm, or advertising agency to handle hall promotion. In other circumstances, the hall owner might handle this project. As a rule, the Concert Hall Manager has the authority to hire people and fire them. In directing the activities of all these workers, the Manager tries to ensure the most efficient operations possible for the theater.

Another function of the Concert Hall Manager is to oversee the financial business of the hall. The

individual must try to keep the hall or theater booked. Sometimes the Manager will buy the talent; other times he or she will rent out the hall to various promoters. Whichever system is used, the individual must negotiate to get the best price. When promoters rent the hall, the individual must attempt to obtain the best rental fee, giving away the fewest possible extras.

The Concert Hall Manager may be responsible for payroll. In some cases, if a union is involved (and they frequently are, the individual must see that all union regulations are enforced at the hall. Unions involved might include the musicians union, the electricians union, and others.

After an event has been planned, the Manager is in charge of advertising it and publicizing it to maximize the attendance. This might be accomplished with the assistance of an advertising agency and a public relations firm. The hall may have its own in-house advertising agency and/or publicist.

The Hall Manager must be knowledgeable about obtaining the most exposure for an event for the least amount of money.

It is the responsibility of the Hall Manager to make sure that the facility is in good condition and clean at all times. If there are things that need repair, the individual oversees the work. On occasion, the hall may be refurbished or completely done over. The Hall Manager, once again, is in charge of these work projects.

The Hall Manager must be ready to handle all types of crises effectively and without panicking. Potential problems include an act not showing up for a performance, union workers going on strike before a show, inclement weather on the night of a performance when tickets are being sold at the door, or a patron getting unruly during a show. There are, of course, many other things that can occur.

The Concert Hall Manager must see to it that the money that is to be paid to acts is available on the night of a show. He or she must also be sure to fulfill any contract riders exactly as they are written.

The individual must work closely with all the media in the immediate area. Most of the time these press people will be offered press passes or backstage passes. Maintaining a good relationship with the press and other media goes a long way toward helping the theater become successful.

The Concert Hall Manager works long, irregular hours. He or she is responsible to the owner of the theater, hall, or arena.

Salaries

The salary of a Concert Hall or Arena Manager or Director varies greatly depending on the size of the venue, the location, the prestige of the hall, qualifications of the individual, and the duties.

A person managing a small concert theater in an out of the way location will not make as much as one who is managing a large, prestigious hall in a major metropolitan area. The individual managing a small theater might earn from $12,500 to $22,500 yearly. Those who manage larger, more prestigious halls in major metropolitan areas earn from $20,000 to $38,000+ annually.

Employment Prospects

Employment prospects for a Concert Hall Manager are fair. There are different types of halls, a range of sizes, and various locations. Major cities have the greatest number of concert halls and/or arenas. However, it may be more difficult to obtain a job in these locations.

Smaller cities have fewer opportunities, but jobs are usually easier to obtain.

Advancement Prospects

Advancement is difficult for Concert Hall Managers. Those who seek to stay in that field usually need to find jobs in larger facilities or more prestigious halls. There seems to be a correlation between the size and prestige of a concert hall and the difficulty of obtaining a job there.

Individuals who do move into better positions, however, are usually able to continue advancing their careers.

Education and Training

Most positions as Concert Hall Managers only require a high school diploma. There are, however, jobs that require additional education. Many people who hold these positions have degrees in music, theater, or business. A good many of these individuals originally aspired to be musicians, actors, or actresses. When that fell through, they went into managing concert halls as a way of maintaining contact with the industry.

Courses that may prove useful include theater management, business, bookkeeping, accounting, communications, marketing, and other music business-oriented subjects.

Experience/Skills/Personality Traits

Concert Hall Managers cannot just walk into a job without experience. Usually the individuals have worked in the music business or at least in some type of theater for a period of time. A job as an assistant manager of a concert hall is often extremely helpful to the individual.

Managing a concert hall, one must be adept at reading concert contracts and the long riders that sometimes accompany them. One must have the ability to handle crises effectively. The individual must also be totally knowledgeable about the music business and concert hall and arena affairs.

Being responsible and having supervisory skills are musts.

Unions/Associations

Concert Hall Managers may belong to the Musical Theaters Association (MTA) and/or the International Association of Auditorium Managers (IAAM). Concert Hall Managers may have to deal with a variety of unions, including the American Federation of Musicians (AFM).

Tips for Entry

1. Your chances of obtaining a job, if you are not experienced, are better in a smaller facility and/or a smaller city.
2. Jobs for theater or Concert Hall Managers are often advertised in the classified or display sections of newspapers.
3. Try to find a job as an assistant manager in a small venue. The employee turnover is higher in these halls, and you will have a better chance of promotion in a shorter span of time.
4. Many openings are advertised in a word-of-mouth fashion. Get friendly with Hall Managers in other facilities.

STAGE MANAGER

CAREER PROFILE

Duties: Supervising and overseeing all activities occuring onstage in a theater, club, concert hall, arena, etc.; may be responsible for lighting, curtain changes, etc.; in charge of backstage area

Alternate Title(s): None

Salary Ranges: $8,500 to $35,000+

Employment Prospects: Fair

Advancement Prospects: Poor

Best Geographical Location(s) for Position: Large metropolitan cities

Prerequisites:

Education or Training—No education required; training in lighting, sound, and/or electronics helpful

Experience—Lighting technician; sound person; assistant stage manager

Special Skills and Personality Traits—Responsibility; dependability; enjoyment of music; knowledge of lighting technology; cognizance of sound and/or electronics; supervisory skills; ability to get along with people

CAREER LADDER

```
┌─────────────────────────────────────┐
│  Stage Manager in Large, Prestigious │
│   Concert Hall, Club, Theater, etc.; │
│        Hall or Club Manager          │
└─────────────────────────────────────┘

┌─────────────────────────────────────┐
│                                      │
│           Stage Manager              │
│                                      │
└─────────────────────────────────────┘

┌─────────────────────────────────────┐
│          Sound Technician;           │
│         Lighting Technician;         │
│       Assistant Stage Manager;       │
│              Student                 │
└─────────────────────────────────────┘
```

Position Description

The Stage Manager is the individual in charge of much that occurs onstage in a concert hall, theater, arena, club, etc. Depending on the situation, he or she may work alone or oversee the work of an assistant and/or an entire staff.

The Stage Manager must be present during rehearsals and concerts. His or her duties depend on the type of venue, its size, and the kind of concert.

If the Stage Manager is working in a very large concert hall or theater, he or she might be responsible for supervising or controlling the lighting of the stage and the room. For example, during a show the Stage Manager might have the house or room lights off and the stage lit brightly. Or the stage may be dark, illuminated by a spotlight. The Stage Manager must find out during the rehearsal exactly when the act wants each kind of lighting. He or she probably will go over the show concept with the act or their management, road management, or lighting technician.

Many of the top rock acts travel with their own lighting technician and/or light show. In these instances the Stage Manager works with the act's technician, helping and advising. The Stage Manager may or may not be responsible for the lighting in these circumstances.

The Stage Manager may also be responsible for controlling the volume on the microphones. Once again, if an act comes in with their own sound people, the Stage Manager may just help and advise these people. In other situations, the Stage Manager might oversee a resident sound technician.

The Stage Manager is in charge of curtain changes. This includes making sure that the curtains are opened at the proper times and closed when there is an intermission or the show is finished.

The Stage Manager is also responsible for keeping the backstage area as clear as possible. Many times, with very well-known acts, the backstage area gets crowded and noisy. It is up to the individual to check for backstage passes and enforce any rules and regulations necessary to clear the area of unnecessary people.

At times, the Stage Manager may have the responsibility of making sure that the act has water, soda, juice, towels, etc. in their dressing room.

The Stage Manager might be the one who tells the act when to begin or when they should go on stage. He or she may also signal to the act when their show should be over.

The individual works late hours in this job. He or she is usually responsible to the facility manager or owner.

Salaries

Salaries of Stage Managers vary according to the type of venue, the geographical location, and the qualifications and duties of the individual.

Generally, the larger and more prestigious a theater, club, concert hall, arena, etc. is, the larger the Stage Manager's salary.

Individuals working as Stage Managers may earn from $8,500 to $35,000+ annually.

Employment Prospects

Employment prospects for Stage Managers are fair. Almost every theater, concert hall, and arena hires a Stage Manager. Clubs might hire individuals for this position or may delegate their responsibilities to other people.

If an individual works in a smaller venue, he or she may be hired as a Stage Manager and also have additional duties.

Metropolitan areas tend to have more positions.

Advancement Prospects

It is difficult for a Stage Manager to advance his or her career. The individual may obtain a position in a larger or more prestigious concert hall, club, theater, etc. In some situations, the individual may go on to become a club or theater manager or talent buyer. In other situations, the Stage Manager is just working in that position to be close to the live music business. He or she may be an aspiring musician, songwriter, etc.

Education and Training

No formal education is required for the position of Stage Manager. The individual may require training in sound, lighting, electronics, etc., depending on the position. If he or she is hoping to advance to club or theater manager, the Stage Manager may consider taking some business classes.

Experience/Skills/Personality Traits

The Stage Manager must enjoy music. He or she will probably have to listen to quite a bit of it. The individual must be dependable and reliable. He or she needs the ability to get along with others. Supervisory skills may be necessary.

The Stage Manager should also know as much as possible about electronics, lighting, and sound equipment.

The individual in this position may have been a sound technician, a lighting technician, or an assistant Stage Manager, or might just have finished school.

Unions/Associations

Stage Managers may belong to the International Alliance of Theatrical Stage Employees (IATSE). They may also belong to the American Guild of Musical Artists (AGMA) under certain conditions.

Tips for Entry

1. Stage Manager jobs are often advertised in the classified sections of newspapers.
2. You might consider visiting clubs, theaters, concert halls, etc. Speak to the manager of any of these venues. Tell him or her of your qualifications and leave a resumé. Follow up by writing a letter thanking the person for talking to you.
3. Volunteer your services as a Stage Manager in a community, school, or church concert or play. It will give you useful experience.
4. The more skills you have, the better your chances are to find a job. Learn all you can about lighting, sound, electronics, stage techniques, etc.
5. You might consider taking a theater course to learn concepts that might be helpful to you.

RESIDENT SOUND TECHNICIAN

CAREER PROFILE

Duties: Providing sound for concerts; working sound board; keeping sound equipment in good working order

Alternate Title(s): Sound Man (or Woman); Audio Technician; Sound Engineer

Salary Range: $7,000 to $18,000

Employment Prospects: Fair

Advancement Prospects: Poor

Best Geographical Location(s) for Position: Any city that houses concert halls, arenas, clubs, etc.

Prerequisites:

Education or Training—No educational requirement; formal or informal electronic and/or sound training

Experience—Experience working sound boards, sound equipment, and electrical equipment

Special Skills and Personality Traits—Ability to work with people; knowledge of electronics; knowledge of sound board; responsible attitude; good musical "ear"; enjoyment of music

CAREER LADDER

```
┌─────────────────────────────────────┐
│  Sound Technician at Major Venue;    │
│  Director of Audio Department        │
└─────────────────────────────────────┘

┌─────────────────────────────────────┐
│                                     │
│  Sound Technician                   │
│                                     │
└─────────────────────────────────────┘

┌─────────────────────────────────────┐
│  Roadie;                            │
│  Usher                              │
└─────────────────────────────────────┘
```

Position Description

The Resident Sound Technician of a hall is responsible for the basic sound engineering of a concert. The technician may work in a club, theater, concert hall, arena, school, or any similar location. The individual may be a full-time or a part-time employee.

The Sound Technician oversees the set-up of the sound equipment. The objective is to have everything in just the right place in order to produce the best possible sound. As the Resident Sound Technician, the individual must be aware of any acoustical problems in the room. Understanding the acoustical problems is just the beginning of a Sound Technician's chore. Solving the problem is the prime responsibility. The more familiar the person is with the room and its problems, the better he or she can counsel the touring technician employed by the act or the act's road manager.

In the position of Resident Sound Technician, the individual must attend all sound checks scheduled before a concert. During these sound checks, the individual will talk to the act's road manager or act members in order to determine exactly what type of sound they require. The technician will also discuss any special effects the act likes to have with their sound during the show.

The Resident Sound Technician might ask questions involving how the act wants their music balanced. The individual might advise the act on the volume requirement of the hall and should be prepared to regulate the sound.

During a concert or show the Resident Sound Technician is responsible for running the sound board. The sound board is usually set up somewhere in the middle of the front of the stage. From this location the technician can best hear the sound and make the proper adjustments.

After the concert, the Resident Sound Technician will go over the equipment and check for any problems. If repairs are required, the technician will either make them or arrange for others to take care of them immediately.

The Resident Sound Technician works closely with the act's road manager. In some cases, the act appearing at the club or hall will travel with their own sound technician. Under these circumstances, the Resident Sound Technician will act as an advisor and overseer.

People in these positions must usually work late evening hours. Work schedules do not begin, however, until the afternoon.

Salaries

Resident Sound Technicians may work either part-time or full-time. On a part-time basis, they will probably be paid by the hour or the show. Rates can vary from minimum wages to approximately $25 per hour.

Sound Technicians who work full-time may earn $7,000 to $18,000+ annually, depending on the type and size of the club, arena, hall, etc. that they are involved with.

Employment Prospects

Employment prospects for Resident Sound Technicians are fair. Qualified individuals may find employment in a variety of clubs, halls, areans, schools, or theaters. Some of these positions may be part-time. People seeking employment in this type of job category may have to relocate to areas where there are greater opportunities.

Advancement Prospects

It is difficult to advance in this career. It can be done, however. A number of Resident Sound Technicians who work in halls are picked up by major touring groups seeking a qualified sound technician.

Sound Technicians may advance their careers by locating a position at a larger, more prestigious hall. Others in this field are promoted to a director position in a theater or hall's audio department.

Education and Training

There is no formal educational requirement for a position as a Resident Sound Technician. Different halls or clubs may require that applicants have some training, either formal or informal, in electronics and sound recording. There are a variety of technical and vocational schools that teach electronics. Most people, however, pick up the basics of sound engineering by watching and listening to others.

Experience/Skills/Personality Traits

A Sound Technician working in a hall, club, arena, etc. must be able to work well with people. Many times the Sound Technician who travels with an act will accompany the group to the hall. The Resident Sound Technician may have to advise or consult with this individual. It is imperative that the individual be a responsible type of person. He or she must be at sound checks on time to oversee things, even if there is another technician hired by the group working the sound equipment at a concert.

The Sound Technician must have a good knowledge of electronics, the sound board, and other sound equipment. The individual must have a good musical "ear" and enjoy music.

Unions/Associations

Resident Sound Technicians may belong to the International Alliance of Theatrical Stage Employees (IATSE). This is a bargaining union for individuals working in theater situations.

Tips for Entry

1. Sound Technician positions are often advertised in the help wanted sections of newspapers. Check under "Sound Technician", "sound engineer", or "audio technician".
2. Check the clubs and theaters in your area that employ Resident Sound Technicians. Talk to the managers of these clubs and theaters and tell them of your qualifications. Follow up the discussion by sending them your resumé to keep on file.
3. You might consider a short stint as an apprentice to a Resident Sound Technician. This will provide you with added on-the-job experience. The Sound Technician may leave the job or know of other openings. All this can be useful to you.

NIGHTCLUB MANAGER

CAREER PROFILE

Duties: Managing the day-to-day operations of a nightclub

Alternate Title(s): Club Manager

Salary Range: $10,000 to $55,000+

Employment Prospects: Fair

Advancement Prospects: Fair

Best Geographical Location(s) for Position: All cities have opportunities as well as many smaller locations

Prerequisites:

Education or Training—No formal education required; training in food service or the hospitality industry helpful

Experience—Working as assistant nightclub manager; positions as bartender, host or hostess

Special Skills and Personality Traits—Supervisory skills; aggressiveness; personableness; knowledge of the entertainment and/or music business, booking acts, negotiating, and contracts; ability to deal under pressure

CAREER LADDER

```
┌─────────────────────────────┐
│   Nightclub Manager in      │
│ Large, Prestigious Nightclub; │
│     Nightclub Owner         │
└─────────────────────────────┘

┌─────────────────────────────┐
│                             │
│     Nightclub Manager       │
│                             │
└─────────────────────────────┘

┌─────────────────────────────┐
│                             │
│  Assistant Nightclub Manager │
│                             │
└─────────────────────────────┘
```

Position Description

A Nightclub Manager is responsible for overseeing the day-to-day (or night-to-night) functions of a nightclub. Duties may differ depending on the type of club an individual manages. In many instances, the Nightclub Manager is also the club owner.

As the Nightclub Manager, a person may be responsible for not only hiring the entertainment, but deciding what type of entertainment the club will use. For example, should the club cater to country fans, disco fans, or rock-and-rollers? The Manager must also decide whether the club should use live entertainment, disco D.J.'s, or jukeboxes. In making these decisions, the individual must often do research. Other clubs in the area may be checked out. Clubs that have been unsuccessful as well as those that are doing well may be looked into. Often, if a Nightclub Manager sees why a certain club isn't doing well, he or she knows what changes must be made in order to be successful.

The Nightclub Manager must choose what types of advertising to use. In certain areas, radio works well. In other areas, TV advertising or the print media may work better. The individual must develop an advertising budget and decide where his or her advertising dollar can best be spent.

The Nightclub Manager may call local media, trying to build good relationships between editors, disc jockeys, TV producers, and the club.

When the club hires live entertainment, the Nightclub Manager may be responsible for negotiating and signing contracts, or this responsibility may fall to the club owner.

The individual must run the nightclub. This includes hiring and training personnel. The Nightclub Manager may hire bartenders, waitresses, hosts, hostesses, chefs, cooks, security people, lighting technicians, sound people, etc., depending on the type of establishment.

As the Nightclub Manager, the individual may be responsible for buying food and liquor. He or she may also be in charge of controlling the liquor and making sure that all state and local alcohol laws are observed.

The Nightclub Manager must make sure that all accounts are paid. The individual may be responsible for tallying nightly totals and receipts.

If there are any problems in the club, the Manager is in charge of taking care of them. The Nightclub Manager works long hours. He or she may begin working in the afternoon and not get home until 4:00 or 5:00 A.M. The Nightclub Manager is responsible to the club owner.

Salaries

Salaries for Nightclub Managers depend on the type of club, its location, its popularity, and the experience and duties of the individual.

Salaries run from around $10,000 to $55,000+. If the Club Manager is also the club owner, he or she may receive a salary plus a share of profits from the club or the individual might just receive a share of the profits.

Employment Prospects

Employment prospects for Nightclub Managers are fair. The individual might have to work in a very small club, or an establishment specializing in a different form of entertainment or music than the Manager's choice. He or she might have to move to another location to find a job.

There are nightclubs all over the country. However, many of these are so small they don't use the services of a Manager.

Advancement Prospects

Advancement prospects are fair for a Nightclub Manager. After obtaining some experience in a small nightclub, an individual may move into a job as Nightclub Manager in a larger, more prestigious club. The Nightclub Manager might also open up his or her own nightclub.

Education and Training

There is no formal educational requirement to become a Nightclub Manager. Some training in business is helpful. Training in food service or the hospitality field might also be useful.

Experience/Skills/Personality Traits

Any type of experience in running a business is a plus. Usually a Nightclub Manager has worked as either an assistant manager or a supervisor in a nightclub, bar, or restaurant.

The individual must be knowledgeable about the music business, booking talent, negotiating, and contracts. Much of this is learned on the job.

The Nightclub Manager needs the ability to deal well with people and to deal effectively under pressure.

Being aggressive and personable helps. The individual in this position needs good supervisory skills.

Unions/Associations

Nightclub Managers may work with any number of local unions, depending on what variety of club they manage. Individuals may also represent their clubs in the National Federation of Music Clubs.

Tips for Entry

1. You might begin by working as a bartender, host, or hostess. Then move on to a job as an assistant nightclub manager.
2. These jobs are often listed in the help wanted sections of newspapers.
3. The more skills you have, the better your position. If you have managed a restaurant or bar and have an understanding of the entertainment business, put these things in your resumé.
4. You may consider sending a resumé and cover letter to a number of nightclubs. Ask them to keep your resumé on file.
5. Think about trying to obtain a job as a Nightclub Manager in a hotel/motel club. These clubs can be found all over the country and turnover is high. You may go directly to the hotel/motel or send a letter and resumé to the main office of a hotel/motel chain.

EDUCATION

MUSIC SUPERVISOR

CAREER PROFILE

Duties: Directing and coordinating activities of teaching personnel engaged in instructing students in vocal and instrumental music in school system

Alternate Title(s): Music Administrator

Salary Range: $13,000 to $45,000

Employment Prospects: Fair

Advancement Prospects: Fair

Best Geographical Location(s) for Position: All areas throughout the country have opportunities

Prerequisites:

Education or Training—Bachelor's degree in music education; master's degree or additional graduate courses in supervision and administration

Experience—Teaching music in school system

Special Skills and Personality Traits—Ability to administer; ability to lead; enjoyment of music; tolerance, ability to relate to others on all levels

CAREER LADDER

```
┌─────────────────────────────────┐
│                                 │
│     State Music Supervisor      │
│                                 │
└─────────────────────────────────┘

┌─────────────────────────────────┐
│                                 │
│       Music Supervisor          │
│                                 │
└─────────────────────────────────┘

┌─────────────────────────────────┐
│                                 │
│       Music Teacher;            │
│     Music Department Head        │
│                                 │
└─────────────────────────────────┘
```

Position Description

The school Music Supervisor may work in a variety of situations. He or she may work as a school Supervisor, a district Supervisor, or a state Music Supervisor.

In this position, the individual is responsible for directing and coordinating activities of teaching personnel who are engaged in instructing students in vocal and instrumental music in a specific school or school system.

As a supervisor, the person probably will not teach on a day-to-day basis. There are, however, positions in which the person teaches a few days a week and administers a program the remaining days.

One of the duties of a Music Supervisor is to plan and develop the music education curriculum for the school, district, or state. This is accomplished by meeting and consulting with teachers and others on the administrative staff to get input. Working closely with these people, the supervisor can tell which programs work, which do not, which should be eliminated.

The Music Supervisor will visit classrooms while other teachers are giving classes and observe and evaluate them. If the Supervisor has any comments on their teaching, he or she may set up a meeting. During this meeting, the Supervisor will talk about the evaluation and recommend possible changes in teaching methods.

The Supervisor will analyze the music education program in the school, district, or state. The individual may evaluate both the instructional methods and/or the materials used in teaching.

As many schools are currently experiencing cutbacks in funds, the supervisor may have to decide which programs to continue and which to cut out.

The Music Supervisor might order any instructional materials, books, supplies, equipment, and/or visual aids needed by the music department. In this position, he or she is authorized to order and purchase musical instruments required for instruction or for the school band.

Additionally, the school Music Supervisor would help establish interschool bands, choruses, and orchestras to represent the various schools at civic and community events.

The Music Supervisor's hours are usually regular working or school hours. He or she is responsible to either the principal, the superintendent, or the Commissioner of Education.

Salaries

Salaries of Music Supervisors depend largely on the location of the school district and the position. Supervisors generally have salaries that parallel those of teachers in the area. If, for example, teachers' salaries are low in a particular community, the supervisor's salary, too, will be low. Conversely, if the supervisor works in a district in which teachers' salaries are relatively high, his or hers will be correspondingly higher.

The salary range for Music Supervisors runs from $13,000 to $45,000 yearly.

Employment Prospects

Employment prospects are fair for Music Supervisors. Applicants may have to relocate to another area in order to obtain a position.

There is not a high turnover rate in these jobs.

Advancement Prospects

Individuals in the position of school Music Supervisor can be promoted to District Music Supervisor. District Supervisors can be promoted to state Music Supervisor positions.

Advancement is possible if there is an opening. As noted above, there isn't a great deal of turnover in this job category.

Individuals with education in supervision and administration may additionally go on to positions as assistant principal or principal.

Education and Training

Music Supervisors are required to have bachelor's degrees with a major in music education.

As a rule, they would have to complete a semester of student teaching in order to become a music teacher.

Music Supervisors are generally required to have additional courses in supervision and administration and/or master's degrees depending on the state regulations.

Experience/Skills/Personality Traits

Music Supervisors must like music. Generally, they have held positions as music teachers for a few years prior to applying for a job as a Music Supervisor.

As a supervisor, an individual must know how to teach and be able to evaluate others. He or she must also have the ability to lead others, administer a program, and, most important, enjoy music and instructing others in it.

Unions/Associations

Music Supervisors may belong to the National Federation of Teachers (NFT). Individuals may belong to the National Association of State Supervisors of Music (NASSM). The Music Supervisor might also be a member of the Music Educators National Conference (MENC) or the National Association of Schools of Music (NASM).

Tips for Entry

1. There are specialty employment agencies that deal specifically with educational jobs. These are usually located in larger cities.
2. Major cities usually have Sunday newspapers that publish sections on educational job openings.
3. Check with your local school district for openings.

COLLEGE, CONSERVATORY, or UNIVERSITY MUSIC EDUCATOR

CAREER PROFILE

Duties: Teaching music instruction, theory, history, composition, and/or instrumental or vocal training and performance; coaching chamber music groups

Alternate Title(s): Music Teacher; Professor; Instructor

Salary Range: $15,000 to $45,000

Employment Prospects: Fair

Advancement Prospects: Fair

Best Geographical Location(s) for Position: Locations with colleges, conservatories, and/or universities may have positions available

Prerequisites:

Education or Training—Master's degree minimum; many positions require doctoral degree

Experience—Teaching at some level; instrumental or vocal performance experience (if applicable)

Special Skills and Personality Traits—Knowledge of many facets of music; desire to continue learning, studying, and researching; ability to communicate ideas to students

CAREER LADDER

```
┌─────────────────────────────┐
│                             │
│         Professor           │
│                             │
└─────────────────────────────┘

┌─────────────────────────────┐
│                             │
│     Associate Professor     │
│                             │
└─────────────────────────────┘

┌─────────────────────────────┐
│                             │
│     Assistant Professor     │
│                             │
└─────────────────────────────┘
```

Position Description

College, Conservatory, and/or University Music Educators may be hired for a variety of different positions. They may be brought into a school as a general music educator to teach areas of music theory, music arranging, and/or music history, or they may teach vocal or instrumental performance. Educators are also hired to coach chamber music groups or to conduct choruses or orchestras.

Applicants for positions that require some performance skills are usually given auditions. These types of positions may include any area of instrumental instruction, coaching, or conducting.

Educators at higher learning institutions, especially those which specialize in music degrees, generally teach students who want to learn all they can from the curriculum. Most of these students are seriously considering professional careers in music.

It is the duty of the Educator to be as knowledgeable and informed about his or her subject matter as possible. He or she must help the students learn all they can during their educational careers.

Most Educators also delve into research areas of special interest to them. They take the research and write papers for publication. Published works help Educators advance their careers and increase the demand for their services.

Working in a school setting, the Educator may participate in many of the cultural and educational programs, events, and benefits available.

The Educator cannot walk into a classroom or lecture hall and begin teaching without preparation. Preparation for classes takes a great deal of time. This is especially true for the beginning Educator or for the individual who is teaching a course for the first time.

Educators who solely teach voice or instrumental performance or coach or conduct music groups usually require less preparation time.

The Educator must have specific hours set aside each week to meet with his or her students. He or she must read student's papers and grade any tests or exams.

The Educator working in a community college setting will probably teach about eighteen hours a week. An Educator working at a four-year university, college, or conservatory spends considerably fewer hours teaching. Teaching time usually runs from nine to twelve hours per week. Keep in mind, though, the amount of time that is spent in preparation, student meetings, and grading. Total working time may be more than forty-five hours per week.

The Educator is responsible to the head of his or her department or to the administrator of the school.

Salaries

Salaries for College, Conservatory, or University Music Educators depend on the school, its reputation, and its location. Salaries also depend on the professional status of the Educator.

Salaries for assistant professors can start at $15,000 yearly. As the Educator gains more experience, the salary may go to $18,000.

Associate professors earn from $18,000 to $25,000 yearly. Professors' salaries range from $20,000 to $45,000 yearly. As noted above, however, salaries depend heavily on the school where the Educator is employed. A professor working at a prestigious university would undoubtedly earn more than a professor teaching at a small college.

Employment Prospects

There is a fair chance for employment as a Music Educator at a conservatory, college, or university. Applicants, however, must be willing to relocate to areas that have openings.

Applicants additionally must be willing to teach in more than one specialization.

Advancement Prospects

Educators in higher learning institutions can advance their careers in a number of ways. They can start out as assistant professors and teach for a few years. Eventually they may be promoted to associate professors. During the years as an assistant professor, the Educator is evaluated. He or she may or may not receive tenure. Associate professors can also be promoted to full professors.

The Educator can also advance his or her career by taking a position in a college and then seeking a better position in a more prestigious university.

Education and Training

The majority of positions as College, Conservatory, and/or University Music Educators require at least a master's degree. Many of the positions also demand a doctoral degree.

There are Educators currently teaching at conservatories and universities who hold no degree. Individuals such as symphony orchestra members are accepted as Educators on the basis of exceptional musical acclaim.

Experience/Skills/Personality Traits

Most Educators have some type of teaching experience previous to their appointment at a college, university, or conservatory.

The individual must have a tremendous knowledge of many facets of music, not only his or her specialization. He or she usually has an ongoing desire to learn more, whether through study or research.

Most important, the College, University, or Conservatory Music Educator must be able to effectively communicate ideas and theories to their students.

Unions/Associations

College, University, or Conservatory Educators may belong to the College Music Society and the American Musicological Society. These organizations sponsor a number of conferences and programs during the year. They also publish newsletters.

Individuals may also be members of the College Band Directors National Association, the College Music Society, and/or the National Association of College Wind and Percussion Instructors.

Tips for Entry

1. There is a list of openings at a variety of schools, colleges, and universities called the "Music Faculty List". This list is published by the College Music Society (CMS) and the American Musicological Society (AMS). The list is available to their members.

2. Openings are usually sent to college placement offices.

3. Many positions are advertised in the classified sections of Sunday newspapers. Some positions are advertised in display ads.

4. You may send your resumé with a cover letter directly to a college or university and ask to have it kept on file in case an opening arises.

SECONDARY SCHOOL MUSIC TEACHER

CAREER PROFILE

Duties: Teaching instrumental and/or vocal music and theory to high school or junior high students

Alternate Title(s): High School Music Teacher or Instructor; Junior High School Music Teacher or Instructor; Instrument Teacher; Voice Teacher

Salary Range: $11,000 to $42,000

Employment Prospects: Fair

Advancement Prospects: Good

Best Geographical Location(s) for Position: Areas throughout the country have opportunities

Prerequisites:

Education or Training—Bachelor's degree in music education; some schools require additional education for permanent certification

Experience—Student teaching

Special Skills and Personality Traits—Ability to teach; enjoyment of music; ability to play instrument(s); ability to read music

CAREER LADDER

```
┌─────────────────────────────┐
│                             │
│   Tenured Music Teacher     │
│                             │
└─────────────────────────────┘

┌─────────────────────────────┐
│                             │
│ Secondary School Music Teacher │
│                             │
└─────────────────────────────┘

┌─────────────────────────────┐
│                             │
│     Student Teacher         │
│                             │
└─────────────────────────────┘
```

Position Description

Secondary School Music Teachers can work in junior high or high schools and at public, private, or parochial institutions. Their duties vary depending on the type of job they are hired for.

A Secondary School Music Teacher might fill a position in instrumental teaching. This teacher would be responsible for giving lessons to students, organizing and conducting a school band and/or orchestra, and teaching basic music theory. The instrument teacher is also responsible for putting on school concerts. He or she might work with students to get them ready for competitions or auditions for summer music festivals. In addition, the instrumental Music Teacher could be in charge of putting together a marching band. In this case, he or she would not only be responsible for rehearsals and conducting, but also for performances in parades and at various events after school hours and on weekends or holidays.

A Secondary School Music Teacher might conversely fill a position in vocal instruction. This teacher would be responsible for giving vocal lessons, putting together and conducting school choruses and choirs, and teaching basic music theory. The vocal teacher is usually in charge of putting on all vocal concerts. He or she might be involved in musicals or plays put on by the school.

The vocal teacher works with students preparing them for school and state vocal competitions. He or she might also be in charge of a school glee club.

Secondary School Music Teachers, like all teachers, usually go through a period of student teaching. Through student teaching they can better evaluate what area of specialization they prefer. They get the important chance for hands-on training with students while they are still under supervision.

The Secondary School Music Teacher is evaluated after a certain number of years in a school system. If his or her evaluation is positive, he or she will receive tenure. After receiving tenure, the teacher cannot be fired from the school system under normal conditions and circumstances. This gives the job a great degree of security. The school system can, however, terminate the teacher's position and move him or her to another area of music specialization.

In addition to the Secondary School Music Teacher's teaching and leading responsibilities, he or she must be available for parent/teacher/student conferences.

He or she is responsible for making up lesson plans and grading student work.

Teachers usually work only ten months a year. If they work in summer school positions, they are paid extra. Teachers do not work during school vacations.

Music Teachers are responsible to the music department head, the school principal, or the superintendent of the school system.

Salaries

Salaries for teachers depend on the location of the school, the type of school, and the teacher's qualifications.

Teachers working in large metropolitan areas earn more than teachers in small communities. Teachers who work in private or parochial schools usually start out at around $11,000 per school year. Their salaries can go up to $23,000 yearly.

Teachers who work in public schools usually start out at around $15,000 per school year. Their salary can go up to $42,000 annually. In addition, most school systems have fringe benefits and pension plans.

Salaries in public schools are usually paid on a system called "steps". Each time an individual reaches a certain step, his or her salary is raised. Steps relate to the amount of education (degrees, credits, etc.) a teacher has accumulated. Steps also relate to the amount of experience that a teacher has.

Employment Prospects

Employment prospects are not good, but positions may be found if the applicant is willing to relocate to other areas. Teachers who get tenure often do not leave their jobs, so school system turnover is not great. Once a teacher gets tenure, he or she is likely to stay in the system until retirement.

Advancement Prospects

Teachers advance their careers in a number of ways. First, there is the monetary advancement. This is attained through the step system noted above.

Second, teachers who have proven themselves are given tenures. This means that they cannot be fired under normal circumstances. This gives the individual a great deal of security.

Third, teachers can take additional courses and become department heads, district music supervisors, or state music supervisors.

Education and Training

Secondary School Music Teachers are required to have at least a bachelor's degree with a major in music education. They are usually required to complete a semester of student teaching.

The individual who plans on teaching in a public school must have a teaching certificate or license. These are granted to qualified individuals by state education departments.

In order to get permanent certification, many states require additional credits or even a master's degree.

Experience/Skills/Personality Traits

Secondary School Music Teachers must like to teach and have good teaching skills.

As a Secondary School Music Teacher, an individual usually specializes in either vocal or instrumental music. However, he or she needs a broad background and knowledge of music.

He or she must also have at least a limited knowledge of conducting either a vocal or band ensemble.

Unions/Associations

Teachers may belong to the National Educators Association (NEA) or the National Federation of Teachers (NFT). Both of these organizations work on behalf of the Teacher to obtain better benefits, working conditions, and salaries.

Teachers may also belong to the Music Educators National Conference, the Music Teachers National Associations, Inc., the National Association of Schools of Music, the American Choral Directors Association, and a host of others. These associations work toward good music education in the schools and offer seminars, conferences, booklets, and other information on various subjects.

Tips for Entry

1. There are employment agencies (usually located in major cities) that specialize in locating positions for teachers. Check these out.
2. College placement offices receive notices of openings at schools.

3. Get letters of recommendation from several of your professors at school as well as your student teaching supervisor.

4. Apply for summer school positions. These are often easier to obtain, and they help you get your foot in the door of a school system.

ELEMENTARY SCHOOL MUSIC TEACHER

CAREER PROFILE

Duties: Teaching singing, listening, and music theory to elementary school students

Alternate Title(s): Music Instructor

Salary Range: $11,000 to $42,000

Employment Prospects Fair

Advancement Prospects: Good

Best Geographical Location(s) for Position: Areas throughout the country have opportunities

Prerequisites:

Education or Training—Bachelor's degree in music education; some schools require additional education for permanent certification

Experience—Student teaching

Special Skills and Personality Traits—Enjoyment of children; enjoyment of music; ability to play an instrument; ability to teach

CAREER LADDER

```
┌─────────────────────────────────┐
│      Tenured Music Teacher       │
└─────────────────────────────────┘

┌─────────────────────────────────┐
│  Elementary School Music Teacher │
└─────────────────────────────────┘

┌─────────────────────────────────┐
│         Student Teacher          │
└─────────────────────────────────┘
```

Position Description

Elementary School Music Teachers work in public, private, or parochial schools. Their duties vary depending on the school and the ages and grades they teach.

Music Teachers must often follow guidelines for what they teach students. These are set up by the school music department heads, district music supervisors, and state music supervisors.

Very young children, such as those in kindergarten and the first grade, are often taught simple things, like singing songs or rhythmic movements. This singing, clapping, and stamping is considered fun by most children. The teacher also might play records or show films about music.

As the age and grade of the children increases the Music Teacher can teach such things as music theory, singing fundamentals, and group singing. He or she might also get the students interested in instruments and possibly give lessons.

Music Teachers learn many of the teaching methods that they use as student teachers. Student teaching gives the individual a chance for hands-on training with supervision.

A Music Teacher is evaluated after a certain number of years working in the school system (usually three or four), and he or she may receive tenure. After receiving tenure, a teacher cannot be fired from the school system under normal circumstances. This gives the job a tremendous amount of stability.

Good Elementary Music Teachers are creative and enthusiastic. They come up with unique ways of teaching. For example, the teacher might have the class make instruments out of everyday materials or have the students write their own lyrics and music for a song.

In addition to the normal teaching responsibilities, Music Teachers might also direct the school's choral group, be involved in plays, shows, concerts, etc. in the school.

Teachers usually work only ten months a year. If they work in summer school, they receive additional remuneration. Teachers also have time off during all school vacations.

Teachers are responsible to the department head, principal, or superintendent of the school system.

Salaries

Salaries for Music Teachers depend on the location of the school, the type of school, and the teacher's qualifications.

Teachers in large metropolitan areas earn more than teachers in small communities. Teachers in private or parochial schools usually start out at around $11,000 per school year. Their salaries can go up to $23,000 yearly.

Teachers in public schools usually start out at around $15,000 per school year. Their salary can go up to $42,000 annually.

Salaries in public schools are usually paid on a system called "steps". Each time a teacher reaches a certain step, his or her salary is raised. Steps relate to the amount of education (degrees, credits, etc.) a teacher accumulates. Steps also relate to the amount of experience a teacher has.

Employment Prospects

Employment prospects for Music Teachers are not as good as they were a few years ago. There are still positions available, however. Teachers may have to relocate to areas in which openings occur.

Teachers who get tenure tend not to leave their jobs, so the turnover in a school system is low.

Advancement Prospects

Teachers advance their careers in a number of ways. First, there is a monetary advancement. This is attained through the step system mentioned above. Second, Teachers who have proven themselves are given tenure. This means that they cannot, under normal circumstances, be fired. This provides job stability.

Third, Teachers can take additional courses and become department heads, district music supervisors, or state music supervisors.

Education and Training

Teachers are required to have at least a bachelor's degree. Most Music Teachers major in music education. Usually individuals are required to take a semester of student teaching.

As a rule, if the individual is planning on teaching in a public school, he or she must also obtain a teaching certificate or license. These are granted by state education departments to qualified individuals.

In order to get permanent certification, many states require a master's degree or additional credits in music education.

Experience/Skills/Personality Traits

Elementary School Music Teachers must have both the ability and the patience to teach children. They are usually required to play at least one instrument, either piano or guitar.

The Elementary School Music Teacher must also be able to read music and must have a broad knowledge of the subject.

Elementary School Music Teachers must be creative and enthusiastic in order to guide children into an interest in this subject.

Unions/Associations

Teachers may belong to the National Educators Association (NEA) or the National Federation of Teachers (NFT). Both of these organizations work on behalf of the Teacher to obtain better benefits, working conditions, and salaries.

Teachers may also belong to a host of associations, depending on their interests. These include the Music Educators National Conference, the Music Teachers National Association, Inc., the National Association of Schools of Music, the American Choral Directors Association, and others. These groups work toward having good music education in the schools and offer seminars, conferences, pamphlets, booklets, and other valuable information.

Tips for Entry

1. There are employment agencies (usually located in major cities) that specialize in locating positions for teachers. Check these out.
2. Colleges usually have placement offices that receive notices of openings at schools.
3. Get letters of recommendation from several of your professors at college as well as your student teacher supervisor.

PRIVATE INSTRUMENT TEACHER

CAREER PROFILE

Duties: Instructing and teaching a student how to play a specific instrument on a private or semiprivate basis

Alternate Title(s): Studio Teacher

Salary Range: $7,500 to $25,000+

Employment Prospects: Good

Advancement Prospects: Fair

Best Geographical Location(s) for Position: Cities and metropolitan areas with large enough populations to support a number of private teachers

Prerequisites:

Education or Training—Extensive training and/or study in specific instrument

Experience—Playing instrument

Special Skills and Personality Traits—Ability to teach; ability to play one or more instruments; patience; enthusiasm

CAREER LADDER

```
┌─────────────────────────────────┐
│  Owner of Private Teaching Studio │
└─────────────────────────────────┘

┌─────────────────────────────────┐
│   Private Instrument Teacher     │
└─────────────────────────────────┘

┌─────────────────────────────────┐
│          Performer;              │
│         Schoolteacher;           │
│           Student                │
└─────────────────────────────────┘
```

Position Description

A Private Instrument Teacher teaches students how to play a specific instrument. Sometimes the student is eager to learn the instrument; at other times he or she is being forced to take lessons. This can be quite frustrating for the teacher.

Good instrument teachers have the ability to make the instrument exciting and make learning to play a good experience. Expertise in a certain instrument alone does not make a good teacher.

Private Instrument Teachers can teach in a number of different locations, including their home, the student's home, a music instrument store, a private studio, or a community room.

Private Instrument Teachers often teach groups of three or four students at one time in addition to giving private lessons to individual students. Lessons run from forty-five minutes to an hour and are usually scheduled once a week. Students must be encouraged not to miss lessons and to practice in between.

Instructors may teach beginners or advanced students. There are also expert instructors who teach professionals.

Private Instrument Teachers must be reliable and dependable. Nothing hurts a new teacher's reputation more than forgetting a lesson or habitually cancelling.

If the Private Instrument teacher is self-employed (as opposed to working on staff in a studio or shop), he or she must decide how much will be charged per lesson, how and when the fee will be paid, and what policies to develop on the way his or her business will be run.

If the instructor is teaching in a studio or shop, he or she might put the students together for a group recital or a program of solo performances.

The Private Instrument Teacher is responsible directly to the student (or, in the case of children, to the parents). To be successful, the teacher must be easy to get along with, congenial, and professional, as well as be a good teacher.

Most often, a successful teacher is one who struggled through technical problems in his or her own training. These individuals have frequently developed new and easier ways to conquer these problems and can pass the methods on to their students.

Private Instrument Teachers usually have irregular working hours because of students' jobs and/or school times.

Salaries

Salaries vary depending on the instrument being taught and the expertise of the teacher. Fees usually range from $10 to $20 per hour. Fees naturally go up for experts in the field, such as jazz greats, orchestra musicians, etc. These fees can run from $30 to $100 and up per lesson.

Private Instrument Teachers are often on staff in music stores or studios. In cases such as this, the instructor is either paid a fee per student, a weekly salary, or a combination of the two. Studio teachers may earn from $7,500 to $25,000 annually.

Employment Prospects

A talented Private Instrument Teacher is always in demand on staff at a studio or music store or as a self-employed private instructor. Once a teacher obtains a few students who are satisfied, word travels fast.

There are many Private Instrument Teachers who work full-time as schoolteachers and part-time giving lessons after school. The individual may obtain quite a few private students as a result of the school position.

Advancement Prospects

Advancement prospects are fair for a Private Instrument Teacher. As noted above, it doesn't take long for word to travel about a good teacher.

Eventually, the teacher may have so many students that he or she wants to open a private teaching studio. The individual may employ other Private Music Teachers of the same instrument or diversify, offering instruction in other instruments. When hiring other teachers, the owner must screen the teachers carefully in order to uphold the reputation of the studio.

Education and Training

The main requirement for a Private Instrument Teacher is the ability to play an instrument well enough to show a student the techniques of playing. Extensive training and/or study in the specific instrument or group of instruments is necessary. This may be professional training from a conservatory or college, private lessons, or self-taught skills.

Experience/Skills/Personality Traits

Private Instrument Teachers must have the ability to play an instrument or instruments and to teach it as well. It does not follow that if an individual plays an instrument he or she can necessarily teach someone else to play it.

One of the most important traits a teacher can have is patience. Often, it takes new students a while to pick up new techniques on an instrument. The teacher must be enthusiastic enough to communicate the excitement of new techniques to the student.

Unions/Associations

Private Music Teachers do not have a union. They can belong to the American Federation of Musicians (AFM) if they are also performers.

Private Music Teachers might also belong to The Music Teachers National Association, Inc., the Music Educators National Conference, or the National Association of Schools of Music. These organizations promote music education of all varieties.

Tips for Entry

1. Talk to all the music, record, and instrument shops in the area. Discuss your credentials and the instrument or instruments you can teach.
2. Leave business cards and/or flyers in all the music, record, and instrument shops. Include information such as your name, phone number, any accomplishment with your instrument, and any other pertinent information.
3. Contact the churches, temples, and synagogues in your area as well as all the school systems and colleges. It is usually best to visit all the places in person instead of calling or writing. Have your credentials with you.

MUSIC THERAPIST

CAREER PROFILE

Duties: Using music or musical activities to treat physical, mental, and/or emotional disabilities in patients

Alternate Title(s): None

Salary Range: $10,000 to $35,000

Employment Prospects: Excellent

Advancement Prospects: Fair

Best Geographical Location(s) for Position: Positions may be found in every major city in the country as well as in smaller communities

Prerequisites:

Education or Training—Undergraduate degree in music therapy required; master's degree may be required

Experience—Some experience working with handicapped or disabled individuals

Special Skills and Personality Traits—Ability to work with handicapped and/or disabled individuals; compassion; ability to play piano and/or guitar; emotional stability

CAREER LADDER

```
┌─────────────────────────────┐
│  Music Therapist Consultant; │
│  Music Therapist Supervisor  │
└─────────────────────────────┘

┌─────────────────────────────┐
│       Music Therapist        │
└─────────────────────────────┘

┌─────────────────────────────┐
│       College Student        │
└─────────────────────────────┘
```

Position Description

The Music Therapist works to restore a patient's health, working with a number of other individuals. These might include doctors, nurses, teachers, physical therapists, psychologists, psychiatrists, and/or the patient's family. Together the team decides what course of action to take for the patient's therapy.

Often, when all else has failed, the Music Therapist can make a breakthrough with a patient. The Music Therapist uses different forms of music as therapy for patients who have physical, mental, or emotional disabilities or illnesses.

The Music Therapist plans musical activities for an individual or a group. For example, the therapist may teach a group of elderly patients a new song or play a record or tape of tunes that were popular when they were younger. This often helps a withdrawn nursing home patient remember and reminisce. The patient might start talking about what was going on in his or her life when the song was popular.

The Music Therapist might teach a blind child how to play an instrument. This gives the child a sense of accomplishment that he or she might not have had before. Once again, the therapist has accomplished something of value.

The Music Therapist is often responsible for selecting pieces to be used as background music in certain rooms in a facility. Through training, the therapist knows what type of music might evoke a reaction and what type might be soothing.

The Music Therapist in a hospital might put together a group of patients to sing or play instruments for hospital staff and other patients.

He or she works with a patient on either a one-to-one basis or in a group, depending on the patient and his or her needs. Conferences are often held with other members of the team. At these conferences the Music Therapist discusses the patient's needs and progress. The Music Therapist is usually happy if the patient makes even the slightest amount of progress. Progress is usually slow, and the therapist must be extremely patient.

The result of music therapy really doesn't have anything to do with music. The therapist hopes to reach his or her patient through music and have the patient become healthier emotionally, mentally, and/or physically.

Salaries

A Music Therapist just entering the field usually makes from $10,000 to $12,500 yearly. A more experienced therapist at a larger institution or facility may have a salary of $18,000 to $23,000 yearly. Supervisory positions in the field of music therapy often offer yearly salaries of $35,000 and up.

Employment Prospects

With the growing number of health care facilities, the music therapy field is wide open. There are currently more positions than there are Music Therapists. A qualified individual should have no problem finding a job.

Advancement Prospects

Music Therapists can move up to supervisory or administrative positions. These positions, however, usually reduce the contact therapists have with patients. They also require additional training and education.

Other Music Therapists move into research or university teaching. These positions also limit contact with patients.

Many therapists go into private practice and consulting after working in institutions or facilities for a period of time.

Education and Training

Music Therapists need bachelor's degrees in music therapy. There are many colleges that offer this degree program. Courses usually include music theory, voice studies, instrument lessons, pyschology, sociology, and biology in addition to the general courses. A Music Therapist who plans on working in a public school system must also have a teaching degree.

Many positions require a master's degree. These, too, can be obtained at colleges and universities around the country.

In addition, Music Therapists must go through a six-month internship before getting their licenses.

Experience/Skills/Personality Traits

A good Music Therapist must be able to work with handicapped and/or disabled people. He or she must have patience, compassion, and emotional stability.

A Music Therapist must be able to play the piano and/or guitar. Ability to play other instruments is a plus. He or she must also be able to teach others to either play an instrument or sing. A good knowledge of music is essential.

Many Music Therapists work at a health facility or school as a summer job or as a volunteer before deciding to become a therapist. This gives them the opportunity to gain some experience in the field.

Unions/Associations

Two associations that Music Therapists may belong to are the National Association for Music Therapy, Inc. and the American Association for Music Therapy. These organizations help place qualified Music Therapists, do research, and act as liaisons for colleges that have music therapy programs.

Tips for Entry

1. Go to the college job placement office. Often facilities or schools looking for Music Therapists will send a list of openings to colleges and universities that grant degrees in music therapy.
2. Both the National Association for Music Therapy, Inc. and the American Association for Music Therapy have registration and placement services for their members. Join the organizations. In addition, their newsletters list various openings.
3. Many positions for Music Therapists are available through the Federal Government. These civil service positions can be located through your state employment service.

MUSIC LIBRARIAN

CAREER PROFILE

Duties: Cataloging music, recordings, musical books, etc.; doing reference work on music-related subjects

Alternate Title(s): Record Librarian (in radio stations)

Salary Range: $10,500 to $24,000

Employment Prospects: Poor

Advancement Prospects: Poor

Best Geographical Location(s) for Position: Large cities housing conservatories, symphonies, large public libraries, and many radio stations

Prerequisites:

Education or Training—Bachelor's degree in music history or theory and/or library science; some positions require a master's degree

Experience—Library assistant position

Special Skills and Personality Traits—Interest in music recordings, books, and research; extensive knowledge of music history and theory; library research training; foreign language helpful

CAREER LADDER

```
┌─────────────────────────────────┐
│                                 │
│   Music Library Administrator   │
│                                 │
└─────────────────────────────────┘

┌─────────────────────────────────┐
│                                 │
│        Music Librarian          │
│                                 │
└─────────────────────────────────┘

┌─────────────────────────────────┐
│                                 │
│            Student              │
│                                 │
└─────────────────────────────────┘
```

Position Description

A Music Librarian combines his or her skills as a librarian with an extensive knowledge of music. Duties vary depending on the type of position. Usually, however, the Music Librarian is responsible for cataloging all musical materials. These might include records, tapes, printed music, books on music-oriented subjects, etc.

The Music Librarian must do all reference work. He or she often looks up or finds information for a student, library patron, or professor. The individual must constantly be reading reviews of new music books, records, and tapes. The person in this position often writes reviews of books and music. The Music Librarian is in charge of ordering or recommending new materials for the library to purchase.

At times, the Music Librarian's duties also include arranging for courses on music-related subjects or lecturing on music. Depending on the position, the Music Librarian might also be respon-

sible for putting together concerts, recitals, and other music-related activities or locating sponsors for these activities.

A Music Librarian may work in a library or school, for an orchestra, or at a television or radio station. At a TV station, the librarian is not only responsible for cataloging the music, but is also often responsible for helping choose music for programs.

The Music Librarian working at a radio station must catalog all the station's records and tapes. He or she is usually responsible for pulling the records that the disc jockey or program director has chosen prior to a show. At stations that have live request shows, the Music Librarian may be on hand to pull the requested records from the library. The radio station Music Librarian is usually responsible for putting used records and tapes back in their proper places. He or she keeps track of any broken, scratched, or warped records that need replacement. In addition, the librarian works with the program director choosing and purchasing new music.

The Music Librarian must be an extremely organized individual. His or her memory must be good enough to remember vintage tapes, records, books, etc.

The Music Librarian usually works regular hours. If the Music Librarian works in a public library, conservatory, or university library position, he or she is usually responsible to the library director. If the position is in a TV or radio station, the individual is usually responsible to the program director and/or station manager. Music Librarians working in music stores or record shops are responsible to the store manager or owner.

Salaries

A Music Librarian at a mid-sized radio station might make a starting salary of $11,500 yearly. His or her salary at a larger station might range from $15,000 to $19,000 annually.

Music Librarians working in libraries, schools, conservatories, etc. can make from $10,500 for a beginning position to $24,000 in a position that requires experience.

Employment Prospects

There are more Music Librarians than there are jobs to fill. A Music Librarian can choose from a variety of different settings, including schools, conservatories, colleges, universities, public libraries, sheet music stores, record stores, radio or TV stations, orchestras, and music research libraries.

Positions in symphonies and/or choirs are limited. There is a low rate of turnover of Music Librarians in schools, conservatories, colleges, universities, and public libraries. The best place to look for a job is in a mid-sized radio station. Individuals in these stations often leave for jobs with bigger stations.

Advancement Prospects

There is almost no possibility for advancement as a Music Librarian. The competition for jobs in this field is very tough. The main way to advance as a Music Librarian is to find a job at a bigger radio station, better college or university, or more extensive library.

Music Librarians can also be promoted to administrative positions at the facility or institution for which they work.

Education and Training

The education required of a Music Librarian varies according to the type of position desired. All positions require at least an undergraduate degree in music theory or history. Some positions require a dual major in music and library sciences. Other positions require a master's degree in either music or library sciences. Jobs at very large libraries often require a master's in both disciplines.

Experience/Skills/Personality Traits

Most Music Librarians work in libraries before and during their training. Picking up the basic library science skills makes training for the position easier. Prior experience in a sheet music store or large record store is also helpful.

Music Librarians must like to do research and have a great interest in music, recordings, and books.

This position also requires an ability to get along with people. Depending on the type of position, some Music Librarians must also be knowledgeable in a foreign language.

Unions/Associations

There are a number of associations for Music Librarians to belong to. These include the American Library Association (ALA) and the Special Libraries Association (SLA). Music Librarians might additionally belong to the Music Library Association (MLA) and the American Federation of Musicians (AFM).

Tips for Entry

1. As competition is very stiff, secure as much education as possible.
2. In addition to required courses, take specialized classes in specific areas such as ethnic music. Become an expert in at least one specialty.
3. Try to obtain a job as a library assistant while you're still in school.

TALENT AND WRITING

RECORDING GROUP

Duties: Recording tunes for singles and albums

Alternate Title(s): Recording Act; Recording Artist(s)

Salary Range: It is impossible to estimate earnings

Employment Prospects: Poor

Advancement Prospects: Fair

Best Geographical Location(s) for Position: New York City, Los Angeles, Nashville

Prerequisites:

Education or Training—No formal educational requirement; musical and/or vocal training may be helpful

Experience—Writing songs; playing music; singing

Special Skills and Personality Traits—Musical and/or vocal talent; creativity; understanding of music and recording industry; professionalism; good stage appearance; charisma; ability to persevere; luck

```
┌─────────────────────────────────┐
│                                 │
│     Top Recording Group         │
│                                 │
└─────────────────────────────────┘

┌─────────────────────────────────┐
│                                 │
│     Recording Group             │
│                                 │
└─────────────────────────────────┘

┌─────────────────────────────────┐
│     Musical Artists;            │
│     Songwriters;                │
│     Aspiring Recording Group    │
└─────────────────────────────────┘
```

Position Description

A Recording Group is a group that is currently recording their music professionally or that has done so in the past. For the sake of this section, Recording Group will mean a group or an individual artist.

Recording Groups may be involved with any type of music, including rock, pop, folk, country, R & B, disco, classical, and orchestral.

The Recording Group may evolve in a number of ways. Many Groups start out as bar bands, lounge groups, show groups, etc. Other Groups begin their careers by writing music and making demos, never really setting foot on stage.

Once the Group receives a recording contract, they need to find something to record. A Recording Group may or may not write their own material. If they don't, they must find suitable songs to record. These might be located through the help of an A&R person, a music publisher, the group's manager, etc.

After a Group finds songs that might be potential hits, they learn them, rehearse until perfect, and record. This is done with the help of engineers, arrangers, studio musicians, and/or background vocalists.

The Recording Act will work with all the different departments in a record company to get ready for the release of the record. The Group and/or their representative may sit down with the publicity and press department to give them information for press kits, news releases, etc. They may work with the promotion department setting up promotional appearances. The Group may talk to the art department about ideas for the album cover.

Once the record is released, one or more members of a Recording Group may visit key radio stations and meet with program directors, music directors, and disc jockeys. A concert tour to promote the release of the record will probably be scheduled. The Group may give interviews to various print media and appear on TV talk and variety shows.

The Recording Group must set aside time for rehearsals both before concert tours and while on the road. Once they have made it, the Group must always sound their best.

As a successful Recording Group, the members may enjoy some fame and fortune. To keep the fame and build up the fortune, the Group must constantly come up with new tunes to record that become hits.

Becoming a top Recording Group is the ultimate goal for most musical artists. Staying at the top is never easy.

Salaries

Earnings for Recording Groups are impossible to estimate. There are too many factors that can influence finances: how the Group splits up the money, how popular the Group is, the type of recording contract, etc.

Many Groups do not make big money on their first recording, even if it is a hit. It depends how much was spent making the record. Record companies usually recoup their expenses from the record's profits.

Successful Recording Groups can make hundreds of thousands or even millions of dollars. Some of these monies are earned from the sale of the record. Other monies might come from concert tours, public appearances, and merchandising of the Group's name and products.

Employment Prospects

Realistically, it is very difficult to become a top Recording Group. For every Group that gets a recording contract, there are hundreds that don't. However, a group with talent, perseverance, and a lot of luck can make it eventually. Many Groups that fail may just give up too soon.

Advancement Prospects

Once a Group has obtained a bona fide recording contract, they have a fair chance of advancing their career. The first step in advancement for a Recording Group is getting a record on the charts. The second is moving it up the charts. Moving into the top ten on the charts is next. A Recording Group whose record holds the number one position for one or more weeks is achieving the goal. Having a string of tunes hit this position is even better.

None of this is easy, but it is attainable.

Education and Training

Members of Recording Groups are not required to have any educational training, although many individuals do have a college background. Some type of music and/or vocal training is necessary. This might come through private study or schooling or be self-taught.

Experience/Skills/Personality Traits

Members of Recording Groups should have good stage presence and charisma. This is important for the Group when they do promotional tours and appearances. Members should be talented musically and/or vocally. An understanding of the music and recording industry is necessary. An ability to deal with business situations is helpful. Perseverance, luck, and being at the right place at the right time are a must.

Unions/Associations

Recording Groups may be members of the American Federation of Musicians (AFM). They might also belong to the National Academy of Recording Arts and Sciences (NARAS). This is the association which gives out the Grammy awards each year. Depending on the type of music the Group records, they might belong to the Country Music Association (CMA), the Black Music Association (BMA), or the Gospel Music Association (GMA).

Tips for Entry

1. Make the most professional demo possible.
2. Try to have original songs on the demo.
3. Many members of successful Recording Groups start out as session musicians. After they are recognized as having talent, they strike out on their own.
4. Never send your demos out without first querying interest. Either call the record company or write them a note. Try to send your demo to a specific person, not just a title. For example, address it to "Mr. John Jones, A&R Director," not just "A&R Director".

FLOOR SHOW BAND

CAREER PROFILE

Duties: Performing in nightclubs, hotels, bars, concert halls, etc.; putting on shows; entertaining people

Alternate Title(s): Show Group

Salary Range: $100 to $5,000+ per engagement

Employment Prospects: Fair

Advancement Prospects: Poor

Best Geographical Location(s) for Position: Larger cities have more opportunities

Prerequisites:

Education or Training—No educational requirements; musical training helpful

Experience—Performing; working in bands

Special Skills and Personality Traits—Good stage appearance; musical and/or vocal skills; knowledge of musical trends; ability to travel; charisma

CAREER LADDER

```
┌─────────────────────────────────────┐
│  Well-Paid, Well-Known Show Band;    │
│  Recording Act                       │
└─────────────────────────────────────┘

┌─────────────────────────────────────┐
│                                      │
│  Floor Show Band                     │
│                                      │
└─────────────────────────────────────┘

┌─────────────────────────────────────┐
│  Bar Band;                           │
│  Lounge Act                          │
└─────────────────────────────────────┘
```

Position Description

Floor Show Bands work in nightclubs, hotels, cruise ships, cafés, bars, and concert halls putting on shows for patrons. They not only perform, they entertain. Show Groups may perform all different types of music in their act.

Show Bands have to play a specific number of sets per night. Generally, Show Bands will be required to perform two shows. They may also have to play one or two dance sets during the course of the engagement.

The dance set will consist of popular and old tunes the group plays so that patrons can get out on the floor and dance. Shows, on the other hand, must be developed and put together. During show sets, members of the audience stay seated and watch and listen to the act on stage. The act may include any number of songs, melodies, skits, jokes, etc. The show may also contain dancers, light shows, sound effects, or any number of other special effects.

Show Groups have pizzazz. The show set is usually planned quite extensively. Ad-libs may sound like ad-libs to the audience, but they have usually been repeated time and time again. The

show must be flexible. At times, a Show Group will change their opening and their closing and leave the rest of the act as is. As new songs become hits, the group may wish to take out some of their old material and replace it. Usually, Floor Show Groups have exciting finales. They wear costumes on stage. Key members of the group may change costumes for each set.

Between sets or after the engagement, the musicians and vocalists may mingle with patrons.

Floor Show Groups may work in one place for two or three weeks before moving on to the next gig.

Fees are paid weekly or semi-weekly for this type of work. Hotel rooms and, on occasion, food may be part of the deal.

The Floor Show Group travels quite a lot. If the club manager likes their show, they will be booked back again. This is how Show Groups build up followings in specific areas. Individuals must not only be free to travel, but also like living out of a suitcase for months at a time.

The Show Group must appear professional at all times. They must arrive at the correct times for their sets, dressed appropriately. Working hours are usually at night. In order to attain success, it helps for the group to develop good working relationships with managers and agents of clubs where they work. The group is responsible directly to the club manager. It is he or she who controls whether or not the group is invited back. Members of Show Groups often acquire a bit of stardom, at least on the club circuit where they perform.

Salaries

It is difficult to determine a salary range for members of Show Groups. There are quite a number of factors that can affect salaries: the way the group splits up fees, how popular the act is, whether they are working under a union contract, how many members are in the act, expenses, etc.

As a rule, Show Bands earn more per engagement than lounge acts. According to the American Federation of Musicians (AFM) union, leaders earn more than the other members of groups.

There are Show Groups that work sporadically and earn minimum fees (according to union contracts). There are also Show Groups that tour fifty weeks a year, zipping back and forth across the country (or sections of it) earning large fees.

Fees for Show Bands run from $100 to $5,000+ per engagement.

Employment Prospects

Once a group attracts a following, employment prospects are fair. Until a Show Band has a following, employment is difficult. Show Groups usually work with agents who book them in specific areas of the country. Some Show Groups also try to book themselves, but this task can be extremely difficult. There are agents who work specifically with Show Bands and have contracts with various rooms around the country. Groups of this type may also open for better-known acts.

Advancement Prospects

It is difficult to advance as a Show Band. Most groups of this kind aspire to be recording artists. This transition is tough to make.

Show Groups can, however, build up a tremendous following. By doing this, they assure themselves of constant bookings and larger fees.

Advancement in any part of the music business depends on talent, the ability to persevere, and a lot of luck.

Education and Training

There are no educational requirements for members of Show Bands. What is required is the ability to play and/or sing very well. This may be acquired through high school training, college or university education, private study, or self-teaching.

Experience/Skills/Personality Traits

Show Groups must be exciting. Their members need to have a good stage presence and charisma. It goes without saying that members of these groups must have musical and/or vocal skills.

Show Groups must not only perform, but also entertain. They need the ability to play dance sets and show sets. In order to do this, someone in the group or their entourage must put shows together creatively. The group needs to keep in mind the current musical trends. It is often required that the group have a variety of different sets, enabling patrons to come back to the club, see the show, and not be bored.

Unions/Associations

Members of Show Bands may belong to the American Federation of Musicians (AFM). This union bargains for musicians on fees, terms of contracts, etc. It also helps protect the musician from being fired unjustly, treated badly, etc.

Not all musicians belong to the union. However, most major clubs work with the union and do not hire any nonunion groups.

Tips for Entry

1. Join the union. They often know of openings. Hanging around their offices or talking to other union members helps build a contact list.
2. Be professional. If you have an interview with a club manager or agent, show up on time. If you cannot get to an interview on time, chances are you will be late for gigs.
3. Have a professional photographer take pictures of the group. Make sure the group is shown in the picture as they will be on stage (e.g., don't take pictures in costumes and go on stage in jeans).
4. Have the group's name printed on the picture. Don't forget to include your agent's or manager's phone number. If you don't have either yet, use a number where you know someone will answer the phone most of the time. If you don't answer, someone else will get a call for the job.
5. Print up a list of clubs where you have worked previously. You might want to get recommendations in writing from club owners you have worked for.
6. Print up a list of tunes you can perform for both dance sets and show sets.

7. You might want to make up a small brochure (or a letter with the group's picture) letting people know that you are available. Send this to clubs, agents, organizations, etc.

8. When you do get gigs, get the commitment in writing in the form of a contract. Make sure dates, times, monies, and any other pertinent information are included. Make sure that the contract is signed by both parties.

DANCE BAND

CAREER PROFILE

Duties: Playing music and singing in clubs, bars, schools, etc. so that patrons can dance

Alternate Title(s): Bar Band; Lounge Band

Salary Range: It is impossible to estimate earnings of Dance Bands

Employment Prospects: Fair

Advancement Prospects: Poor

Best Geographical Location(s) for Position: Any location has possible openings

Prerequisites:

Education or Training—Musical training helpful

Experience—Performing; member of school band

Special Skills and Personality Traits—Musical ability and talent; good stage appearance; knowledge of all type of music; ability to read music helpful

CAREER LADDER

```
┌─────────────────────────────┐
│     Floor Show Band;        │
│      Recording Act          │
└─────────────────────────────┘

┌─────────────────────────────┐
│        Dance Band           │
└─────────────────────────────┘

┌─────────────────────────────┐
│         Musician            │
└─────────────────────────────┘
```

Position Description

Dance Bands may work in schools, bars, clubs cafes, or hotels, or for private parties. The Dance Band's main function is to provide music for people to dance to and listen to.

When Dance Bands are employed by a specific person, they contract to play a certain number of sets. These sets are usually from forty-five minutes to one hour in length. The Band may play from two to five sets nightly, taking breaks in between.

Dance Bands may consist of guitarists, bass players, pianists, organists or synthesizer players, drummers, singers, horn players, etc. They may have any number of people in them.

Dance Bands usually specialize in one or two varieties of music. Rock, pop, Top 40, disco, jazz, country, swing, etc. are all possibilities. When the band is hired they need to ask what type of music will be required for the engagement.

Dance Bands must set aside specific periods of time for rehearsals. Good Dance Bands know most of the current hits in their variety of music. Additionally, most Dance Bands know an assortment of other tunes. It is important for the dance band to have a big playlist. This will enable them to perform sets without repeating songs.

Dance Bands may take requests from the audience. These requests may be made in a written form or face-to-face. Dance Bands often have specific parts of their sets in which they take requests. In this way, the structure of their show will not be disturbed.

It is usual for Bands to know ahead of time which songs will be played at what time during the set. There may be a group leader who calls out the songs during the show. The sets may be peppered with ad-libs by members of the group.

Dance Bands may work on either a part-time or a full-time basis. Frequently, the first paying job a musician has is in a Dance Band. Dance Bands usually work nights, although they may be hired for affairs and functions in the daytime.

Members of Dance Bands often hold day jobs or teach on the side in order to earn additional income.

When working, the group is responsible to the individual or club who has hired them. The Dance

Band may work with an agent, manager, road manager, or other personnel. They may perform popular tunes as well as their own compositions.

Salaries

Salaries and/or fees for Dance Bands and their members vary greatly depending on the popularity of the group, their location, experience, etc.

Groups playing in school situations earn from $50 to $500+ per engagement. Dance Bands with large followings may earn considerably more.

If the members of the band belong to the musicians union (AFM), their base pay will be set by the union.

Dance Bands working in bars earn between $50 and $500+ per night. A Group playing in a lounge or nightclub setting might earn from $150 to $500 per engagement.

Employment Prospects

Dance Bands looking for part-time work on weekends have a fair chance of finding gigs if they are good. These groups usually have fairly large followings within their community.

Dance Bands seeking full-time employment have a more difficult time. There are many more bands looking for work than there are openings.

Advancement Prospects

It is very hard for a Dance Band to advance their career. The most these groups can reasonably hope for is that they will attract such a large following that they will stay booked constantly and can demand and receive bigger fees.

A group may decide to put together a show and try to work as a show group. Most groups, however, break up before this occurs.

If the band is very talented, very lucky, and in the right place at the right time, they may become a top recording group. The odds are against this.

Education and Training

Members of Dance Bands are not required to have any type of specialized education. The ability to play an instrument or sing well is essential. Training for this may be picked up in school or in private study, or it may be self-taught.

This is not to indicate that members of Dance Bands are uneducated. Many are highly educated. Some have degrees or backgrounds in music, while others hold degrees in other majors. Some Dance Band members are still in school.

Experience/Skills/Personality Traits

Dance Bands must have, or be able to build, large followings. The group must have musical talent and ability. Members of the group should be able to work well together, giving and taking. They must want to persevere and stay together. Dance Bands that play during their college years know that they will probably only be together until graduation. Other groups may stay together for years on end. As long as all the members want the same thing, it usually works out.

Many members of Dance Bands begin playing their instrument or singing while in school. They find that they can earn money while enjoying themselves playing in a school group for a dance or prom.

Members of Dance Bands need a good stage presence. Professional behavior at all times is important. Bands that are familiar with all types of music will have more flexibility in finding jobs.

Unions/Associations

Members of Dance Bands may belong to the American Federation of Musicians (AFM), which is a bargaining union. It helps the musician in all phases of his or her career, from setting guidelines on base salaries for performing to providing health insurance plans.

Tips for Entry

1. Openings for Dance Bands may be found in local papers in the help wanted section.
2. Other openings are learned about by word-of-mouth through members of organizations, schools, associations, firms, etc.
3. Be as professional as possible. Show up on time for all interviews and gigs.
4. Have pictures taken by a professional photographer.
5. Have the group's name, representative, and phone number printed on the pictures so that people know how to locate you for jobs.
6. Set up adequate time for rehearsals *before* a job, not during it.
7. You may consider making up a small brochure or printed piece to mail to potential talent buyers (schools, clubs, agents, etc.).
8. Try to get job commitments in writing in the form of contracts. There are standard contract forms available if you don't have one. Read the contract thoroughly before signing and make sure all information is correct.
9. Make up business cards and give them out. Tell everyone you have a group. Put cards on bulletin boards in stores, schools, malls, etc.
10. You might want to put an ad in a local paper indicating your group's availability. Make sure to put down a phone number where people can locate you or your representative.
11. Make up a press package. Include a resumé and an 8" X 10" glossy photo. Make it as professional and neat as possible.

SESSION MUSICIAN

CAREER PROFILE

Duties: Playing background music for a recording artist in a studio

Alternate Title(s): Studio Musician; Session Player; Sideman or Woman; Freelance Musician; Backup Musician

Salary Range: $0 to $75,000+

Employment Prospects: Fair

Advancement Prospects: Poor

Best Geographical Location(s) for Position: New York, Los Angeles, Nashville; other cities may also have opportunities

Prerequisites:

Education or Training—Musical training helpful

Experience—Performing in bands and groups

Special Skills and Personality Traits—Proficiency in at least one instrument; dependability; ability to read music; versatility

CAREER LADDER

```
┌─────────────────────────────┐
│   Recording Artist;         │
│                             │
│   Group Leader              │
└─────────────────────────────┘

┌─────────────────────────────┐
│                             │
│   Session Musician          │
│                             │
└─────────────────────────────┘

┌─────────────────────────────┐
│                             │
│   Musical Group Member      │
│                             │
└─────────────────────────────┘
```

Position Description

The Session Musician may be known as a studio musician, a session player, a sideman or woman, a freelance musician, or a backup musician. The job, however, stays the same.

The main responsibility of a Session Musician is to back up the leader of a group in the recording studio. He or she might also play music for commercials. At times, the individual may back up the leader of the group in a live concert.

It is important for the Session Musician to have the ability to sight-read. There is usually not a lot of time for rehearsals, and because of the high cost of studio personnel and time, mistakes are not tolerated.

In order for the Session Musician to get as much work as possible, it is in his or her best interest to know how to play a number of different styles and to be proficient in more than one instrument.

Session Musicians are usually hired by a contractor. This individual most often calls musicians he or she knows and has worked with before. The contractor tells the individual the date, time, and whom they will be backing up. The Session Musician either accepts the job or rejects it. After a few job rejections, the contractor probably won't call that particular Session Musician back, no matter what the reason for the rejections.

It is the responsibility of the Session Musician to play what he or she is told and in the manner that the leader of the group or the producer wants it played. He or she must be responsible, reliable, and easy to get along with, in addition to being a good musician.

Session Musicians are usually paid by the hour. Their minimum fee is set by the union (AFM). If they are in great demand, they can usually negotiate higher fees. Session Musicians often work with a number of different groups over a short time span. Each job is called a gig or a session.

A Studio Musician can make a good living. However, one thing that bothers many Studio Musicians is that this job stifles their creativity. Another problem for some is that the individual playing on the recording does not always get credit for his or her work. This means that the Studio Musician works in the shadow of another musician.

Salaries

Salaries of Session Musicians depend on how much work they do, their geographical location, and whether they are in great demand.

The American Federation of Musicians (AFM) specifies the minimum rate Session Musicians should receive. The basic scale is $196.41 for a minimum three-hour call per Musician. A leader or contractor can get double that amount.

When Session Musicians are in demand and well-known, they can negotiate for more than the minimum rates. Individuals who play more than one instrument during a session will usually be paid additional monies.

Talented Session Musicians who are in constant demand may earn $75,000+ annually. Naturally, those who are called less frequently will make considerably less.

Employment Prospects

Employment prospects for Session Musicians are fair if the musician is extremely talented. He or she needs a lot of contacts to get his or her foot in the door. Unfortunately, talent alone doesn't make it.

Session Musicians are often hired through contractors. If an individual is hired and turns out to be not only talented, but responsible and easy to work with, too, he or she will continue receiving assignments from the contractor.

The majority of studio work is found in New York, Los Angeles and Nashville, although there are studios located all over the country.

Advancement Prospects

Session Musicians can advance their careers in a number of ways. They can become group leaders—not always an easy move—or they can become top Session Musicians. To become a top Studio Musician, one must be more talented, more versatile, and better connected than other musicians around.

Although there are many who have moved from being Session Musicians to top positions in the music business, it is a tough hill to climb.

Education and Training

There is no formal educational requirement for Session Musicians. Individuals have usually had extensive private study in their instruments. However, there are also many successful Session Musicians who are self-taught. The ability to read music is not always necessary, but makes the musician more flexible.

Many musicians have college degrees in music or an unrelated subject. This way, they feel they have something to fall back on in case they can't make a living in music.

Experience/Skills/Personality Traits

It is essential for the Session Musician to be a great musician. Most Session Musicians begin their careers playing in local bands while in high school. Any performance experience at all is useful for a Session Musician.

As noted above, it is not always necessary to read music, but the ability to do so is a plus. Another advantage is the ability to play more than one instrument.

Unions/Associations

Session Musicians may be members of the American Federation of Musicians (AFM). This union stipulates the minimum wages that can be paid to musicians in addition to performing a variety of other functions.

Tips for Entry

1. Begin your career by working in a local band.
2. When you feel experienced enough, put an ad for work as a Session Musician in either a music-oriented newspaper or one of the trade magazines.
3. If you want to get into recording studio work and no one will let you put your foot in the door musically, try to get a job doing anything in the studio (studio assistant, receptionist, gofer, etc). You will learn a lot and make the contacts you need.

BACKGROUND VOCALIST

Duties: Backing up other singers or musicians on recordings or in live performance

Alternate Title(s): Singer, Studio Singer; Studio Vocalist; Background Singer; Chorus Member; Jingle Singer; Vocalist

Salary Range: It is impossible to estimate earnings for Background Vocalists

Employment Prospects: Fair

Advancement Prospects: Poor

Best Geographical Location(s) for Position: New York City, Los Angeles, Nashville for major jobs; other locations for smaller jobs

Prerequisites:

Education or Training—No educational requirement; private vocal study useful

Experience—Singing or performing; working in music groups; singing in choruses

Special Skills and Personality Traits—Ability to sight-read; flexible singing style; ability to harmonize; excellent singing ability; good vocal range

```
┌─────────────────────────────┐
│   Major Recording Artist;   │
│        Solo Singer          │
└─────────────────────────────┘

┌─────────────────────────────┐
│     Background Vocalist     │
└─────────────────────────────┘

┌─────────────────────────────┐
│      Unemployed Singer      │
└─────────────────────────────┘
```

Position Description

Background Vocalists back up other singers or musicians on recordings, in jingles, on television commercials, or in live performance. Background Vocalists may have full-time jobs or may freelance.

An individual working as a Background Vocalist in a lounge or show group travels with the act to all their performances. He or she is responsible for singing background music in all the shows. The person must also learn all the songs in the repertoire and attend all the rehearsals.

Background Vocalists working in the theater may sing in the chorus. They must attend all rehearsals, learn parts, and sing in shows.

Background Vocalists who freelance on recordings, jingles, or television commercials have slightly different functions. Such an individual must build up a reputation as a great singer and be flexible, responsible, and available when needed.

The world of singing backup on recordings is unique. A Background Vocalist must be able to walk into a studio, pick up some music, go over it quickly, and be ready to record without a mistake. The Vocalist may be asked to harmonize with other singers with whom he or she has never sung. The individual may also be asked to improvise. The singer who can pick up on what the producers want and sound good is the one who will be called on again.

The Background Vocalist must be versatile. An individual may have a job in the morning doing the background vocals for a pop tune and another gig that night singing background for an R & B tune. The more flexible the singer is, the more opportunities there are.

The Background Vocalist who works on television commercials or radio jingles performs much the same as when doing a recording. Individuals in this type of work often have more time to rehearse the tunes.

People involved in singing background vocals may work long, irregular hours on some days and not at all on others. As a matter of fact, Background Vocalists who rely only on recording dates might not work for weeks or months at a time.

Jobs are often obtained through contractors or producers in the recording field. The Background Vocalist needs many contracts to become successful.

The Background Vocalist working in a group or chorus finds work either through an agent or by auditioning.

Salaries

Salaries of Background Vocalists depend on a number of variables. These include how much the singer works, what type of work he or she performs, geographical location of the singer, and general success. Base salaries of union members are set by the various unions. Background vocalists who work as singers with bands may not belong to a union.

Background Vocalists working in recording studios are paid according to how long the finished product will be, what day and time the individual works, how long the Vocalist is in the studio, etc. A basic rate of $46 is paid to a Vocalist for each song he or she works on. Another $46 is added for each hour that it takes to complete the song. The Background Vocalist will earn additional monies for overtime, other songs, etc. If the completed song is more than 3½ minutes, the individual is paid extra.

It is impossible to estimate the earnings of a Background Vocalist because of the variables involved. Those who are successful may earn up to $100,000+ in the studio.

Employment Prospects

Employment prospects are fair for a Background Vocalist working as a singer within a band. Employment opportunities become more difficult for vocalists seeking work with very well-known acts or in recordings or jingles.

Generally, Background Vocalists must audition for a position in a major act. Competition is keen. Some Background Vocalists audition for agents who find them jobs.

Locating jobs as Background Vocalists for recordings or jingles is much more difficult. One must develop a reputation in order to get a foot in the door.

Advancement Prospects

Advancement is difficult for a Background Vocalist. One of the problems is that the individual rarely possesses the qualities needed to be a soloist. Another possible reason for poor career advancement is the lack of jobs for soloists. Many Background Vocalists aspire to become major recording artists in their own right. This is possible, but the odds are against it.

For those who get their foot in the door as Background Vocalists for recording sessions or jingles, however, there are better advancement prospects. Many of these individuals are offered more work than they can handle. Many a jingle singer has achieved financial security.

Education and Training

There is a school of thought that says that individuals who aspire to be musicians or singers should be educated in a field other than music in order to have something to fall back on. This is up to the individual.

There is no formal education needed to become a singer. Some singers have a broad background in music and others do not. Many Background Vocalists have graduated from conservatories. Still others go to vocal coaches or other private teachers. Many singers are self-taught.

Experience/Skills/Personality Traits

A Background Vocalist needs a good voice and the ability to sing. This is not as silly as it sounds, for many great singers do not possess the confidence to sing well in front of others.

Other qualifications for a good Background Vocalist include the ability to harmonize, possession of a good vocal range, and the ability to sing all styles of music. This permits the Background Vocalist to obtain more jobs.

Although it is not always necessary, it is helpful for a Background Vocalist to be able to sight-read. Many recording jobs specify this.

Additionally, the person in this position must be reliable, show up on time for jobs, and have the perseverance necessary to make a living in this type of job.

Unions/Associations

Background Vocalists may belong to a number of different unions, depending on where they are working. If the Singer is doing a recording session or a radio jingle, he or she may belong to the American Federation of Television and Radio Artists (AFTRA). Individuals singing in theatrical jobs will belong to the American Guild of Musical Artists (AGMA) or the Actors Equity Association, commonly referred to as Equity (AEA). The singer who works on a television commercial may belong to either the Screen Actors Guild (SAG) or AFTRA. Individuals may belong to more than one union.

Tips for Entry

1. Background Vocalists often advertise their specialty in the trades or in the classified sections of newspapers.
2. Read the trades on a regular basis. See what is happening and where there are possible openings.
3. Local groups may advertise for a Background Vocalist in the newspaper's classified section.
4. The various union offices are full of information on openings. You might have to hang around there or become friendly with the people who run the office.
5. Visit different recording studios. Get to know people who book studio time, producers, engineers, etc. These people can help you find work. Make sure you tell them what you do and leave a phone number.
6. The telephone is your lifeline, especially if you are looking for freelance recording dates. Make sure someone answers your phone at all times. If this isn't possible, get an answering service or answering machine. Don't keep the line busy with unnecessary talking. If your number is busy, important people may call someone else for a job.
7. Sing at every possible opportunity. Get your name (and your voice) around.

SONGWRITER

CAREER PROFILE

Duties: Writing lyrics, music, or both

Alternate Title(s): Composer; Lyricist; Writer

Salary Range: 0 to $1,000,000+

Employment Prospects: Fair

Advancement Prospects: Poor

Best Geographical Location(s) for Position: Any location is suitable for writing songs; staff positions are usually located in New York, Los Angeles, and Nashville

Prerequisites:

Educations or Training—No formal education required; songwriter workshops, seminars, and books are helpful; music training may be useful

Experience—Writing music, lyrics, poetry, etc.

Special Skills and Personality Traits—Creativity; musical talent; knowledge of music business helpful; good work habits; persistence; perseverance; cognizance of music theory

CAREER LADDER

```
┌─────────────────────────┐
│                         │
│  Successful Songwriter   │
│                         │
└─────────────────────────┘

┌─────────────────────────┐
│                         │
│       Songwriter         │
│                         │
└─────────────────────────┘

┌─────────────────────────┐
│                         │
│   Aspiring Songwriter    │
│                         │
└─────────────────────────┘
```

Position Description

A Songwriter writes songs. He or she may write the lyrics, the melody, or both. Songwriters who work with others are called collaborators.

Songwriters work in many different ways. Some people sit down at the same time every day and try to create music and/or lyrics. Others wait until they are inspired by an idea, a person, a thought, an occasion, a feeling, etc. Some may write the music first, then try to create or find the perfect lyrics. Others develop lyrics and then try to find the perfect tune.

Songwriters may also be called composers, writers, or lyricists. Once the individual has finished a song, either alone or with another person, he or she must find a way to market it. The main goal of most professional Songwriters is to write a song that is not only recorded, but also turns into a number one hit or a standard.

Before the Songwriter does anything, he or she should make sure that the song is protected. This can be done in a number of ways. The individual can copyright the song. Another method of protection is to put the finished music and words into an envelope, address it, and send it to him or herself via certified registered mail. Once the person receives the song back from the post office, he or she should put it away without opening it. The official postmark is a type of protection. Some individuals feel that if they are dealing with reputable music publishers these procedures are not necessary. However, it is better to be safe than sorry. Many industry professionals feel that the only real protection is to copyright.

The Songwriter must find a music publisher or recording act to work with the song. The person should use any contacts he or she has to get the song listened to. As many publishers, recording acts, producers, A&R people, managers, etc. as possible should be contacted. If the Songwriter does not know such people, he or she must make calls, knock on doors, and write letters.

In order for the song to be listened to, the Songwriter must make up a demo record or cassette. These demos should accurately showcase the song. There is no need to make a very elaborate demo, although it should be as professional as possible. After a demo master is made, copies must be made to send to the important listeners. If the Songwriter makes his or her own demo, the individual should be sure that the tapes are clean and of good quality. Each tape should be labeled with the Songwriter's name, address, phone number, and the names and times of each song included on the demo. Incidentally, if there is more than one song on a tape, the person should note where each song ends and the next begins. There shouldn't be more than three or four songs on a tape.

It is always better to send a query letter prior to sending a demo. Many music publishers and A&R people don't accept unsolicited material. When the Songwriter does send tapes, they should always be sent first class.

The Songwriter may get lucky and have one of his or her songs accepted by a music publisher, recording group, A&R person, etc. Depending on the deal made, the Songwriter may sell the song outright or just sell the rights to it. At this point, the individual should seek the advice of an attorney to go over any details, contracts, etc.

Although the Songwriter receives credit on a record, he or she does not often receive a lot of attention for writing a song.

The individual may work long hours trying to create something unique. The Songwriter may develop a block. Some people write one hit song and are never heard from again. Others have a long stream of hits and standards. There are also many people who write good songs but are never discovered.

Salaries

Earnings of Songwriters depend on a number of factors. These include the number of songs published and/or sold, the number of times each song is played, used, etc., the general popularity of the tune, and the type of agreement made for each song. For example, songs may be sold outright, pay writer's royalties, and/or pay publisher's royalties.

Songwriters may write the tune, the lyrics, or both. If individuals collaborate on songs, monies must be shared. The split will differ depending on the individuals and the tunes.

Songwriters may write songs for years and never sell or publish them. On the other hand, one of these individuals might wake up one day, write a song, have a recording act record it, and have it turn into a monster hit. Financial success can occur at any time in this profession. Once a song is published, a Songwriter may receive royalties from it for the rest of his or her life.

Successful Songwriters can earn $500,000+ yearly. Very successful individuals may earn over a million dollars each year.

Employment Prospects

Almost anyone can write a song. Selling it or publishing it is a different matter. Songwriters may write songs for performers to sing in concert or on records. They may write radio or television jingles or music for plays, films, or TV.

The exciting thing about being a Songwriter is that an individual can write a song that will turn into a hit at any time.

In this profession, a person can work full- or part-time. He or she might be a musician who prefers to write his or her own tunes.

Songwriters usually work for themselves or work with a collaborator. There are numerous opportunities for an individual to be employed by a record company, producer, recording group, etc. as a staff Songwriter. Competition for these jobs is tough.

Advancement Prospects

The way a Songwriter advances is by writing songs that turn into hits. As noted before, this can happen at any time in a Songwriter's career.

Education and Training

There is no formal education needed to be a Songwriter. Depending on whether one writes lyrics, music, or both, he or she might study music theory, harmony, orchestration, and/or ear training. The individal may have studied one or more instruments through private lessons or be self-taught.

The Songwriter might take courses in lyric writing. Again, this is not a requirement.

There are many Songwriter workshops, seminars, and books that may be helpful and provide inspiration.

Experience/Skills/Personality Traits

Songwriters need to be talented, creative people. A knowledge of the music business is helpful in marketing, selling, or publishing the song. The ability to play one or more instruments and/or musical talent is helpful, although not necessary for every Songwriter.

As most Songwriters work on their own, good work habits are useful in getting things accomplished. Persistence is a must in writing new songs and selling and/or publishing them.

Luck and being in the right place at the right time are important factors.

Unions/Associations

Songwriters may belong to a variety of organizations, including the American Society of Composers, Authors, and Publishers (ASCAP), Broadcast Music, Inc. (BMI), and/or the Society of European Stage Authors and Composers (SESAC). These performing rights organizations pay Songwriters royalties for public performances of their song.

An individual might be a member of the American Guild of Authors and Composers (AGAC). This association represents composers and lyricists. The Songwriter may be a member of the Nashville Songwriters Association International, the Country Music Association (CMA), the Gospel Music Association (GMA), and the Black Music Association (BMA). Songwriters might additionally be members of the National Academy of Recording Arts and Sciences (NARAS).

Tips for Entry

1. Write as much as you can. Practice does not always make perfect, but it helps develop the craft.
2. Try to find some songwriting workshops. These not only give helpful advice and tips, but also provide inspiration.
3. Protect your songs. Either copyright them or send them to yourself by registered, certified mail. Copyrighting is best.
4. Do not get involved with any individual who wants you to pay to publish your songs. Publishers are supposed to pay *you* for the songs.
5. Learn as much as possible about every aspect of the music business. It will help you sell, publish, and market your songs more effectively.
6. Try to get your songs listened to by as many people as possible. You might consider letting local club acts, disc jockeys, and music directors hear your tunes. Get their opinions and advice on how to better your work.
7. Have persistence and perseverance.

CHURCH MUSIC

CHOIR DIRECTOR

CAREER PROFILE

Duties: Recruiting and directing choirs; developing and maintaining music budget; planning music programs

Alternate Title(s): Music Director; Minister of Music; Administrator of Music Program; Church Musician

Salary Range: $13,000 to $60,000

Employment Prospects: Good

Advancement Prospects: Fair

Best Geographical Location(s) for Position: Cities with a number of large churches tend to have more positions available

Prerequisites:

Education or Training—Bachelor's degree in church music usually required; master's degree in church music preferred

Experience—Experience working in church music situations helpful

Special Skills and Personality Traits—Ability to work well within the congregational hierarchy and politics; knowledge of choral techniques; familiarity with liturgical practice

CAREER LADDER

Choir Director of Large Church

Choir Director

Organist

Position Description

The Choir Director's prime responsibility is to prepare the church's choir for services. In some jobs, the Choir Director may be the only paid person involved in the music department of the church. In this situation, the Choir Director might not be only in charge of the choir, but might also be the organist accompanying the group during services.

In other positions, the Choir Director acts as the music director, supervising others in the music department of the church and coordinating their efforts.

As a Choir Director, an individual must conduct and lead the choir. This may include auditioning members of the congregation who would like to sing in the choir as well as soliciting potential members who would be assets to the group. The director also auditions singers to act as section leaders, assistant conductors, or soloists.

The Choir Director sets times each week for rehearsals. He or she is responsible for leading and supervising rehearsals so that time is spent most effectively.

Another duty of the director is to choose the music that will be used during services, making sure that it is appropriate to the sermon, holiday, or special occasion. As director, the individual will be in charge of the church's music library and might recruit a volunteer to act as music librarian. The Choir Director must often recruit volunteers to care for vestments and help with music programs as well.

Special programs, concerts, and other musical activities are the responsibility of the choir director. He or she must plan them, orchestrate them, and rehearse them.

The director works closely with all the members of the music department of the church as well as with the minister of the congregation. If any of them have a particular musical need, they will go to the director. The Choir Director is, in essence, the music resource person for the church.

The Music or Choir Director must work out a budget for the music program. This budget is presented to the appropriate members of the congregation for approval. It then becomes the responsibility of the Choir Director to stay within the budget. The budget might include items such as robes for the choir, music for the group, trips for special concerts, staging for plays, etc. The director analyzes the needs and sets budget priorities.

Certain churches have more than one choir. For example, the church may have a regular choir and a children's choir. The director must provide leadership for both. At times, the Choir Director will be asked to have extra concerts or lead the choir at special events, weddings, funerals, etc. The director may also be required to coordinate additional music-oriented activities in the church and community.

In addition to his or her music responsibilities, the Choir Director is usually expected to maintain office hours each week to discuss problems, work with small groups of singers, help the organist, write music, and handle administrative chores. The Music or Choir Director may be expected to attend a variety of workshops, conferences, and seminars each year.

The Choir Director is responsible to a church committee or to the minister of the church. Whatever the case, the Choir Director works very closely with the minister and the congregation to help fulfill their musical requirements.

Salaries

Salaries of church musicians vary depending on their experience, the type of position held, and the size, location, and budget of the church. Salaries for full-time Choir Directors begin at around $13,000 yearly. Salaries go up to $60,000 per year, and may be slightly higher at very large metropolitan churches.

Employment Prospects

Employment prospects for church musicians are good. The Choir Director must have sound training to get into any major position. A bachelor's degree in church music helps land a job; a master's or doctorate in church music makes a person even more employable in this field.

While educational qualifications are helpful, an applicant must also demonstrate an enthusiastic, positive attitude to pass the interview process many church committees require.

Advancement Prospects

Depending on the job a Choir Director holds, he or she has a fair chance of advancement. Small churches do not usually have large music departments. An individual who holds a position in such a church has limited upward mobility in that institution.

In larger metropolitan churches, however, the Choir Director may have a lot of money to put into a music program. The Director can build up the music department of the church and may gain some recognition for doing so. He or she may then move on to a position in an even larger and more prestigious church.

This is not to say that a church musician cannot do well in a smaller church. He or she may institute and supervise a number of music programs, choirs, etc. for the church and be quite happy doing so.

Education

Education requirements for the position of Choir Director differ from church to church. Most churches, however, require at least a bachelor's degree in music with a major in church music. Some churches are now requiring that a Choir Director hold a master's degree.

Experience/Skills/Personality Traits

Church musicians, as a rule, work in churches in one capacity or another throughout most of their lives. The aspiring Choir Director was probably a member of the choir at his or her own church.

It is important that the Choir or Music Director have the ability to work well within the politics of the congregational hierarchy. From the time the person is interviewed, and throughout his or her tenure the Choir Director will be working closely with these people.

The Choir Director must be familiar with liturgical practice. A knowledge of choral techniques and an ability to teach and/or lead is essential. Additionally, most church musicians know how to play the organ, piano, and/or guitar.

Unions/Associations

Among the helpful and useful groups a Choir Director may belong to are the AGO (The American Guild of Organists), the Choristers Guild, the American Choral Directors Association, the Presbyterian Association of Musicians, the Pastoral Association of Musicians (R.C.), the Association of Anglican Musicians, and various other denominational groups.

Tips for Entry

1. Schools of religious music have placement centers at which graduates may register. Churches in need of musical personnel usually advise these placement agencies about openings and opportunities.
2. Your church's Music/Choir Director may know of openings in other churches. Ask around.
3. In certain positions, auditions are necessary (especially if organ playing is part of the job). Check the requirements before an interview so that you can prepare properly.
4. Get involved in church music situations while you're in school. Offer to act as the choir's music librarian; help the Choir Director rehearse groups that are having trouble with a piece. Obtain as much experience as possible.
5. Many of the organizations that church musicians belong to know of openings and opportunities. Check with them about placement.

CANTOR

CAREER PROFILE

Duties: Leading prayers in synagogue or temple; teaching music; pastoral duties

Alternate Title(s): Hazzan; Reverend

Salary Range: $25,000 to $60,000

Employment Prospects: Excellent

Advancement Prospects: Good

Best Geographical Location(s) for Position: Any area that has synagogues and temples

Prerequisites:

Education or Training—College degree required; music major preferred; degree from a Cantorial college

Experience—Taking part in synagogue functions; participation in Jewish youth groups; involvement with junior congregational services

Special Skills and Personality Traits—Knowledge of Hebrew and all Hebraic disciplines; broad musical knowledge; possession of cultured voice; ability to get along with people

CAREER LADDER

```
┌─────────────────────────────────────┐
│  Cantor of Large Synagogue or Temple │
└─────────────────────────────────────┘

┌─────────────────────────────────────┐
│               Cantor                 │
└─────────────────────────────────────┘

┌─────────────────────────────────────┐
│          Cantorial Student           │
└─────────────────────────────────────┘
```

Position Description

The Cantor of a temple or synagogue has a very important position. The prime responsibility of the individual is to present liturgical music that will help clarify the prayers and studies of the religion. The objective is to enrich the religious experience of the worshipers.

As the Cantor of a temple or synagogue, the individual leads the congregation in prayer during services. The Cantor's cultured and melodic voice can usually be heard clearly above everyone else's.

The Cantor may teach music in the religious school of the synagogue. If the temple has a choir, the Cantor will lead them, supervise their rehearsals, etc. The Cantor is responsible for preparing the choir for all services. Special attention is given to the Jewish High Holy Days services. Any musical activity that occurs in the synagogue becomes the Cantor's responsibility.

In the Cantorial position, the individual may teach various courses in the synagogue's adult education classes. One of the main teaching responsibilities is that of preparing youngsters to sing or chant their Bar or Bat Mitzvah services. This responsibility is often shared with other members of the synagogue, depending on how many young people must be trained at any one time.

The Cantor is, in essence, a minister of his or her faith. Although the job is structured in part by the Cantor's duties at all Sabbath worship services, it is unstructured in other ways. Many Cantors maintain schedules that give them time for additional study of the Jewish religion and liturgical music.

The Cantor works closely with the rabbi of the congregation. At times, he or she will be involved in pastoral duties, which might include visiting members of the congregation who are sick or comforting members who are in mourning. The individual may officiate at weddings and funerals as well as at regular weekly services and holidays.

Before becoming a Cantor, one usually chooses the branch of Judaism in which he or she will study and officiate. Individuals may select the Reform branch, the Conservative branch, or the Orthodox branch. Training varies slightly in the various Judaic philosophies.

The job is generally a service position in that the Cantor helps and guides people. Cantors in both small and large congregations are, in fact, public figures in the community. On occasion, they will be asked to serve on community boards, as members of associations, and as speakers at functions.

Cantors additionally have the option during their career of becoming concert artists. In this position, Cantors sing liturgical music in a variety of concert settings, ranging from local functions to full-scale concerts at major halls.

Salaries

Cantors' salaries depend on the location and size of the synagogue or temple. Salaries usually range from $25,000 to $60,000 yearly. Most Cantors also receive living allowances from the congregation.

Cantors may have an opportunity to earn additional income by performing at concerts.

Employment Prospects

The employment prospects for Cantors are excellent. As of this writing, there is a shortage of qualified individuals to fill cantorial positions.

As a rule, Cantors work with congregations close to their branch of Judaic preference. They may work with either Reform, Conservative, or Orthodox congregations.

Advancement Prospects

As noted above, there is a shortage of trained Cantors. Individuals who have gained experience in the cantorate can move into positions in larger synagogues or temples.

Cantors who have established themselves as great singers may become guest Cantors for special services and/or give concerts of Jewish music. There are a number of Cantors who have attained great prestige in this way.

Education and Training

In order to become a trained Cantor one must obtain a college degree. A degree in music is, of course, preferable. There are a limited number of schools available to prepare the individual for a position as a Cantor. Schools differ in the branch of Judaism they follow. One may become a Cantor in the Reform, Conservative, or Orthodox branch of the religion.

Study in one of these schools varies in length from three to five years. As a graduate of a Cantorial college, an individual will receive a diploma certifying him or her a Cantor or Hazzan.

Incidentally, both secular and religious studies must be completed before graduation.

Experience/Skills/Personality Traits

An individual aspiring to become a Cantor must possess a cultured voice. They must have a knowledge of Hebrew and all Hebraic disciplines. Cantors need to be adept at reading Torah.

Musical knowledge is a must and the ability to play an instrument is a plus.

Before an individual decides to become a Cantor, he or she generally participates in a variety of synagogue functions, taking part in various Jewish youth groups and junior congregational services.

Unions/Associations

Depending on the branch of Judaism the Cantor is involved with, he or she may belong to different organizations. Those working in a Conservative congregation might belong to the Cantors Assembly of America. Cantors involved with a Reform congregation may belong to the American Conference of Cantors. Individuals with an Orthodox congregation would belong to the Cantorial Council of America.

Tips for Entry

1. Talk to the Cantor at a synagogue or temple in the branch of Judaism with which you hope to be involved. Ask questions you have about the occupation.
2. The B'nai B'rith Vocational Service has trained people to counsel you in a career as a Cantor.
3. If you require financial aid for your education in this field, there are a number of options. Check out the college of your choice for financial assistance, scholarships, etc. Local community groups and synagogues often offer financial help in this area.
4. There are part-time Cantorial positions available for Cantorial students. Check synagogues, temples, and the school you attend for positions.

ORGANIST

Duties: Playing the organ at religious services

Alternate Title(s): Musician; Church Musician

Salary Range: $10,000 to $25,000

Employment Prospects: Fair

Advancement Prospects: Fair

Best Geographical Location(s) for Position: Cities with a large number of religious institutions tend to have more positions available

Prerequisites:

Education or Training—Organ training; educational requirements vary

Experience—Performance experience playing the organ

Special Skills and Personality Traits—Ability as an organ player; knowledge of religious music; ability to read and write music; ability to get along with congregation

```
┌─────────────────────────────┐
│                             │
│   Choir or Music Director   │
│                             │
└─────────────────────────────┘

┌─────────────────────────────┐
│                             │
│         Organist            │
│                             │
└─────────────────────────────┘

┌─────────────────────────────┐
│                             │
│    Freelance Organist;      │
│         Student             │
│                             │
└─────────────────────────────┘
```

Position Description

An Organist working for a religious institution provides the music during the services. The Organist may be in charge of choosing the music to accompany prayers or may work closely with the choir or music director in accomplishing this task. In some houses of worship, the individual may act as both the Organist and the choir director.

Depending on the size and the budget of the hiring institution, the job may be either full-time or part-time. In a small, rural church, for instance, the organist may work only on Sunday. In a larger metropolitan church, the Organist might be responsible not only for Sunday service music, but also for accompanying choirs, rehearsals, or playing for church services for TV or radio broadcasts.

The Organist may also be required to play for special services, including wedding and funerals. If the individual is working on a part-time basis, he or she is usually paid for the extra workload.

In this position, a person may teach other students the instrument as a way of earning additional income. The Organist is usually allowed to use the organ and the space at no charge. Occasion-

ally, the Organist will find musically talented youngsters in the congregation. It is up to him or her to encourage the students and possibly have them participate in services.

The Organist may be responsible for giving recitals. These are mainly presented as part of the institution's music program. However, it is not unusual to find Organists performing in a setting totally apart from their job.

In a full-time position, the Organist is expected to supervise the maintenance of the organ and make sure that it is always in proper working order.

As a member of the house of worship's music committee, the Organist might advise the congregation on music-related matters. He or she usually has regular office hours or at least time in which practice and rehearsal take place.

The Organist working for a house of worship may play in a church, synagogue, or temple. The individual need not be of the same religious belief as the congregation for which he or she is providing music. The Organist is responsible to the institution's music or choir director, the music committee, or directly to the minister, priest or rabbi.

Salaries

Salaries of Organists in religious institutions vary. Some jobs are part-time, some are full-time. Part-time positions are usually paid by the service. Fees range from $15 to $100 per service.

Depending on duties, location of the church or temple, size of the institution, budget, etc., Organists working full-time may make between $10,000 and $25,000 yearly.

Employment Prospects

There are quite a few opportunities to work as an Organist in a church, temple, or synagogue. Many of these positions are only part-time. (A number of churches, temples, and synagogues have Organists within the congregation who donate their services.)

Full-time positions are available in larger metropolitan areas. The more education and experience an individual has, the better opportunity he or she will have to obtain a full-time position.

Advancement Prospects

Advancement for an Organist is possible. In this position, an individual may be promoted in a number of directions. For example, the Organist may go from a part-time to a full-time position. The individual may find a position at a larger institution that pays a higher salary. An Organist might advance to the position of Organist/Choir Director or to that of music director.

Education or Training

Educational requirements for Organists vary according to the position. In a small town church or temple, often all that is required is the ability to play the organ well.

Conversely, Organists who are hired to work in large metropolitan houses of worship in full-time positions may be required to hold not only a bachelor's degree, but possibly a master's degree. If the Organist's position is one which also encompasses the duties of a musical or choir director, a degree will generally be required.

In lieu of college education (although training is most certainly needed), Organists may apply for an Associates Certificate. This is given by the American Guild of Organists. The organization gives a series of tests and certifies church musicians at various levels.

Experience/Skills/Personality Traits

The Organist must be accomplished on the instrument. He or she must be able to read and write music. A knowledge of religious music is a must.

The Organist may need to know how to maintain the organ or at least be able to supervise service on it.

Organists must get along well with the congregation and be reliable.

Unions/Associations

Organists may belong to the musicians union (AFM) if they play outside the the church, synagogue, or temple. They may also belong to a number of organizations, including the AGO (the American Guild of Organists), the Choristers Guild, the American Choral Directors Association, the Presbyterian Association of Musicians, the Pastoral Association of Musicians (R.C.), The Association of Anglican Musicians, or a host of other denominational groups.

Tips for Entry

1. There are often ads in the classified sections of newspapers from religious institutions looking for organists. Most of these jobs are part-time.
2. The American Guild of Organists has a placement service for church organists. Churches let the organization know of any openings they have.
3. The music director or choir director of any institution usually knows about job openings or opportunities in other institutions. Speak to these individuals.

MISCELLANEOUS CAREER OPPORTUNITIES IN MUSIC

MUSIC JOURNALIST

CAREER PROFILE

Duties: Writing articles, reviews, and critiques on music acts, concerts, shows, records, videos, etc.

Alternate Title(s): Writer; Music Critic; Music Reviewer

Salary Range: $7,500 to $100,000+

Employment Prospects: Good

Advancement Prospects: Fair

Best Geographical Location(s) for Position: New York City and Los Angeles for major music publications; other large cities with moderate-sized publications and smaller locations for individuals just starting out

Prerequisites:

Education and Training—College degree required or preferred for most jobs

Experience—Writing for school paper; reviewing local concerts or records for local papers

Special Skills and Personality Traits—Writing skill; knowledge of music; typing skill; objectivity; ability to work under pressure

CAREER LADDER

```
┌─────────────────────────────────────┐
│ Music Journalist for Major Publication │
└─────────────────────────────────────┘

┌─────────────────────────────────────┐
│          Music Journalist            │
└─────────────────────────────────────┘

┌─────────────────────────────────────┐
│ Entertainment Journalist for Local Paper; │
│ Nonmusic-Oriented Reporter or Journalist; │
│               Student                │
└─────────────────────────────────────┘
```

Position Description

Music Journalists work in many different situations. A Music Journalist might be on staff at a local or small circulation weekly newspaper. In this case, he or she might write a daily, biweekly, or weekly column about happenings in the music business. The Music Journalist would also be responsible for reviewing any concerts, shows, and artists passing through the area. The Music Journalist might review new records or music products on the market. In small circulation newspapers, he or she might write about other entertainment-oriented subjects. A Music Journalist may also have to report on nonentertainment subjects.

As Music Journalists move into positions on larger papers or magazines, their jobs become more specialized. For instance, one might be a classical reviewer, a rock writer, a jazz writer, a record reviewer, etc.

The life of a Music Journalist is often exciting. He or she is expected to be knowledgeable about the field of music being covered. Usually the individual also enjoys the music. As a Music Journalist reviewing concerts or acts, the individual might first receive a press kit on the artist. A phone interview may take place for additional background material. Music Journalists receive press passes to the shows covered.

Prior to the event, he or she may have much of the background story developed and written. After the show, the journalist writes a review of the actual act. The ability to work under pressure is a must, as the finished review may have to be completed and handed in just an hour after the show ends to make a deadline. The journalist must also be careful to be as objective as possible. For example, if the journalist is writing a review of a group of which he or she is not particularly fond, this feeling may enter the review. It must not be allowed to color the piece.

Music Journalists interview musical acts for short features or in-depth articles. The ability to delve below the surface to seek information is necessary to Music Journalists. The Music Journalist who will move up and succeed is the one who asks the questions that no one else has thought of and develops a really interesting story.

Reviewers often have to review semiprofessional concerts, such as student symphonies. The reviewer must try to write a review in which the symphony is judged on its own merits and not the same basis as a major orchestra.

Music Journalists gather material in a variety of ways. They may research prior stories about a group in other magazines or publications. They may interview the act either personally or by phone. During the interview, the Music Journalist may either take notes or record the interview session (with the permission of the act). The journalist may talk with people who are close to the act (the manager, a songwriter, family members, friends, etc.). It is important to end up with a factual and interesting story.

Music Journalists may work full-time and part-time. They can work as stringers for publications on a concert-to-concert basis or work on a freelance basis doing stories by commission or writing articles to sell.

A Music Journalist is responsible to the editor of the publication for which he or she writes. Many Music Journalists become editors after a few years in writing.

Salaries

Salaries for Music Journalists depend on where they are employed, how experienced they are, and what they do.

A beginning journalist writing reviews and/or music news for a local paper can earn between minimum wage and $15,000 yearly. As he or she gains more experience, yearly salaries go up to $20,000 or $25,000.

Journalists writing for major publications or newspapers make between $17,500 and $100,000+ yearly. The higher figure, of course, is for those who have made it in the field. Salaries usually average between $35,000 and $50,000 annually for a Music Journalist working for a good publication.

Employment Prospects

Employment prospects are good for the individual who doesn't mind starting at the bottom and/or moving to a location where a job is available.

Nearly all newspapers have some type of entertainment or music section, including local newspapers and magazines. The reporter-journalist may often have other duties besides writing about music.

After one gains experience writing professionally, he or she may seek employment anywhere. Employers usually require writing samples.

Advancement Prospects

If a Music Journalist has a good writing style, is responsible, and develops good contacts and a good reputation, he or she can advance. Music Journalists generally advance by obtaining positions at more prestigious publications. For example, they can go from a job on a local paper to a position on a regional newspaper. They can advance from this point to a major city newspaper as a music reviewer, reporter or journalist. Or they can obtain a position at a prestigious music-oriented magazine.

Education and Training

Most jobs on newspapers require a college education. Individuals might, however, be able to obtain a position on a local newspaper without a college degree, but advancement is difficult.

There are journalism degrees offered at many colleges, although this does not have to be the specific degree obtained. A general liberal arts education is usually sufficient. If individuals are interested in this type of career, they should take a variety of journalism, communications, and writing courses.

Experience/Skills/Personality Traits

Music Journalists usually begin writing for their high school papers. During their college years, they obtain positions on their school papers or part-time for local newspapers reviewing concerts, writing music columns, and critiquing records.

The Music Journalist must have good writing skills as well as a solid knowledge of the type of music he or she is writing about. The journalist must be a responsible individual who can get things done on time. Newspapers and magazines cannot wait for someone to finish articles.

Unions/Associations

Music Journalists might belong to a number of associations or organizations depending on their interests. One of the most important is the Music Critics Association. This organization sponsors seminars, conferences, etc. for those in the industry.

Tips for Entry

1. Get experience locally reviewing music events, concerts, records, etc.

2. You may consider proposing a music column to a local newspaper or magazine that doesn't already have one.
3. Names and addresses of daily newspapers are available in the *Editor and Publisher International Year Book*. This publication is available in many libraries and larger newspaper offices. You might use this as a starting point to send out your resumés and writing samples. Pick a geographical area you want to work in and send your resumé to all the newspapers in that region.

4. There are a number of fellowships, assistantships, scholarships, and internships available in the journalism field. You might have to begin your career in an area of journalism other than music.
5. If you are in college, try to get on the college paper. Every bit of experience is important.
6. The Music Critic Association of America sponsors seminars and other interesting programs for those in the field.

APPENDIX I
DEGREE AND NONDEGREE PROGRAMS

A. COLLEGES AND UNIVERSITIES THAT OFFER MAJORS RELATED TO THE MUSIC INDUSTRY

Although possession of a college degree does not guarantee a job in the field of music, many people feel that it is in their best interest to pursue an education after high school to learn additional information, gain new skills, and make important contacts. As the music industry is so competitive, a higher education may give one person an edge over another who doesn't continue his or her schooling.

The following is a list of four-year schools that grant degrees that relate to the music indus-try. They are grouped by state.

More colleges are beginning to grant degrees in this area every year. Check the newest copy of *Lovejoy's* (found in the reference section of libraries or in guidance or counseling centers) for additions of schools giving degrees in this field.

There are also numerous two-year schools that offer study in the music industry, as well as four year-schools that have courses in the music indus-try but do not offer a degree in the field.

ALABAMA

University of North Alabama
Wesleyan Avenue
Florence, AL   35632

CALIFORNIA

**California State
   University/Dominguez Hills**
Carson, CA   90747

FLORIDA

Florida Southern College
Lakeland, FL   33802

Jacksonville University
2800 University Boulevard
Jacksonville, FL   32211

ILLINOIS

Bradley University
1501 West Bradley
Peoria, IL   61625

Columbia College
600 South Michigan
Chicago, IL   60605

Elmhurst College
190 Prospect Avenue
Elmhurst, IL   60126

Lewis University
Route 53
Romeoville, IL   60661

North Park College
5125 North Spaulding Avenue
Chicago, IL   60625

Quincy College
1831 College Avenue
Quincy, IL   62301

INDIANA

Anderson College
Anderson, IN   46012

De Pauw University
South Locust Street
Greencastle, IN   46135

Valparaiso University
East Union Street
Valparaiso, IN   46383

IOWA

Drake University
25th and University Streets
Des Moines, IA   50311

KANSAS

Southwestern College
110 North College
Winfield, KS   67156

Sterling College
North Broadway
Sterling, KS   67579

KENTUCKY

Union College
College Street
Barbourville, KY   40906

MASSACHUSETTS

**Anna Marina College for Men and
   Women**
Sunset Lane
Paxton, MA   01612

MICHIGAN

Aquinas College
1607 Robinson Road, SE
Grand Rapids, MI   49506

Madonna College
36600 Schoolcraft Road
Livonia, MI   48150

Wayne State University
Detroit, MI   48202

MINNESOTA

College of St. Catherine
2004 Randolph Avenue
St. Paul, MN   55105

St. Mary's College
Terrace Heights
Winona, MN   55987

MISSOURI

Fontbonne College
6800 Wydown Boulevard
St. Louis, MO   63105

School of the Ozarks
Point Lookout, MO   65726

NEBRASKA

Kearney State College
905 West 25th Street
Kearney, NE   68849

Peru State College
Peru, NE   68421

NEW JERSEY

Jersey City State College
2039 Kennedy Boulevard
Jersey City, NJ   07305

NEW MEXICO

Eastern New Mexico University
Station 7
Portales, NM   88130

NEW YORK

New York University
25 West 4th Street
New York, NY   10003

Syracuse University
200 Administration Building
Syracuse, NY   13210

NORTH CAROLINA

Elizabeth City State University
Parkview Drive
Elizabeth City, NC   27909

**University of North
    Carolina/Asheville**
One University Heights
Asheville, NC   28804

OHIO

**College of Mount St. Joseph on the
    Ohio**
Mount St. Joseph, OH   45051

Heidelberg College
Tiffin, OH   44883

OREGON

Warner Pacific College
2219 Southeast 68th Avenue
Portland, OR   97215

PENNSYLVANIA

Clarion University of Pennsylvania
Clarion, PA   16214

MANSFIELD UNIVERSITY
Alumni Hall
Mansfield, PA   16933

TENNESSEE

Belmont College
1900 Belmont Boulevard
Nashville, TN   37203

Memphis State University
Memphis, TN   38152

Middle Tennessee State University
Murfreesboro, TN   37132

TEXAS

Abilene Christian University
ACU Station
Box 7988
Abilene, TX   79699

VIRGINIA

**Shenandoah College and
    Conservatory of Music**
Winchester, VA   22601

WASHINGTON

Evergreen State College
Olympia, WA   98505

University of Puget Sound
1500 North Warner
Tacoma, WA   98416

Whitworth College
Spokane, WA   99251

WISCONSIN

Carroll College
100 North East Avenue
Waukesha, WI   53186

Mount Senario College
College Avenue West
Ladysmith, WI   54848

Northland College
1411 Ellis Avenue
Ashland, WI   54806

University of Wisconsin/Oshkosh
135 Dempsey Hall
Oshkosh, WI   54901

B. COLLEGES AND UNIVERSITIES THAT OFFER DEGREES IN MUSIC THERAPY

The following list contains colleges and universities that grant degrees in music therapy. The list was provided by the National Association for Music Therapy, Inc. Schools are arranged by state.

ALABAMA

University of Alabama
University, AL   34486

ARIZONA

Arizona State University
Tempe, AZ   85281

ARKANSAS

Henderson State University
Arkadelphia, AR   71923

CALIFORNIA

California State University
Long Beach, CA   90840

University of the Pacific
Stockton, CA   95211

COLORADO

Colorado State University
Fort Collins, CO   80523

DISTRICT OF COLUMBIA

Catholic University of America
Washington, DC   20064

Howard University
Washington, DC   20056

FLORIDA

Florida State University
Tallahassee, FL   32306

University of Miami
Coral Gables, FL   33124

GEORGIA

Georgia College
Milledgeville, GA   31061

University of Georgia
Athens, GA   30602

ILLINOIS

DePaul University
804 West Belden Avenue
Chicago, IL   60614

Illinois State University
Normal, IL   61761

Western Illinois University
Macomb, IL   61455

INDIANA

Indiana University
Fort Wayne, IN   46815

University of Evansville
Evansville, IN   47702

IOWA

University of Iowa
Iowa City, IA   52242

Wartburg College
Waverly, IA   50677

KANSAS

University of Kansas
Lawrence, KS   66045

LOUISIANA

Loyola University
New Orleans, LA   70118

MASSACHUSETTS

Anna Maria College
Paxton, MA   01612

MICHIGAN

Eastern Michigan University
Ypsilanti, MI   48197

Michigan State University
East Lansing, MI   48824

Wayne State University
Detroit, MI   48202

Western Michigan University
Kalamazoo, MI   49008

MINNESOTA

Augsburg College
Minneapolis, MN   55454

College of Saint Teresa
Winona, MN 55987

University of Minnesota
Minneapolis, MN   55455

MISSISSIPPI

William Carey College
Hatticsburg, MS   39401

MISSOURI

Maryville College
13550 Coway Road
St. Louis, MO   63141

University of Missouri/Kansas City
Kansas City, MO   64111

MONTANA

Eastern Montana College
Billings, MT   59101

NEW JERSEY

Montclair State College
Upper Montclair, NJ   07043

NEW MEXICO

Eastern New Mexico University
Portales, NM   88130

NEW YORK

Nazareth College of Rochester
4245 East Avenue
Rochester, NY   14610

State University College/Fredonia
Fredonia, NY   14063

State University College/New Paltz
New Paltz, NY   12561

NORTH CAROLINA

East Carolina University
Greenville, NC   27834

Owens College
Charlotte, NC   28274

OHIO

Baldwin-Wallace College
Berea, OH   44017

Case Western Reserve University
Cleveland, OH   44106

Cleveland State University
Euclid at East 24th St.
Cleveland, OH   44114

College of Wooster
Wooster, OH   44691

Oberlin College
Oberlin, OH   44074

**College of Mt. St. Joseph on the
   Ohio**
Mt. St. Joseph, OH   44051

Ohio University
Athens, OH   45701

University of Dayton
Dayton, OH   45469

OKLAHOMA

Phillips University
Enid, OK   73701

**Southwestern Oklahoma State
   University**
Weatherford, OK   73096

OREGON

Willamette University
Salem, OR   97301

PENNSYLVANIA

Combs College of Music
Philadelphia, PA   19119

College Misericordia
Dallas, PA   18612

Duquesne University
Pittsburgh, PA   15282

Hahnemann University
230 North Broad Street
Philadelphia, PA   19102

Mansfield University
Mansfield, PA   16933

Marywood College
Scranton, PA   18509

Slippery Rock State College
Slippery Rock, PA   16057

SOUTH CAROLINA

Baptist College at Charleston
Charleston, SC   29411

TENNESSEE

Tennessee Technological University
Box 5045
Cookeville, TN   38501

TEXAS

Sam Houston State University
Huntsville, TX   77341

Southern Methodist University
Dallas, TX   75275

Texas Woman's University
Denton, TX   76204

West Texas State University
Canyon, TX   79016

UTAH

Utah State University
Logan, UT   84322

VIRGINIA

Radford University
Radford, VA   24142

**Shenandoah College and
   Conservatory of Music**
Winchester, VA   22601

WISCONSIN

Alverno College
Milwaukee, WI   53215

University of Wisconsin/Eau Claire
Eau Claire, WI   54701

University of Wisconsin/Milwaukee
Milwaukee, WI   53201

University of Wisconsin/Oshkosh
Oshkosh, WI   54901

C. COLLEGES AND UNIVERSITIES THAT OFFER DEGREES IN MUSIC EDUCATION

The following list contains colleges and universities that offer degrees in music education. The schools are arranged by state.

ALABAMA

Alabama State University
915 Jackson Street
Montgomery, AL   36195

Auburn University
201 Martin Hall
Auburn University, AL   36849

Jacksonville State University
Jacksonville, AL   36265

Samford University
800 Lakeshore Drive
Birmingham, AL   35229

Troy State University
University Avenue
Troy, AL   36082

University of Montevallo
Montevallo, AL   35115

ARIZONA

Arizona State University
Tempe, AZ 85281

ARKANSAS

Arkansas State University
P.O. Box 1630
State University, AR   72467

COLORADO

Metropolitan State College
1006 11th Street
Denver, CO   80204

University of Colorado
Boulder, CO   90309

University of Northern Colorado
Greeley, CO

CONNECTICUT

University of Hartford
200 Bloomfield Avenue
West Hartford, CT   06117

**Western Connecticut State
   University**
181 White Street
Danbury, CT   06810

FLORIDA

Florida State University
Tallahasse, FL   32306

University of Florida
Gainsville, FL   32601

University of Miami
Coral Gables, FL   33124

GEORGIA

Georgia State University
University Plaza
Atlanta, GA   30303

ILLINOIS

De Paul University
Chicago, IL   60614

Easten Illinois University
Charleston, IL   61920

State University of Illinois
Normal, IL   61761

Wesleyan University of Illinois
Bloomington, IL   61701

INDIANA

Indiana University
Bloomington, IN   46401

KANSAS

Kansas State University
Manhattan, KS   66506

University of Kansas
Lawrence, KS   66045

KENTUCKY

Eastern Kentucky University
Richmond, KY   40475

University of Kentucky
Lexington, KY   40560

LOUISIANA

Louisiana Tech University
P.O. Box 5266
Tech Station
Ruston, LA   71272

MARYLAND

Towson State University
Baltimore, MD   21204

University of Maryland
College Park, MD   20742

MASSACHUSETTS

Berklee School of Music
Boston, MA   02215

Boston University
121 Bay Stale Road
Boston, MA   02215

University of Lowell
Lowell, MA   01854

MICHIGAN

Central Michigan University
100 Warriner Hall
Mount Pleasant, MI   48859

Eastern Michigan University
214 Pierce Hall
Ypsilanti, MI   48197

Michigan State University
250 Administration Building
East Lansing, MI   48824

Western Michigan University
Kalamazoo, MI   49008

MINNESOTA

Mankato State University
Mankato, MN   56001

University of Minnesota
Duluth, MN   55812

MISSISSIPPI

Mississippi State University
P.O. Drawer 5268
Mississippi State, MS   39762

NEBRASKA

University of Nebraska
Lincoln, NE   68508

NEW JERSEY

Westminster Choir College
Princeton, NJ   08540

William Paterson College
Wayne, NJ   07470

NEW YORK

Ithaca College
Ithaca, NY   14850

State University of New York/Potsdam
Potsdam, NY   13676

Syracuse University
Syracuse, NY   13210

NORTH CAROLINA

Appalachian State University
Boone, NC   28608

OHIO

Bowling Green State University
Bowling Green, OH   43403

Capital University
2199 East Main Street
Columbus, OH   43209

Kent State University
145 Rockwell Hall
Kent, OH   44242

Ohio State University
Ada, OH   45810

OKLAHOMA

Central State University
100 North University Drive
Edmond, OK   73034

PENNSYLVANIA

Clarion University of Pennsylvania
Clarion, PA   16214

Duquesne University
600 Forbes Avenue
Pittsburgh, PA   15219

Edinboro University of Pennsylvania
Edinboro, PA   16444

Indiana University of Pennsylvania
Indiana, PA   15705

Lebanon Valley College
Annville, PA   17003

Mansfield University of Pennsylvania
Mansfield, PA   16933

Millersville University of Pennsylvania
Millersville, PA   17551

SOUTH CAROLINA

Bob Jones University
Greenville, SC   29614

TEXAS

Baylor University
P.O. Box 6367
Waco, TX   76706

East Texas State University
East Texas Station
Commerce, TX   75428

UTAH

Brigham Young University
A-153 ASB
Provo, UT   84602

VIRGINIA

James Madison University
Harrisburg, VA   22807

D. WORKSHOPS, SEMINARS, ETC.

The following is a listing of workshops, seminars, courses, and symposiums and the subjects that they cover. This is by no means a complete listing. Many associations, schools, and companies offer other workshops. As subject matter changes frequently, a good number of the people running these workshops and seminars did not wish to have their programs listed. You may want to contact associations dealing with the employment area in which you are interested to obtain more information on programs not listed here.

This listing is for your information. It is offered to help you find programs of interest to you. The author does not endorse any one program over another and is not responsible for subject content.

American Society of Composers and Publishers (ASCAP)
1 Lincoln Plaza
New York, NY   10023
212-595-3050
ASCAP offers a variety of workshops for songwriters.

American Symphony Orchestra League (ASOL)
633 E Street N.W.
Washington, DC   20004
202-628-0099
The ASOL offers regional workshops, seminars and symposiums in every phase of orchestra business and craft including orchestra management, marketing, fund-raising, and conducting. The ASOL holds an annual conference that presents many informative programs.

Dick Grove School of Music
12754 Ventura Boulevard
Studio City, CA   91604
213-985-0905
800-423-2283
The Dick Grove School of Music has courses in lyric writing and composition as well as a variety of workshops and seminars for musicians.

NACA (National Association for Campus Activities)
P.O. Box 6828
Columbia, SC   29260
803-782-7121
NACA offers workshops and educational sessions of interest to those seeking careers in the music business at their annual conventions. They also hold a variety of workshops on concert management and promotion in various locations throughout the country.

National Association of Music Merchants
5040 Avenida Encinas
Carlsbad, CA   92008
619-438-8001
The NAMM offers a variety of seminars at their conventions and expositions. Programs change every year but always revolve around better business methods, selling, etc.

National Association of Recording Merchandisers (NARM)
1008-F Astoria Boulevard
Cherry Hill, NJ   08003
609-424-7404
NARM holds an annual convention with seminars on various subjects.

National Music Publishers Association (NMPA)
205 East 42nd Street
New York, NY   10017
212-370-5330
The NMPA holds periodic forums for people involved in music publishing. Forums are put together by the Los Angeles and Nashville chapters as well as the New York chapter.

Piano Technicians Guild
9140 Ward Parkway
Kansas City, MO   64114
816-444-3500
The Piano Technicians Guild holds an annual convention that features three and a half days of technical sessions. Seminars of interest to piano technicians are also offered throughout the year by the Guild's various chapters.

Practising Law Institute
810 Seventh Avenue
New York, NY   10019
212-765-5700
The Practising Law Institute gives programs throughout the year on a variety of subjects of interest to attorneys and management. Programs include such subjects as "Counseling Clients in the Entertainment Industry."

Songwriter Seminars and Workshops
928 Broadway
New York, NY   10010
212-505-7332
This group gives workshops for songwriters.

Songwriting Workshop and the Business of Music
Rustron Music Productions
200 Westmoreland Avenue
White Plains, NY   10606
914-946-1689
Workshops here encompass songwriting and the music industry.

The Recording Workshop
455 Massieville Road
Chillicothe, OH   45601
800-848-9900
614-663-2544
The Recording Workshop gives seminars and workshops in music video production, recording engineering, and music production.

The Songwriter Advocate (TSA)
47 Maplehurst Road
Rochester, NY   14617
716-266-0679
TSA offers courses, workshops, etc. in songwriting, theory,
copyright, publishing, and evaluation of songs.

The Songwriters Guild
276 Fifth Avenue
N.Y., NY   10001
212-686-6820

The Songwriters Guild offers workshops in both the business
and the craft of songwriting. These are held throughout the
year. The Guild has an "Ask A Pro" workshop, a song
critique workshop, and courses in all phases of songwriting.
Courses and workshops are held in New York, Nashville,
and Los Angeles.

E. SCHOLARSHIPS AND FELLOWSHIPS

The following is a listing of selected scholarships
and fellowships. Use this list as a beginning. There
are many, many more available.

American Symphony Orchestra League (ASOL)
633 E Street N.W.
Washington, DC   20004
202-628-0099
The ASOL holds an orchestra management fellowship
program annually.

NACA (National Association For Campus Activities)
P.O. Box 6828
Columbia, SC   29260
803-782-7121
NACA has a newly developed educational foundation which
raises funds for scholarships and grants in various areas of
the music industry.

National Association of Music Merchants (NAMM)
5040 Avenida Encinas
Carlsbad, CA   92008
619-438-8001

The NAMM offers $1,000 scholarship grants to schools in the
U.S. that meet their curriculum eligibility. Money is
disbursed to worthy students in these schools.

National Association of Recording Merchandisers
10008-F Astoria Boulevard
Cherry Hills, NJ   08003
609-424-7404
NARM awards a variety of scholarships each year.

National Federation of Music Clubs
1336 N. Delaware Street
Indianapolis, IN   46202
317-638-4003
The National Federation of Music Clubs offers scholarships
and awards in various fields.

APPENDIX II
UNIONS AND ASSOCIATIONS

The following is a list of the unions and
associations discussed in the book. There are
numerous other associations listed here as well that
might be useful to you.

The names, addresses, and phone numbers are
included so that you can get in touch with any of
the unions or associations for information you
might want.

The national offices of the unions will be able to
get you the phone number and/or address of the
closest local office.

Academy of Country Music (ACM)
6255 Sunset Boulevard
Suite 915
Hollywood, CA   90028
213–462–2351

**Acoustical Society of America
   (ASA)**
335 E. 45th Street
New York, NY
212–661–9404

Actors Equity Association (Equity)
165 West 46th Street
New York, NY   10036
212–869–8530

American Advertising Federation (AAF)
1400 K Street N.W.
Suite 1000
Washington, DC   20005
202–898–0089

American Association for Music Therapy (AAMT)
211 E. 43rd Street
Suite 1601
New York, NY   10017
212–867–4480

American Bar Association (ABA)
1155 E. 60th Street
Chicago, IL   60637
312–947–4000

American Choral Directors Association (ACDA)
P.O. Box 5310
Lawton, OK   73504
405–355–8161

American Composers Alliance
170 West 74th Street
New York, NY   10023
212–362–8900

American Conference of Cantors (ACC)
838 Fifth Avenue
New York, NY   10021
212–249–0100

American Federation of Musicians (AFM)
1500 Broadway
New York, NY   10036
212–869–1330

American Federation of Teachers (AFT)
11 Dupont Circle N.W.
Washington, DC   20036
202–797–4400

American Federation of Television and Radio Artists (AFTRA)
1350 Avenue of the Americas
New York, NY   10019
212–265–7700

American Guild of Authors and Composers (AGAC)
(see **The Songwriters Guild**)

American Guild of Music (AGM)
Box 3
Downers Grove, IL   60515
312–968–0173

American Guild of Music Artists (AGMA)
1841 Broadway
New York, NY   10023
212–265–3687

American Guild of Organists (AGO)
815 2nd Avenue
Suite 318
New York, NY   10017
212–687–9188

American Guild of Variety Artists (AGVA)
184 Fifth Avenue
New York, NY   10010
212–675–1003

American Institute of Certified Public Accountants (AICPA)
1211 Avenue of the Americas
New York, NY   10019
212–575–6200

American Library Association (ALA)
50 E. Huron Street
Chicago, IL   60611
312–944–6780

American Marketing Association (AMA)
250 S. Wacker Drive
Suite 200
Chicago, IL   60606
312–648–0536

American Music Conference (AMC)
1000 Skokie Boulevard
Wilmette, IL   60091
312–251–1600

American Musicological Society
201 South 34th Street
Philadelphia, PA   19104
215–898–8698

American Society of Composers and Publishers (ASCAP)
1 Lincoln Plaza
New York, NY   10023
212–595–3050

American Society of Music Arrangers (ASMA)
P.O. Box 11
Hollywood, CA   90078
213–462–2161

American Society of Music Copyists (ASMC)
Box 41
Radio City Station
New York, NY   10101
212–586–2140

American Symphony Orchestra League (ASOL)
633 E Street N.W.
Washington, DC   20004
202–628–0099

Associated Councils of the Arts
570 7th Avenue
New York, NY   10018
212–345–6655

Association of Theatrical Press Agents and Managers (ATPAM)
165 W. 46th Street
New York, NY   10036
212–719–3666

Black Music Association (BMA)
1500 Locust Street
Philadelphia, PA   19102
215–545–8600

B'nai B'rith Vocational Service
1640 Rhode Island Avenue N.W.
Washington, DC   20036
202–857–6600

Broadcast Music, Inc. (BMI)
320 W. 57th Street
New York, NY   10019
212–586–2000

Cantors Association of America and Canada
3 W. 16th Street
New York, NY   10011
212–675–6601

Cantors Assembly of America
150 Fifth Avenue
New York, NY   10011
212–691–8020

The Choristers Guild
2834 W. Kingsley Drive
Garland, TX   75041
214–271–1521

College Band Directors National Association (CBDNA)
c/o Richard L. Floyd
Box 8028
University of Texas
Austin, TX   78712

College Music Society
Regent Box 44
University of Colorado
Boulder, CO   80309
303-492-5049

**Conference of Personal Managers
(National)**
c/o Gerald Purcell
964 Second Avenue
New York, NY   10022
212-421-2670

Country Music Association (CMA)
P.O. Box 22299
Seven Music Circle N.
Nashville, TN   37202
615-244-2840

**Electronic Industry Association
(EIA)**
2001 Eye Street N.W.
Washington, DC   20006
202-457-4900

Gospel Music Association (GMA)
38 Music Square W.
Nashville, TN   37203
614-242-0303

**Guitar and Accessories Music
Marketing Association
(GAMMA)**
150 E. Huron
8th Floor
Chicago, IL   60611
312-266-7200

**Institute of Certified Financial
Planners (ICFP)**
3443 S. Galena
Suite 190
Denver, CO   80231
303-751-7600

**International Association of
Financial Planning (IAFP)**
P.O. Box 57051
Washington, DC   20037
202-245-7565

Institute of Internal Auditors (IIA)
249 Maitland Avenue
Altomonte Springs, FL   32701
305-830-7600

**International Alliance of Theatrical
Stage Employees (IATSE)**
1515 Broadway
Suite 601
New York, NY   10036
212-730-1770

**International Association of
Auditorium Managers (IAAM)**
500 N. Michigan Avenue
Suite 1400
Chicago, IL   60611
312-661-1700

Music Critics Association (MCA)
6201 Tuckerman Lane
Rockville, MD   20852
301-530-9527

**Music Educators National
Conference (MENC)**
1902 Association Drive
Reston, VA   22091
703-860-4000

**Music Industry Educators
Association (MIEA)**
c/o Paul Kelly
190 Prospect
Elmhurst College
Elmhurst, IL   60126
312-297-4100

Music Library Association (MLA)
P.O. Box 487
Canton, MA   02021
617-828-8450

**Music Publishers Association
(MPA)**
130 W. 57th Street
New York, NY   10019
212-582-1122

**Music Teachers National
Association Inc.**
2113 Carew Tower
Cincinnati, OH   45202
513-421-1420

**National Academy of Recording
Arts and Sciences (NARAS)**
157 W. 57th Street
New York, NY   10019
212-245-5440

**National Association for Campus
Activities (NACA)**
P.O. Box 11489
Columbus, SC   29211
803-799-0768

**National Association for Music
Theaters**
John F. Kennedy Center
Washington, DC   20566
202-965-2800

**National Association for Music
Therapy, Inc. (NAMT)**
1133 15th Street N.W.
Washington, DC   20005
202-429-9700

**National Association of Accountants
(NAA)**
919 3rd Avenue
New York, NY   10022
212-754-9700

**National Association of Broadcast
Employees and Technicians
(NABET)**
7101 Wisconsin Avenue
Suite 800
Bethesda, MD   20814
301-657-8420

**National Association of
Broadcasters (NAB)**
1771 N Street N.W.
Washington, DC   20036
202-293-3500

**National Association of College
Wind and Percussion Instructors
(NACWPI)**
Division of Fine Arts
Northeast Missouri State University
Kirksville, MO   63501
816-785-4442

**National Association of Music
Merchants (NAMM)**
5140 Avenida Encinas
Carlsbad, CA   92008
619-438-8001

**National Association of Pastoral
Musicians**
225 Sheridan St. N.W.
Washington, DC   20011
202-753-5800

**National Association of Recording
Merchandisers (NARM)**
1008-F Astoria Boulevard
Cherry Hill, NJ   08003
609-424-7404

**National Association of Schools of
Music (NASM)**
11250 Roger Bacon Drive
No. 5
Reston, VA   22090
703-434-0700

National Association of State Supervisors of Music (NASSM)
c/o George R. Neaderhiser
Kansas Department of Education
120 E. Tenth Street
Topeka, KS 66612
913-296-4932

National Council of Accoustical Consultants
66 Morris Avenue
Springfield, NJ 07081
201-379-1100

National Entertainment and Campus Activities Association (NECCA)
(see **National Association for Campus Activities**)

National Entertainment Conference (NEC)
(see **National Association for Campus Activities**)

National Federation of Music Clubs
1336 N. Delaware Street
Indianapolis, IN 46202
317-683-4003

National Music Publishers Association (NMPA)
205 E. 42nd Street
New York, NY 10017
212-370-5330

National Piano Manufacturers Association (NPMA)
130 W. 57th Street
New York, NY 10019
212-582-1122

National Society of Public Accountants (NSPA)
1010 N. Fairfax Street
Alexandria, VA 22314
703-549-6400

National Songwriters Association International
803 18th Avenue S.
Nashville, TN 37203
615-321-5004

National Orchestra Association (NOA)
111 W. 57th Street
Suite 1400
New York, NY 10019
212-247-1228

Piano Technicians Guild
9140 Ward Parkway
Kansas City, MO 64114
816-444-3500

Practising Law Institute (PLI)
810 Seventh Avenue
New York, NY 10019
212-765-5700

Professional Secretaries International
301 E. Armour Boulevard
Kansas City, MO 64111
816-531-7010

Organization of Women in Music
229 Shupley Street
San Francisco, CA 94107

Public Relations Society of America (PRSA)
845 Third Avenue
New York, NY
212-826-1750

Recording Industry Association of America Inc. (RIAA)
888 Seventh Avenue
New York, NY 10106
212-765-4330

Recording Institute of America (RIA)
15 Columbus Circle
New York, NY 10023
212-582-0400

San Francisco Bay Lawyers Association
Room 255
Building C
Fort Mason
San Francisco, CA 94123
415-775-7200

Screen Actors Guild (SAG)
3629 Cahuenga Boulevard W.
Los Angeles, CA 90068
213-876-3030

SESAC, Inc.
10 Columbus Circle
New York, NY 10019
212-586-3450

Society of Professional Audio Recording Studios (SPARS)
P.O. Box 11333
Beverly Hills, CA 90213
213-651-4944

The Songwriters Guild (formerly American Guild of Authors and Composers)
276 Fifth Avenue
New York, NY 10001
212-686-6820

Special Libraries Association (SLA)
235 Park Avenue South
New York, NY 10003
212-477-9250

Touring Entertainment Industry Association (TEIA)
1024 Currie Street
Fort Worth, TX 76107
817-870-9819

Volunteer Lawyers for the Arts
Suite 711
1560 Broadway
New York, NY 10036
212-576-1150

APPENDIX III
BIBLIOGRAPHY

A. BOOKS

There are thousands of books written on all aspects of music. The books listed below are separated into general categories. The subject matter in many of the books overlaps other categories.

These books can be found in bookstores or libraries. If your local library does not have the books you want to read, you might want to ask your librarian to order them for you through the interlibrary loan system.

This list is meant as a beginning. For other books that might interest you, look in the music section of bookstores. You can also check *Books In Print* (found in the reference section of libraries).

RECORDING AND THE RECORD BUSINESS

Davis, Clive. *Clive: Inside the Record Business.* Morrow: New York, 1975.

Gere, Don. *The Record Producers Handbook.* Acrobat Books: Los Angeles, 1978.

Gillett, Charles. *Making Tracks.* E.P. Dutton & Co.: New York, 1974.

Hirsch, Paul. *The Structure of the Popular Music Industry: The Filtering Process by Which Records are Pre-Selected for Consumption.* University of Michigan, Institute for Social Research: Ann Arbor, 1969.

Jahn, Mike. *How to Make a Hit Record.* Bradbury Press: Scarsdale, NY, 1976.

Lambert, Dennis, and Ronald Zalkind. *Producing Hit Records.* Schirmer Books: New York, 1980.

Sadler, Barry. *Everything You Want to Know About the Record Industry.* Aurora Publications: Nashville, 1978.

Stokes, Geoffrey. *Star-Making Machinery.* Bobbs-Merrill: New York, 1976.

Sward Rapaport, Diane. *How to Make and Sell Your Own Records.* Quick Fox: New York, 1979.

Woram, John. *The Recording Studio Handbook.* Sagamore Press: Plainview, NY, 1979.

RADIO

Hall, Claude and Barbara. *This Business of Radio Programming.* Billboard Publications: New York, 1977.

Lujack, Larry. *Super Jock.* Henry Regnery: Chicago, 1975.

Passman, Arnold. *The Deejays.* Macmillan: New York, 1971.

Quaal, Ward L., and James A. Brown. *Broadcast Management.* Hastings House: New York, 1976.

ROAD

Burton, Gary. *A Musician's Guide to the Road.* Billboard Books: New York, 1981.

RETAILING/WHOLESALING

Starting and Managing a Small Retail Music Store. U.S. Government Printing Office: Washington, DC, 1970.

BUSINESS: PUBLISHING

Feist, Leonard. *Introduction to Popular Music Publishing in America.* National Music Publishers Association: New York, 1980.

Warner, Jay. *How to Have Your Hit Song Published.* Music Bank Publications: Murphys, CA, 1978.

BUSINESS: LAW

Biede, Donald. *Legal Business Aspects of the Music Industry.* Practicing Law Institute: New York, 1980.

Gersohn, Fredric B. *Counseling Clients in the Performing Arts.* Practicing Law Institute: New York, 1975.

INSTRUMENT REPAIR AND DESIGN

Reblitz, Arthur. *Piano Servicing, Tuning and Rebuilding.* Vestal: Vestal, NY, 1976.

PUBLICITY AND PROMOTION

Greene, Bob. *Billion Dollar Baby*. Atheneum: New York, 1974.

Hirsch, Abby, and Dale Burg. *The Great Carmen Miranda Look-Alike Contest and Other Bold Faced Lies*. St. Martin's Press: New York, 1974.

Rosenman, Joel, et al. *Young Men With Unlimited Capital*. Harcourt Brace Jovanovich: New York, 1974.

Stein, Howard, and Ronald Zalkind. *Promoting Rock Concerts*. Schirmer Books: New York, 1979.

SYMPHONY ORCHESTRAS

The Gold Book. The American Symphony Orchestra League: Washington, DC (annual).

Baler Carr, Janet. *Evening at Symphony: A Portrait of the Boston Symphony Orchestra*. Houghton Mifflin: Boston, 1977.

Reiss, Alvin H. *The Arts Management Handbook*. Law-Arts Publishers: Santa Monica, CA, 1974.

Seltzer, George. *The Professional Symphony Orchestra in the U.S.* Scarecrow Press: Metuchen, NJ, 1975.

EDUCATION: MUSIC THERAPY

Guston, Thayer E. *Music in Therapy*. Macmillan: New York, 1968.

Michel, Donald E. *Music Therapy: An Introduction to Therapy and Special Education Through Music*. C.C. Thomas: Springfield, IL, 1976.

Priestly, Mary. *Music Therapy in Action*. St. Martin's Press: New York, 1975.

EDUCATION: MUSIC LIBRARIAN

Redfern, Brian. *Organizing Music in Libraries*. Shoestring Press: Hamden, CT, 1978.

TALENT AND WRITING: MUSICIANS

Faulkner, Robert R. *Hollywood Studio Musicians*. Aldine-Atherton: Chicago, 1971.

Lawrence, Sharon. *So You Want to Be a Rock and Roll Star*. Dell Publishing: New York, 1976.

Lieber, Leslie. *How to Form a Rock Group*. Grosset & Dunlap: New York, 1968.

McDonald, Gerald. *Training and Careers for the Professional Musician*. Grebsham Publishing: England, 1979.

TALENT AND WRITING: SONGWRITING

Boyce, Tommy, and Melvin Powers. *How to Write a Hit Song and Sell It*. Wilshire Publishing: North Hollywood, CA, 1974.

Brohough, William. *Songwriter's Market*. Writers Digest: Cincinnati, annual.

Hall, Tom T. *How I Write Songs: Why You Can*. Chappell Music: New York, 1976.

Pincus, Lee. *The Songwriters Success Manual*. Music Press: New York, 1978.

Rachlin, Harvey. *The Songwriters Handbook*. Funk & Wagnalls: New York, 1977.

Whitfield, Jane. *Songwriters Rhyming Dictionary*. Wilshire Book Company: North Hollywood, CA, 1974.

CHURCH MUSIC

Bauman, William A. *The Ministry of Music: A Guide for the Practicing Church Musician*. Liturgical Press: Collegeville, MN, 1975.

Mendelson, Solomon, and Samuel Rosenbaum. *Careers in the Cantorate*. B'nai B'rith Vocational Service: Washington, DC, 1969.

Rhys, Stephen, and King Palmer. *ABC of Church Music*. Crescendo Books: New York, 1969.

Thayer, Lynn W. *The Church Music Handbook*. Zondervan Publishing House: Grand Rapids, MI, 1971.

JOURNALISM

Flippo, Chet. *Rock Journalist and Rolling Stone*. M.A. Thesis, University of Texas at Austin: Austin, 1974.

THE MUSIC INDUSTRY

Chapple, Steve and Rebee Garofalo. *Rock 'N' Roll is Here to Pay*. Nelson Hall: Chicago, 1977.

Denisoff, R. Serge. *Solid Gold—The Popular Recording Industry*. Transaction Books: New Brunswick, NJ, 1975.

Rachlin, Harvey. *The Encyclopedia of the Music Business*. Harper & Row: New York, 1981.

Shemel, Sidney and M. William Krasilovsky. *More About This Business of Music*. Billboard Publications: New York, 1982.

Shemel, Sidney and M. William Krasilovsky. *This Business of Music*. Billboard Publications: New York, 1971.

Spitz, Robert Stephen. *The Making of a Superstar.* Anchor Press/Doubleday: New York, 1978.

Taubman, Jospeh. *In Tune With the Music Business.* Law Arts Publishing: Santa Monica, 1980.

Zalkind, Ronald. *Getting Ahead in the Music Business.* Schirmer Books: New York, 1979.

GENERAL

Belz, Carl. *The Story of Rock.* Oxford University Press: New York, 1972.

Burt, Jessie, and Bob Ferguson. *So You Want to Be in Music.* Abingdon Press: Nashville, 1970.

Csida, Joseph. *The Music Record Career Handbook.* Billboard Books: New York, 1975.

Dagnal, Cynthia. *Starting Your Own Rock Band.* Contemporary Books, Inc.: Chicago, 1983.

Dilello, Richard. *The Longest Cocktail Party: A Personal History of Apple.* Playboy: New York, 1972.

Fong-Torres, Ben. *The Rolling Stone Rock 'N' Roll Reader.* Bantam Books: New York, 1974.

Gelly, David. *The Facts About a Rock Group—Featuring Wings.* Harmony Books: New York, 1976.

Greenfield, Robert. *S.T.P. A Journal Through America With the Rolling Stones.* E.P. Dutton: New York, 1974.

Harris, Herby, and Lucient Farrar. *How to Make Money in Music.* Arco: New York, 1978.

Logan, Nick, and Bob Woffinden. *The Illustrated Encyclopedia of Rock.* Harmony Books: New York, 1977.

Monaco, Bob, and James Riordan. *The Platinum Rainbow.* Swordsman Press: Sherman Oaks, 1981.

Rappoport, Victor D. *Making It in Music.* Prentice-Hall, Inc.: Englewood Cliffs, NJ, 1979.

B. PERIODICALS

Magazines, newspapers, membership bulletins, and newsletters may be helpful for finding information about a specific job category or finding a job in a specific field.

As with the books in the previous section, this list should serve as a beginning. There are many periodicals that are not listed because of space limitations. Periodicals also tend to come and go. Look in your local library or in newspaper/magazine shops for other periodicals that might interest you.

The periodicals in this section are listed in general categories. Subject matter may overlap. Check all categories relevant to the type of career you seek.

THE TRADES

Billboard
1500 Broadway
New York, NY   10036

Cashbox
6363 Sunset Boulevard
Hollywood, CA   90028

Daily Variety
1400 North Cahuenga Boulevard
Los Angeles, CA   90028

Hollywood Reporter
6715 Sunset Boulevard
Hollywood, CA   90028

Variety
154 West 46th Street
New York, NY   10036

RECORDING AND THE RECORD INDUSTRY

NARAS Journal
157 West 57th Street
New York, NY   10019

RADIO

The Album Network
9000 Sunset Boulevard
Hollywood, CA   90069

Broadcasting
1735 De Salle Street
Washington, DC   20018

The Confidential Report
9000 Sunset Boulevard
Hollywood, CA   90069

The Friday Morning Quarterback
Cherry Hill Plaza
1415 East Marlton Pike
Suite 505
Cherry Hill, NJ   08034

The Gavin Report
One Embarcadero Center
Suite 220
San Francisco, CA   94111

Goodphone Weekly
4565 Sherman Oaks Avenue
Sherman Oaks, CA   91403

International Radio Report
7011 Sunset Boulevard
Los Angeles, CA   90028

Music Programmers Guide
233 East Erie Street
Chicago, IL   60611

New on the Charts
1501 Broadway
New York, NY   10036

Radio and Records
1930 Century Park West
Los Angeles, CA   90067

Radio Music Report
6445 Powers Ferry Road
Suite 210
Atlanta, GA   30339

Walrus
Box 35
Narberth, PA   19072

ON THE ROAD

Performance Magazine
1020 Currie Street
Forth Worth, TX   76107

CLUBS AND ARENAS

Amusement Business
Box 24970
Nashville, TN   37202

Music Clubs Magazine
600 South Michigan Avenue
Chicago, IL   60605

RETAILING AND WHOLESALING

Audio Magazine
401 North Broad Street
Philadelphia, PA   19107

High Fidelity
130 East 59th Street
New York, NY   10022

Musical Merchandise Review
370 Lexington Avenue
New York, NY   10017

Music Retailer
210 Boylston Street
Chestnut Hill, MA   02167

Sound Arts Merchandising Journal
14 Vanderventer Avenue
Port Washington, NY   11050

Stereo Review
1 Park Avenue
New York, NY   10016

Upbeat
222 West Adams Street
Chicago, IL   60606

REPAIR AND RESTORATION

Harpsichord
P.O. Box 4323
Denver, CO   80204

Piano Technicians Journal
Box 1813
Seattle, WA   98111

PUBLIC RELATIONS AND PUBLICITY

Public Relations Journal
Public Relations Society of America
   (PRSA)
845 Third Avenue
New York, NY   10022

ORCHESTRAS

Foundation News
888 Seventh Avenue
New York, NY   10019

Orchestra News
1729 Superior Avenue
Cleveland, OH   44114

Symphony News
American Symphony Orchestra
   League (ASOL)
633 E Street N.W.
Washington, DC   20004

EDUCATION

American Music Teacher
408 Carew Tower
Cincinnati, OH   45202

Journal of Music Therapy
1133 15th Street N.W.
Washington, DC   20005

Marching Band Director
725 University Drive
Arlington Heights, IL   60004

Music Educators Journal
Music Educators National
   Conference
1902 Association Drive
Reston, VA   22091

**National Association of College
   Wind and Percussion Instructors
   Journal**
1902 Association Drive
Reston, VA   22091

**School Musician, Director and
   Teacher**
4049 West Peterson Avenue
Chicago, IL   60646

School Music News
P.O. Box 2620
Schenectady, NY   12309

TALENT AND WRITING

ASCAP in Action
One Lincoln Plaza
New York, NY   10023

BMI: The Many Worlds of Music
589 Fifth Avenue
New York, NY   10017

The Composer
317 Nobel Drive
Santa Cruz, CA   95060

Contemporary Keyboard
20605 Lazaneo
Cupertino, CA   95014

Country Music
475 Park Avenue South
New York, NY   10016

Down Beat
222 West Adams Street
Chicago, IL   60606

Frets
20605 Lazaneo Drive
Cupertino, CA   95014

Guitar Player Magazine
20605 Lazaneo Drive
Cupertino, CA   95014

Guitar Review
409 E. 50th Street
New York, NY   10022

Hit Parader
Charlton Publications, Inc.
Charlton Building
Derby, CT   06418

International Musician
1500 Broadway
New York, NY   10036

Keyboard World Magazine
P.O. Box 4399
Downer, CA   90241

Songplugger
P.O. Box 3839
Hollywood, CA   90038

Songwriter
P.O. Box 3510
Hollywood, CA   90028

Songwriter's Review
1697 Broadway
New York, NY   10019

CHURCH MUSIC

The American Organist
630 Fifth Avenue
New York, NY   10020

Church Music
Concordia Teachers College
7500 Augusta Street
River Forest, IL   60305

Church Musician
127 Ninth Avenue North
Nashville, TN   37203

Journal of Church Music
2900 Queen Lane
Philadelphia, PA   19129

Modern Liturgy
7291 Coronado Drive
San Jose, CA   95129

Music Ministry
201 Eighth Avenue South
Nashville, TN   37203

Pastoral Music
1029 Vermont Avenue N.W.
Washington, DC   20005

Sacred Music
Route 2
Box 1
Irving, TX   75061

MISCELLANEOUS MUSIC MAGAZINES

Circus
115 East 57th Street
New York, NY   10022

Crawdaddy
72 Fifth Avenue
New York, NY   10011

Creem
187 South Woodward Avenue
Birmingham, MI   48011

Goodtimes
230 Arlington Circle
East Hills, NY   11548

Rolling Stone
745 Fifth Avenue
New York, NY   10022

APPENDIX IV
RECORD COMPANIES

The following is a list of record companies. As you will note, most of the companies are located in the music capitals of the country. Whenever possible, branch offices have been included.

A & M Records, Inc.
1416 North La Brea
Hollywood, CA   90028
213–469–2411

595 Madison Avenue
New York, NY   10022
212–826–0477

A & M Records of Canada, Ltd.
939 Warden Avenue
Scarborough, Ontario,
    Canada M1L4C5
416–725–7191

Arista Records, Inc.
6 West 57th Street
New York, NY
212–489–7400

1888 Century Park East
Los Angeles, CA   90067
213–553–1777

ATCO Records
75 Rockefeller Plaza
New York, NY   10019
212–489–0955

9229 Sunset Boulevard
Los Angeles, CA   90069
213–273–3763

Atlantic Recording Corporation
9229 Sunset Boulevard
Los Angeles, CA   90069
213–278–9230

75 Rockefeller Plaza
New York, NY   10019
212–484–6000

Backstreet Records (Division of MCA Records)
70 Universal City Plaza
Universal City, CA   90608
213–508–4500

Bearsville Records
Box 135
Bearsville, NY   12409
914–679–7303

Buddah Records, Inc.
1790 Broadway
New York, NY   10019
212–582–6900

Bulldog Records
50 East 42nd Street
New York, NY   10017
212–687–2299

Capitol Records, Inc.
1370 Avenue of the Americas
New York, NY   10019
212–757–7470

1750 North Vine Street
Hollywood, CA   90028
213–462–6252

29 Music Square East
Nashville, TN   32703
615–244–1842

CBS Records
1801 Century Park West
Los Angeles, CA   90067
213–556–4700

51 West 52nd Street
New York, NY   10019
212–975–4321

49 Music Square West
Nashville, TN   37203
615–259–4321

Casablanca Records
8255 Sunset Boulevard
Los Angeles, CA   90046
213–650–8300

137 West 55th Street
New York, NY   10019
212–397–0660

Chrysalis Records
9255 Sunset Boulevard
Los Angeles, CA   90069
213–550–0171

115 East 57th Street
New York, NY   10022
212–935–8750

Columbia Records
51 West 52nd Street
New York, NY   10019
212–975–4321

1901 Century Park West
Los Angeles, CA   90067
213–556–4700

49 Music Square West
Nashville, TN   37203
615–259–4321

De-Lite Records
1733 Broadway
New York, NY   10019
212–757–6770

Electra/Asylum Records
962 North La Cienega Boulevard
Los Angeles, CA   90069
213–655–8280

1216 17th Avenue South
Nashville, TN   37212
615–320–7525

665 Fifth Avenue
New York, NY   10022
212–355–7610

EMI-Americana Records
1370 Avenue of the Americas
New York, NY   10019
212–757–7450

6920 Sunset Boulevard
Los Angeles, CA   90028
213–461–9141

29 Music Square East
Nashville, TN   37203
615–329–9356

Epic Records
51 West 52nd Street
New York, NY   10019
212–975–4321

1801 Century Park West
Los Angeles, CA   90067
213–556–4700

49 Music Square West
Nashville, TN   37203
615–329–4321

Geffen Records
9130 Sunset Boulevard
Los Angeles, CA   90069

Island Records, Inc.
444 Madison Avenue
New York, NY   10022
212–355–6550

K-Tel Int'l Inc.
11311 K-Tel Drive
Minnetonka, MN   55343
612–932–4000

Don Kirshner Entertainment
1370 Avenue of the Americas
New York, NY   10019
212–489–0440

MCA Records
10 East 53rd Street
New York, NY   10022
212–888–9700

27 Music Square East
Nashville, TN   37203
615–244–8944

70 Universal City Plaza
Universal City, CA   90608
213–985–4321

Motown Records Group
6255 Sunset Boulevard
Los Angeles, CA   90028
213–468–3500

Philadelphia International Records
309 South Broad Street
Philadelphia, PA   19107
215–985–0900

Polydor Records, Inc.
810 Seventh Avenue
New York, NY   10019
212–399–7100

6255 Sunset Boulevard
Los Angeles, CA   90028
213–466–9574

Prelude Records
200 West 57th Street
New York, NY   10019

RCA Records
1133 Avenue of the Americas
New York, NY   10036
212–598–5900

6363 Sunset Boulevard
Los Angeles, CA   90028
213–468–4000

30 Music Square West
Nashville, TN   37203
615–244–9880

RSO Records, Inc.
1775 Broadway
New York, NY   10019
212–975–0700

8335 Sunset Boulevard
Los Angeles, CA   90069
213–650–1234

Rolling Stones Records
c/o Atlantic Records
75 Rockefeller Plaza
New York, NY   10019
212–484–6000

Sire Records
3 East 54th Street
New York, NY   10022
212-832-0950

Solar Records
6255 Sunset Boulevard
Hollywood, CA   90028
213-467-6527

Phil Spector International
P.O. Box 69529
Los Angeles, CA   90069
213-846-9900

Spring Records
161 West 54th Street
New York, NY   10019
212-581-5398

Sun International Corp.
3106 Belmont Boulevard
Nashville, TN   37212
615-385-1960

Tamala Records
6255 Sunset Boulevard
Los Angeles, CA   90028
213-468-3500

Twentieth Century Fox Records
8544 Sunset Boulevard
Los Angeles, CA   90059
213-657-8310

United Artists Records
6920 Sunset Boulevard
Los Angeles, CA   90028
213-461-9141

1370 Avenue of the Americas
New York, NY   10019
212-757-7470

50 Music Square West
Nashville, TN   37203
615-329-9356

Warner Brothers Records, Inc.
1706 Grand
Nashville, TN   37203
615-256-4282

3 East 54th Street
New York, NY   10022
212-832-0600

3300 Warner Boulevard
Burbank, CA   91510
213-846-9090

APPENDIX V
BOOKING AGENCIES

The following is a listing of booking agencies found around the country. Although most of the agencies listed are major companies, we have also included some of the regional agencies that may be of value to you.

Agency for the Performing Arts
  (APA)
888 Seventh Avenue
New York, NY   10106
212-582-1500

9000 Sunset Boulevard
Los Angeles, CA   90069
213-273-0744

Willard Alexander, Inc.
660 Madison Avenue
New York, NY   10021
212-751-7070

333 North Michigan Avenue
Chicago, IL   60610
312-236-2460

American Talent International Ltd.
888 Seventh Avenue
New York, NY   10106
212-977-2300

Associated Booking Corporation
  (ABC)
1995 Broadway
New York, NY   10023
212-874-2400

3511 Hall Street
Dallas, TX   75219
214-874-2400

2700 North River Road
Des Plaines, IL   60018
312-269-0930

Banner Talent Associates, Inc.
1650 Broadway
New York, NY   10019
212-581-6900

Dick Blake International, Inc.
P.O. Box 24727
Nashville, TN   37202
615-244-9550

Board Brothers Talent Agency, Inc.
1508 16th Avenue South
Nashville. TN   37212
615-386-8700

Billy Deaton Talent Agency
1300 Division Street
Nashville, TN   37203
615-244-4259

Diversified Management Agency
  (DMA)
17650 W. Twelve Mile Road
Southfield, MI   48076
313-559-2600

Empire Agency, Inc.
P.O. Box 514
Marietta, GA   30061
404-427-1200

Frontier Booking
1776 Broadway
New York, NY   10019
212-246-1505

**The Good Music Agency, Inc.
   (GMA)**
P.O. Box 437
Excelsior, MI   55331
612–474–2581

The Jim Halsey Co.
445 Park Avenue
New York, NY   10022
212–605–2824

3225 South Norwood
Tulsa, OK   74135
918–663–3883

9000 Sunset Boulevard
Hollywood CA   90069
213–278–3397

2 Music Circle South
Nashville, TN   37203
615–242–0902

Hit Attractions, Inc.
P.O. Box 35585
Charlotte, NC   28235
704–372–3955

**International Creative
   Management, Inc. (ICM)**
40 West 57th Street
New York, NY   10019
212–556–5600

8899 Beverly Boulevard
Los Angeles, CA   90048
213–550–4000

International Talent Group (ITG)
200 West 57th Street

New York, NY   10019
212–246–8118

Betty Kaye Productions, Inc.
2701 Cottage Way
Sacramento, CA   95825
916–487–1923

P.O. Box 3448
Santa Monica, CA   90403
213–829–0747

Shorty Lavender Talent Agency
P.O. Box 120789
Nashville, TN   37212
615–327–9595

Buddy Lee Attractions, Inc.
38 Music Square East
Nashville, TN   37203
615–244–4336

100 West 57th Street
New York, NY   10019
212–247–5216

Magna Artist Corporation
595 Madison Avenue
New York, NY   10022
212–752–0363

Monterey Peninsula Artists
P.O. Box 7308
Carmel, CA   93921
404–624–4889

The William Morris Agency
1350 Avenue of the Americas
New York, NY   10019
212–586–5100

151 El Camino Drive
Beverly Hills, CA   90212
213–274–7451

2325 Crestmoor Road
Nashville, TN   37215
615–385–0310

Premier Talent Agency
3 East 54th Street
New York, NY   10022
212–758–4900

Regency Artists, Ltd.
9200 Sunset Boulevard
Los Angeles, CA   90069
213–273–7103

Sutton Artists Corporation
119 West 57th Street
New York, NY   10019
212–977–4870

11777 San Vicente Boulevard
Los Angeles, CA   90049
213–820–8110

Top Billing International
P.O. Box 121089
Nashville, TN   37212
615–327–1133

Norby Walters Associates
200 West 51st Street
New York, NY   10019
212–245–3939

9200 Sunset Boulevard
Beverly Hills, CA   90069
213–275–9449

APPENDIX VI
MUSIC PUBLISHERS

This list contains most of the larger music publishers as well as some of the smaller ones. Larger music publishers may take longer to get back to you because of the high volume of songs they work with. Smaller music publishers may work harder with the songs they have. Try sending your material to both varieties.

Abkco Music, Inc.
1700 Broadway
New York, NY   10019
212–399–0300

Acoustic Music, Inc.
Box 1546

Nashville, TN   37202
615–242–9198

Acuff-Rose Publishing, Inc.
2510 Franklin Road
Nashville, TN   37204
615–385–3031

**American Broadcasting Music,
   Inc.**
4151 Prospect Avenue
Los Angeles, CA   90027
213–663–3311

1330 Avenue of the Americas
New York, NY   10019
212–887–4355

Andustin Music
Box 669
Woodstock, NY   12498
914–679–6069

April/Blackwood Music
1350 Avenue of the Americas
New York, NY   10019
212–975–4886

1930 Century Park West
Los Angeles, CA   90067
213–556–4790

Arista Music Publishing Group
8304 Beverly Boulevard
Los Angeles, CA   90048
213–842–0771

ATV Music Corp.
6255 Sunset Boulevard
Hollywood, CA   90028
213–462–6933

888 Seventh Avenue
New York, NY   10019
212–977–5680

1217 16th Avenue South
Nashville, TN   37212
615–327–2753

Beechwood Music
6255 Sunset Boulevard
Hollywood, CA   90028
213–469–8371

1370 Avenue of the Americas
New York, NY   10019
212–489–6740

Belwin-Mills Publishing Corp.
1776 Broadway
New York, NY   10019
212–245–1100

Blackwood Music
Box 17272
Memphis, TN   38117
901–767–2220

Braintree Music
9200 Sunset Boulevard
Hollywood, CA   90069
213–466–6428

Broadman Press
127 9th Avenue North
Nashville, TN   37234
615–251–2500

Buddah Music
1790 Broadway
New York, NY   10019
212–582–6900

The Cameron Organization, Inc.
822 Hillgrove Avenue
Western Springs, IL   60668
312–246–8222

Glen Campbell Enterprises, Ltd.
1900 Avenue of the Stars
Los Angeles, CA   90067
213–553–8434

Can't Stop Music
65 East 55th Street
Suite 302
New York, NY   10022
212–751–6177

CBS Songs
1015 16th Avenue South
Nashville, TN   37212
615–329–8100

1515 Broadway
New York, NY   10036
212–975–4321

Chappell Music Company
11 Music Circle South
Nashville, TN   37203
615–244–3882

810 Seventh Avenue
New York, NY   10019
212–399–7373

6255 Sunset Boulevard
Hollywood, CA   90028
213–469–5141

**Cherry Lane Music Publishing
   Co., Inc.**
110 Midland Avenue
Port Chester, NY   10573
914–937–8601

Chrysalis Music Corp.
115 East 57th Street
New York, NY   10022
212–935–8750

Coal Miners Music Inc.
7 Music Circle North
Nashville, TN   37203
615–259–9448

Bruce Cohn Music
Box 359
Somona, CA   95476
707–938–4060

Combine Music Group
35 Music Square East
Nashville, TN   37203
615–255–0624

Cream Publishing Group
8025 Melrose Avenue
Los Angeles, CA   90046
213–655–0944

Delightful Music Ltd.
1733 Broadway
New York, NY   10019
212–757–6770

The Drake Music Group
809 18th Avenue South
Nashville, TN   37202
615–327–3211

Fame Publishing Co., Inc.
Box 2527
Muscle Shoals, AL   35660

Famous Music Corp.
6430 Sunset Boulevard
Los Angeles, CA   90028
213–461–3091

2 Music Circle South
Nashville, TN   37203
615–242–3531

1 Gulf & Western Plaza
New York, NY   10023
212–333–3433

Far Out Music, Inc.
7417 Sunset Boulevard
Hollywood, CA   90046

Fort Knox Music Co.
1619 Broadway
New York, NY   10019
212–489–8170

G.G. Music, Inc.
Box 374
Fairview, NJ   07022
201–941–3987

Al Gallico Music Corp.
9255 Sunset Boulevard
Los Angeles, CA   90069
213–274–0165

1111 17th Avenue South
Nashville, TN   37212
615–327–2773

Gaucho Music
161 West 54th Street
New York, NY   10019
212–581–5398

Glenwood Music Corp.
c/o Screen Gems–EMI
1370 Avenue of the Americas
New York, NY   10019
212–489–6740

The Grand Pasha Publisher
5616 Melrose Avenue
Hollywood, CA   90038
213–466–3507

G.Q. Music
c/o Tony Lopez
1860 Grand Concourse
Bronx, NY   10457
212–299–2500

Harrison Music Corp.
6253 Hollywood Boulevard
Hollywood, CA   90028
213–466–3834

Iffin Music Publishing Co.
38 Music Square East
Nashville, TN   37203
615–254–0825

Interworld Music Group
25 West 56th Street
New York, NY   10019
212–582–8810

Island Music
6525 Sunset Boulevard
Hollywood, CA   90028
213–851–1466

Dick James Music, Inc.
24 Music Square East
Nashville, TN   37203
615–242–0600

119 West 57th Street
New York, NY   10019
212–581–3420

JMR Enterprises
1014 16th Avenue South
Nashville, TN   37212
615–244–1630

Kelly & Lloyd Music
1014 16th Avenue South
Nashville, TN   37212
615–244–1630

Kirshner/CBS Music Publishing
1370 West 55th Street
New York, NY   10019
212–489–0440

Kiss Songs
c/o Aucoin Management

645 Madison Avenue
New York, NY   10022
212–826–8800

Lareo Music Inc.
425 Park Avenue
New York, NY   10022
212–371–9400

Manna Music Inc.
2111 Kenmere Avenue
Burbank, CA   91504
213–843–8100

MCA Music
445 Park Avenue
New York, NY   10022
212–759–7500

1106 17th Avenue South
Nashville, TN   37212
615–242–3551

70 Universal City Plaza
Universal City, CA   91608
213–508–4550

Memphis Management Music
Box 17272
Memphis, TN   38187
901–767–2220

Merit Music Corp.
815 18th Avenue South
Nashville, TN   37203
615–327–0518

Midsong Music International
1650 Broadway
New York, NY   10019
212–541–5100

Mighty Three Music Group
309 South Broad Street
Philadelphia, PA   19107
215–546–3510

Multimedia Music Group
110 21st Avenue South
Box 120479
Nashville, TN   37212
615–327–2532

Music Concepts International
9348 Santa Monica Boulevard
Beverly Hills, CA   90210
213–550–6255

**Music Resources International
Corp.**
21 West 39th Street
New York, NY   10018
212–869–2299

**Neverland Music Publishing
Company**
225 East 57th Street
New York, NY   10022
212–888–7711

Nick-O-Val Music
Suite 1A
254 West 72nd Street
New York, NY   10023
212–873–2179

Notable Music Co., Inc.
161 West 54th Street
New York, NY   10019
212–757–9547

O.A.S. Music Group
805 18th Avenue South
Nashville, TN   37203
615–327–3900

O'Lyric Music
11833 Laurelwood Drive
Studio City, CA   91604
213–506–5473

Polish Prince Music
c/o Greene & Reynolds
1900 Avenue of the Stars
Los Angeles, CA   90067
213–553–5434

Jim Reeves Enterprises
Drawer 1
Madison, TN   37115
615–868–1150

Rocket Publishing
125 Kensington High Street
London, W8 3NT England
44–01–938–1741

Brian Ross Music
7120 Sunset Boulevard
Hollywood, CA   90046
213–851–2500

**Scotti Brothers Music
Publishing**
2114 Pico Boulevard
Santa Monica, CA   90405
213–450–4143

**Screen Gems-Colgems/EMI
Music, Inc.**
1370 Avenue of the Americas
New York, NY   10019
212–489–6740

6255 Sunset Boulevard
Los Angeles, CA   90028
213–469–8371

Larry Shayne Enterprises
6362 Hollywood Boulevard
Hollywood, CA   90028
213–462–1603

Robert Stigwood Music
c/o Chappel Music
810 Seventh Avenue
New York, NY   10019
212–399–7373

Stephen Stills Music
5032 Lankersham Boulevard
North Hollywood, CA   91601
213–766–7142

Sulzer Music
Dave Wilson Productions
3505 Kensington Avenue
Philadelphia, PA   19134
215–744–6111

Twitty Bird Music Publishing
   Company
8 Music Square West
Nashville, TN   37203
615–327–3162

United Artists Music
729 Seventh Avenue
New York, NY   10019
212–575–3000

6920 Sunset Boulevard
Los Angeles, CA   90028
213–461–9141

Upstart Music
2210 Rapier Boulevard
Arlington, TX   76013
817–461–8481

Warner Bros. Music
9200 Sunset Boulevard
Los Angeles, CA   90069
213–273–3323

75 Rockefeller Plaza
New York, NY   10019
212–484–8000

APPENDIX VII
RIGHTS SOCIETIES

A. RECORDING RIGHTS SOCIETIES

The following is a list of societies that secure recording rights to music.

American Mechanical Rights
   Association (AMRA)
250 West 57th Street
New York, NY   10019
212–246–4077

Copyright Service Bureau Ltd.
221 West 57th Street
New York, NY   10019
212–582–5030

Harry Fox Agency, Inc.
110 East 59th Street

New York, NY   10022
212–751–1930

SESAC Inc.
10 Columbus Circle
New York, NY   10019
212–586–3450

B. PERFORMING RIGHTS

The following is a list of societies that secure performance rights for music.

American Society of Composers
   (ASCAP)
One Lincoln Plaza
New York, NY   10023
212–595–3050

Broadcast Music, Inc. (BMI)
320 West 57th Street
New York, NY   10019
212–586–2000

SESAC Inc.
10 Columbus Circle
New York, NY   10019
212–586–3450

APPENDIX VIII
PERSONAL MANAGERS AND
MANAGEMENT COMPANIES

Although almost anyone can claim to be a personal manager or have a personal management firm, not everyone can be of service to a new artist or act.

The following is a list of personal managers and management companies who have been successful in the field. Omission from this list does not mean that a manager or management firm is not or cannot be successful with an act. New managers help new acts attain stardom and success on a constant basis. This list is just a beginning.

Acuff-Rose
2510 Franklin Road
Nashville, TN   37204
615–385–3031

Adam's Dad Management
827 Folsom Street
San Francisco, CA   94107
415–777–2930

Buddy Allen Management, Inc.
65 West 55th Street
New York, NY   10019
212–581–8988

Alive Entertainment
9000 Sunset Boulevard
Los Angeles, CA   90069
213–276–4500

Benjamin Ashburn
39 West 55th Street
Penthouse South
New York, NY   10019
212–246–0385

Peter Asher Management
644 North Doheny Drive
Los Angeles, CA   90069
213–273–9433

Aucoin Management, Inc.
645 Madison Avenue
New York, NY   10022
212–826–8800

Sid Bernstein Productions
4 East 75th Street
New York, NY   10021
212–744–9000

Can't Stop Productions
65 East 55th Street
New York, NY   10022
212–751–6177

Paul Cantor Enterprises, Inc.
144 South Beverly Drive
Beverly Hills, CA   90212
213–274–9222

Collins/Barrasso Agency
280 Lincoln Street
Allston, MA   02134
617–783–1100

Day Five Productions
216 Chatworth Drive
San Fernando, CA   91340
213–365–9371

Tony DeLauro
1650 Broadway
New York, NY   10019
212–757–7374

Far Out Management
7417 Sunset Boulevard
Los Angeles, CA   90069
213–874–1300

Freeman and Doff, Inc.
8732 Sunset Boulevard
Los Angeles, CA   90069
213–659–4700

Ken Fritz
444 South San Vincente
Los Angeles, CA   90048
213–651–5350

Gamble, Huff & Bell
309 South Broad Street
Philadelphia, PA   19107
215–985–0900

Shep Gordon
8600 Melrose Avenue
Los Angeles, CA   90069
213–659–7001

Bill Graham Productions
201 Eleventh Street
San Francisco, CA   94103
415–864–0815

Jim Halsey Company, Inc.
3255 South Norwood Avenue
Tulsa, OK   74135
918–663–3883

Jack D. Johnson Talent, Inc.
P.O. Box 40484
Nashville, TN   37204
615–383–6564

Joe Jackson
6255 Sunset Boulevard
Los Angeles, CA   90028
213–466–7315

Quincy Jones Productions
1416 North LaBrea Avenue
Los Angeles, CA   90028
213–469–2411

Don Kelly Organization
1474 North Kins Road
Los Angeles, CA   90069
213–656–4787

Kragen & Company
1112 North Sherbourne
Los Angeles, CA
213–659–7914

Kudo III Management
8250 Wilshire Boulevard
Beverly Hills, CA   90212
213–278–2916

Buddy Lee Attractions. Inc.
38 Music Square East
Nashville, TN   37202
615–244–4336

Leber-Krebs, Inc.
65 West 55th Street
New York, NY   10019
212–765–2600

Donny Linton Management
250 West 57th Street
New York, NY   10017
212–957–9764

Management III Ltd.
9744 Wilshire Boulevard
Beverly Hills, CA
213–550–7100

Ernie Martinelli Management
888 Eighth Avenue
New York, NY   10019
212–JU6–0963

Brian Panella
14020 Old Harbor Lane
Marina Del Ray, CA   90291
213–827–1220

Jess Rand, Inc.
9460 Wilshire Boulevard
Beverly Hills, CA   90212
213–275–6000

Rollins & Joffe
100 Universal Plaza
Universal City, CA   91608
213–985–4321

Sidney A. Seidenberg, Inc.
1414 Avenue of the Americas
New York, NY   10019
212–421–2021

S.I.R. Productions
112 Central Park South
New York, NY   10019
212–489–0950

Scotti Brothers
9229 Sunsct Boulevard
Hollywood, CA   90069
213–550–0120

Starflight Management
2 West 45th Street
New York, NY   10036
212–575–5036

**Robert Stigwood Organization
   (RSO)**
1775 Broadway
New York, NY   10019
212–975–0700

Jeff Wald Associates
9356 Santa Monica Boulevard
Beverly Hills, CA   90210
213–273–2192

Phil Walden & Associates
535 Cotton Avenue
Macon, GA   31201
912–745–8511

Dave Zaan
1650 Broadway
New York, NY   10019
212–581–6900

APPENDIX IX
PUBLIC RELATIONS AND PUBLICITY FIRMS

The following is a list of some of the public relations and publicity firms that handle music and/or entertainment clients.

Bob Abrams & Associates
2030 Prosser Avenue
Los Angeles, CA   90025

Benjamin Ashburn Associates
39 West 55th Street
Penthouse South
New York, NY   10019

Ken Baker Publicity Services
4034 Twentieth Street
San Francisco, CA   94114

Jay Bernstein
9110 Sunset Boulevard
Los Angeles, CA   90069

**Howard Bloom Organization,
   Ltd.**
135 East 55th Street
New York, NY   10022

Brokaw Company
9255 Sunset Boulevard
Los Angeles, CA   90069

Shelly Field Organization
25 Landfield Avenue
Monticello, NY   12701

Freeman & Doff, Inc.
8732 Sunset Boulevard
Los Angeles, CA   90069

Richard Gersh Associates
311 West 57th Street
New York, NY   10019

Ron Grevatt Associates, Ltd.
200 West 57th Street
New York, NY   10019

Harshe-Rotman & Druck, Inc.
3345 Wilshire Boulevard
Los Angeles, CA   90010

Levinson & Associates
927 La Cienega Boulevard
Los Angeles, CA   90069

Peter Levinson Communications
75 East 55th Street
New York, NY   10022

**Mahoney/Wasserman &
   Associates**
510 Madison Avenue
New York, NY   10022

David Mirisch Enterprises
9911 West Pico Boulevard
Los Angeles, CA   90035

Rogers & Cowan
9665 Wilshire Boulevard
Beverly Hills, CA   90212

Steinberg, Lipsman and
Associates Public Relations
8961 Sunset Boulevard
Los Angeles, CA   90069

Solters & Roskin
9255 Sunset Boulevard
Los Angeles, CA   90069

APPENDIX X
GLOSSARY

The following is a list of abbreviations, acronyms, and music business lingo that should prove helpful to individuals interested in the music industry. Entries are listed alphabetically.

AAF	American Advertising Federation
AAMT	American Association for Music Therapy
A & R	Artist & Repertoire (the department in a record company that finds new songs, signs new artists, etc.)
ABA	American Bar Association
ACC	American Conference of Cantors
ACDA	American Choral Directors Association
ACM	Academy of Country Music
advance	A prepayment of monies against future royalties or fees.
AFM	American Federation of Musicians of the United States and Canada (the union that most musicians belong to)
AFT	American Federation of Teachers
AFTRA	American Federation of Television and Radio Artists
AGAC	American Guild of Authors & Composers (now known as The Songwriters Guild)
agent	The person who obtains work for an act or artist
AGM	American Guild of Music
AGMA	American Guild of Musical Artists
AGO	American Guild of Organists
AGVA	American Guild of Variety Artists
AICPA	American Institute of Certified Public Accountants
airplay	The broadcasting of records by radio stations
ALA	American Library Association
AMA	American Marketing Association
AMC	American Music Conference
AOR	Album-oriented rock (a type of music played by radio stations)
ASCAP	American Society of Composers, Authors & Publishers
A-side	The side of a single record that is promoted more actively
ASMA	American Society of Music Arrangers
ASMC	American Society of Music Copyists
ASOL	American Symphony Orchestra League
ATPAM	Association of Theatrical Press Agents & Managers
bio	Biography of artist or act, most commonly used in press kits and for other publicity
BMA	Black Music Association
BMI	Broadcast Music Incorporated
bullet	A printed mark designating songs that have potential on the charts; used in trade magazines, they may look like a bullet, a rocket or a star
B & W glossy	Black and white glossy photograph, also known as an 8 X 10 glossy
B/W	Backed with. The opposite of the A-Side of a record.

C & W	Country and Western
CBDNA	College Band Directors National Association
chart action	The movement of a specific record on the charts
charts	Lists of the current hits, found in the trade magazines
CMA	Country Music Association
commission	A percentage of money paid to an agent, manager, etc. for services
contractor	The person who hires session members for a recording session
copyright	A legal protection granted to an author or composer for the exclusive rights to his or her works
cover record	Another version of a tune that has already been recorded
CPA	Certified public accountant
CPM	Conference of Personal Managers
crossover record	A record that is popular in one type of music and then becomes popular in one or more other markets of music (e.g., a song that becomes a Top 40 hit and then becomes a hit on the country and/or R & B charts)
demo	Demonstration record used for selling a record, tune, or act
D.J.	Disc jockey
EIA	Electronic Industry Association
Equity	Actors Equity Association, the actor's union
fan club	A club made up of people devoted to a specific artist or act
FCC	Federal Communications Commission
format	The style of programming that a radio station uses (e.g. all talk, country, Top 40, etc.)
GAMMA	Guitar and Accessories Music Marketing Association
gig	A job for musicians
GMA	Gospel Music Association
gold album	An LP that has sold 500,000 units
gold record	A single record that has sold one million copies or more
Grammy	One of the most prestigious awards in the music business; given by the NARAS
headliner	The main act people come to see in a concert
hit	A record that is popular and sells a lot of copies
hook	The repetitive part of a song that is most remembered when people think about that tune
hype	Extensive publicity used to promote acts, new records, etc. (Incidentally, hype is not always true.)
IAAM	International Association of Auditorium Managers
IAFP	International Association of Financial Planning
IATSE	International Alliance of Theatrical Stage Employees
ICFP	Institute of Certified Financial Planners
IIA	Institute of Internal Auditors
jingle	Commercial with music
label	Record company
LP	Long-playing record commonly known as an album
lyrics	The words of a song
market	Can refer to a geographical location, such as the East Coast market, the West Coast market, the Southeast market, etc., or may refer to a type of musical market, such as Top 40, R & B, country, etc.
master	The finished tape that is turned into a record
MCA	Music Critics Association
mechanical license	A license obtained from a song publisher, needed to record the song
MENC	Music Educators National Conference
MIEA	Music Industry Educators Association
mix	Putting all the different tracks for a record together electronically

MLA	Music Library Association	**platinum record**	An L.P. that sells at least one million units
MOR	Middle of the road music, also called easy listening music	**platinum single**	A single that sells two million or more copies
Muzak	Canned music such as that heard in dentist's offices, department stores, elevators, etc.	**playlist**	A list of songs that a radio station compiles designating which songs it will play
NAA	National Association of Accountants	**P.R.**	Public relations
NAB	National Association of Broadcasters	**press kit**	A promo kit containing publicity, photos, and other promotional materials on an act
NABET	National Association of Broadcast Employees and Technicians	**PRSA**	Public Relations Society of America
NACA	National Association for Campus Activities	**public domain**	Songs or other works that have no copyright or whose copyright has expired
NACWPI	National Association of College Wind and Percussion Instructors	**R & B**	Rhythm and Blues
NAMM	National Association of Music Merchants	**R & R**	Rock 'n' Roll
NAMT	National Association for Music Therapy, Inc.	**RIA**	Recording Institute of America
NARAS	National Academy of Recording Arts & Sciences	**RIAA**	Recording Industry Association of America, Inc.
NARM	National Association of Record Merchandisers	**royalties**	Monies paid periodically for the sales of records, sheet music, etc.
NASM	National Association of Schools of Music	**royalty statement**	An itemized accounting of earnings for songwriters or recording artists
NASSM	National Association of State Supervisors of Music	**SAG**	Screen Actors Guild
NFMC	National Federation of Music Clubs	**scale**	The minimum union wages
NMPA	National Music Publishers Association	**self-contained act**	A group that has all members included and needs no outside augmentation
NOA	National Orchestra Association	**SESAC**	Society of European Songwriters, Authors and Composers
NPMA	National Piano Manufacturers Association	**single**	A record with one tune on each side
NSPA	National Society of Public Accountants	**SLA**	Special Libraries Association
oldies	Songs that were hits some years ago	**SPARS**	Society of Professional Audio Recording Studios
payola	Money or other "gratuities" given to D.J.'s or program directors in order to have certain records played more often (this is illegal)	**S.R.O.**	Standing room only—all seats for a concert or show are sold out
P.D.	Public domain; program director	**standard**	A song that becomes popular in all markets and then becomes timeless, it may also be known as a classic.
performing rights	The right to license music and collect monies for use by anyone playing that music	**superstar**	Act that is famous, talented, rich, and well known.
personal manager	Person who directs the career of a performer	**supporting act**	Act that opens the show before the main event

TEIA   Touring Entertainment Industry Association

tip sheet   A newspaper, newsletter, or magazine that lists new records and fast-moving tunes (tip sheets are used by program directors and/or music directors at radio stations to help make up the station's playlists)

Top 40   The forty songs in the country that are selling the best and/or requested the most on radio stations (The Top 40 may be found in the trades. Often there is a Top 40 for different categories of music, such as Country, R & B, Albums, etc.)

Top Ten   The top ten songs on the charts

tour   A series of concerts, usually in different geographic areas

tour support   Monies paid to acts to offset the high cost of tours (Tour support is most often paid by the act's label. However, many companies are now underwriting concert tours, including soft drink companies, beer companies, perfume companies, etc.)

trades   Magazines and newspapers that deal with the music/record/entertainment industry.

venue   A hall, auditorium, or club where an act performs

INDEX